A BOLT FROM
THE BLUE

A BOLT FROM
THE BLUE

THE EPIC TRUE STORY OF DANGER, DARING, AND HEROISM AT 13,000 FEET

JENNIFER WOODLIEF

ATRIA PAPERBACK

NEW YORK   LONDON   TORONTO   SYDNEY   NEW DELHI

ATRIA PAPERBACK
A Division of Simon & Schuster, Inc.
1230 Avenue of the Americas
New York, NY 10020

First Atria Paperback edition June 2012

ATRIA PAPERBACK and colophon are trademarks of Simon & Schuster, Inc.

For information about special discounts for bulk purchases, please contact Simon & Schuster Special Sales at 1-866-506-1949 or business@simonandschuster.com.

The Simon & Schuster Speakers Bureau can bring authors to your live event. For more information or to book an event, contact the Simon & Schuster Speakers Bureau at 1-866-248-3049 or visit our website at www.simonspeakers.com.

Manufactured in the United States of America

10   9   8   7   6   5   4   3   2   1

Library of Congress Cataloging-in-Publication Data

Woodlief, Jennifer.
   A bolt from the blue : the epic true story of danger, daring, and heroism at 13,000 feet / by Jennifer Woodlief.
      p. cm.
   1. Mountaineering expeditions—Grand Teton National Park. 2. Mountaineering accidents—Wyoming—Grand Teton National Park. 3. Mountaineering—Search and rescue operations—Wyoming—Grand Teton National Park. I. Title.
   GV199.42.W82G739 2012
   796.52209787'55—dc23
                                                            2012012148
ISBN 978–1–4516–0708–6
ISBN 978–1–4516–0709–3 (ebook)

To Nick,

for both the climb and the view

CAST OF CHARACTERS

Jenny Lake Climbing Rangers

Renny Jackson—head ranger, spotter (in helicopter)

Brandon Torres—incident commander (in rescue cache)

Leo Larson—operations chief (upper scene)

Dan Burgette—medic (lower scene)

Jim Springer—leader (lower scene)

Jack McConnell—at lower scene

Chris Harder (of Gros Ventre subdistrict)—at lower scene

Craig Holm—medic (upper scene)

George Montopoli—at upper scene

Marty Vidak—at upper scene

Helicopter Rescue Pilots

Laurence Perry—2LM

Rick Harmon—4HP

Idaho Climbing Party

Rob Thomas—trip leader, son of Bob, brother of Justin, stepbrother of Reese

Justin Thomas—son of Bob, brother of Rob, stepbrother of Reese

Bob Thomas—father of Rob and Justin, stepfather of Reese

Sherika Thomas—wife of Rob

Steve Oler—father of Sherika

Clint Summers—husband of Erica, Melaleuca employee

Erica Summers—wife of Clint

Rod Liberal—Melaleuca employee

Jake Bancroft—Melaleuca employee

Reagan Lembke—Melaleuca employee

Dave Jordan—friend of Rob

Reese Jackson—stepson of Bob, stepbrother of Rob and Justin

Kip Merrill—friend of Reese

Rob
Sherika
Bob
Steve

**TOP OF
FRICTION PITCH**

Clinton
Erica
Rod

**BOTTOM OF
FRICTION PITCH**

Justin
Jacob
Reagan

**GOLDEN
STAIRCASE**

WALL STREET

ONE

"But mountains do not bow to hopes;
mountains destroy those who have nothing left
but hopes."

—

Pete Sinclair, former Jenny Lake ranger and author of
We Aspired: The Last Innocent Americans

There appeared to be a slight break in the thunderstorm as the pilot approached the summit of the Grand, but high winds continued to swirl the clouds beneath the helicopter, and the sky was darkening off to the west. The aircraft was a Bell 406 Long Ranger L-IV high altitude, meaning that the innards of a Jet Ranger were boosted with a bit more horsepower and the tail rotor enlarged, approximately a $100,000 conversion. The modification gave the pilot more grip at altitude. Few helicopters are able to operate at 14,000 feet, much less with an increased payload capacity—this particular ship was a special piece of equipment, and quite the secret weapon in terms of mountain rescue.

Helicopter N772LM, nicknamed Two-Lima Mike for its call letters, was flown by Laurence Perry, a dashing 50-year-old Brit renowned as much for his flippant attitude on the approach to an accident site as his proficiency at shutting the joking down cold once he arrived on-scene. As one of the few pilots in the world capable of passing the flying exam required by the Jenny Lake rangers—a test that required, in part, a pilot to hold a nearly dead hover for two minutes straight while balancing a 200-pound log on the end of a 100-foot rope—Laurence's eccentricities were roundly accepted.

In more than 18,000 flight hours, Laurence had never operated a helicopter exactly like this one before arriving in the Tetons, but he had become comfortable flying it on rescue operations with the Jenny Lake climbing rangers in the past couple of years. In reality, Laurence could be trusted, and was willing, to fly most any type of aircraft, although technically he was licensed only as a helicopter pilot.

On the afternoon of July 26, 2003, Laurence was transporting two park rangers, both of whom were wholly unmoved by the sweeping, iconic setting of Grand Teton National Park, on a reconnaissance flight. At that moment, the Grand Teton—the highest peak in the Teton range in Jackson, Wyoming, and a mountaineering classic within the climbing community—was nothing more than the extraordinarily unwieldy scene of a tragic accident.

As Laurence climbed closer to the top of the mountain, the rangers' thoughts were already whirling around how to reach the victims, what to pack for the rescue, where best to be inserted into the scene. Much of this analysis was weather-dependent. If the pause in the storm held, Laurence would short-haul the rangers straight to the site, an extremely advanced rescue procedure in which rangers hang underneath a helicopter on the end of a rope the length of two basketball courts and disconnect from that line directly onto the mountainside. Short-hauling minimizes a helicopter's hover time in the air but exposes the rescuer to incredible risk, especially in turbulent weather.

The rangers had received some information from the scene itself, transmitted to the ranger station by cell phone 45 minutes earlier from one of the victims on the mountain. They knew that several climbers had all been struck by a single bolt of lightning just shy of the 13,770-foot summit of the Grand Teton on the Exum Ridge on a 120-foot section of smooth, steep granite known as Friction Pitch.

The rangers were aware that someone in the 13-member climbing party was performing CPR on one of the victims and that there was an array of other burn injuries, including paralysis. They also understood that three of the climbers had hurtled out of sight below Friction Pitch, presumably in a treacherous area of the mountain called the Golden Staircase.

As the helicopter climbed, the rangers searched for figures on or below the brilliant glow of the Golden Staircase, but they couldn't make out any signs of life. About 100 feet below Friction Pitch, in the midst of a vertical sheer rock face by the Jern Crack, they did see three people clinging to the side of the mountain, their ropes apparently tangled in a few rock spurs positioned just above an abyss.

When they reached the top of Friction Pitch, the rangers were momentarily staggered by the sheer scope of the accident site. There were several seemingly dazed climbers wandering above the pitch, a young man with sandy hair and a vacant expression leaning against a large outcropping of rock, a motionless young woman slumped over the top of the ridge, and, most sickening of all, another figure, whom the rangers would come to call the Folded Man, swinging upside-down from a rope about 50 feet down the mountainside. It was completely unclear to them how far he had fallen or how he had ended up in that location. His body was twisted into a sharp inverted V, the back of his head almost touching the heels of his feet, his belly button skyward. He was utterly still.

Leo Larson, something of a Fabio doppelgänger at six-foot-five and 195 pounds, his long blond hair pulled back in a loose ponytail, calmly snapped a few photos to share with the other rangers back in the rescue cache. Both Leo, age 47, and Dan Burgette, the second ranger in the chopper, had been with the Jenny Lake team before they had even begun using short-haul insertions in the mid-1980s. As the day progressed, Dan's duty as spotter in the ship would be taken over by Renny Jackson, head ranger, 27-year Jenny Lake veteran, and all-around legendary climber.

The Folded Man remained limp and unmoving, and both Leo and Dan silently began calculating the safest way to recover the suspended body intact. Watching him rotate in the wind, contorted in the most unnatural of positions with no effort to struggle, the rescuers presumed that he was no longer alive. Still, Laurence kept the helicopter stable, lingering in the air about 60 feet away, as they checked to be sure.

Laurence and Leo were on the side of the aircraft closer to the mountain. Laurence, in particular, was transfixed by the man's torso split in that pose—as he later said, he didn't realize a body could do that—and he felt a wave of sadness wash over him as he flashed on images of forlorn bodies snarled in ropes and swaying in remote and precipitous regions of the Eiger.

It was while he was lamenting the desperate loneliness of epic mountain deaths that Laurence believed he glimpsed the man's hand twitch—or else merely witnessed his fingers flutter in a gust of wind. Laurence looked back at Leo and Dan and, in as unruffled a tone as perhaps only a pilot holding a hover at high altitude can marshal, said, "He's alive."

"Yeah," Leo said. "I saw it, too."

And as simply as that, the mission, at least as it applied to the victim who was hanging, in every true sense, on to his life by a thread, very distinctly took on the heightened urgency of a lifesaving rescue.

Traditionally, in a climbing-related rescue, rangers respond to a single person in trouble. In this situation, the multiple victims alone rendered the operation outrageously complicated, requiring a team of rescuers versed, and secure, in enduring a perpetually fluid and ever-worsening series of circumstances and weather conditions.

In the summer of 2003, the Jenny Lake climbing rangers were faced with several critically injured victims spread over a variety of different locations on the mountain, with turbulent weather, diminishing daylight, and extreme vertical terrain just below the mountain summit. The risk was further ratcheted up with the necessity that the pilot execute precision, high-altitude helicopter maneuvers in the midst of a lightning storm while rangers dangled from the end of a 100-foot rope. Beyond relying on trust, experience, and instinct to execute a flawless—literally flawless—rescue, the rangers would also need every twist of luck to go their way. The chances of the rescuers extricating all of the victims before darkness grounded the helicopter were devastatingly remote and dwindling by the second.

This is the story of the Jenny Lake rangers beating those odds.

It is a rare thing for a ranger to save a life, even in the world of mountain rescue. Given the violent nature of mountaineering injuries and the remoteness of their locations, most serious accidents are fatal. The rangers in Grand Teton National Park confronted several deaths every summer season. This would, however, be the first time a climber had been killed in the park by a lightning strike.

Leo glanced up at the progress of the storm, the fading light. He and Dan made the briefest eye contact. It was unspoken, but they both knew it would take something damn close to a miracle for their team to pluck all of the victims off the mountain before nightfall. Success would necessitate the most complex and sensational operation ever performed in the park. It would require, in fact, what is widely considered the most spectacular rescue in the history of American mountaineering.

For a frozen moment, Leo looked steadily at Laurence, blue eyes meeting blue eyes, then nodded briskly, definitively, at the pilot. In response, he dipped his rotors and veered down to the Saddle.

TWO

"I get paid to do what other people do on their vacations. Except for the training."

—

Jim Springer, Jenny Lake ranger

When Renny received the call about the lightning strike on Friction Pitch on July 26, 2003, a Saturday afternoon, he was home with his daughter, Jane, then age 11. It was instantly clear to him from the information in the call-out—multiple patients, CPR in process on one, several missing climbers, bad weather, high elevation—that it was going to be a huge rescue. It was also apparent to Renny that while the mission would require many of the skills that he and his team regularly trained for every day, that particular tangle of events, at that specific time and place, would be anything but routine. In fact, it quite obviously had the makings of a once-in-a-career sort of rescue.

Renny Jackson's five-foot, 10½-inch frame is 150 pounds of pure, tightly coiled muscle, ideally designed to allow him to scramble up cliffsides Spider-Man-style. At first glance, the combination of his wire-rimmed glasses, his slow and soft voice, and his habit of using as few words as possible to make a point makes him appear bookish, lazy, almost timid. By the second glimpse, it becomes apparent that his brand of self-possessed confidence commands not just respect but also unwavering attention. He exercises in a traditional manner less than might be expected for someone with his exceptional core strength—in the winter, off-season for climbing, he lifts the occasional weight, goes for a run now and then, skis in the backcountry—but, as Renny says, the way you keep in shape for climbing is to climb.

And as a Jenny Lake ranger, climb he did—at work, on his days off from work, on vacation from work. Virtually all of his travels are climbing-related. His wife, Catherine, is a world-class climber herself. Family vacations and family traditions revolve around climbing always. His daughter can barely remember a time when she wasn't climbing with her dad.

When Renny can't get outside in the mountains, in bad weather, for example, the climbing gym in town, which seems as if it might be beneath him, actually provides some hand routes that are as challenging as climbing gets. Another climbing-centric workout he does indoors is chin-ups, despite the tendonitis in his elbows, to maintain his phenomenal arm strength. He knocks them out while drinking strong coffee and listening to rock-and-roll music. Ideally, he hooks up with another ranger, blares some Bob Dylan or Rolling Stones, and works through what he calls Chinese chin-ups. The pattern is Renny doing 10 of them, then the other ranger doing 10, then Renny doing nine, and so on, until they are each down to one, and then they take turns adding one each time until they get up to 10 again. The end result is that both rangers execute more than 100 chin-ups in rapid-fire speed.

By 2003, Renny had been hauling injured hikers and climbers out of the Tetons for more than a quarter of a century, about half as long as the Jenny Lake rangers had been around.

Twenty years before they became the country's most prestigious search-and-rescue climbing team, the Teton park ranger
concept was conceived in 1926, when Fritiof Fryxell came to
Jackson to research his doctorate in glacial geology. He returned the next year with his friend Phil Smith to claim first ascents on many of the range's peaks, and the two of them
became the first seasonal rangers when the area became a national park in 1929.

The park originally opened with only four staff members,
but tourism picked up after World War II, resulting in a slew of
visiting climbers and new routes. In 1948, backcountry rangers
Doug McLaren, Ernie Field, and Dick Emerson, calling on their
experience as veterans of the U.S. Army's 10th Mountain Division, decided to initiate search-and-rescue operations and created the Grand Teton Rescue Team, later renamed the Jenny
Lake climbing rangers. Having come from an Army division of
skiers and climbers who trained in the Colorado Rockies and
on Mount Rainier before heading into combat in the Italian
mountains, these men realized the benefit of hiring experienced climbers for seasonal positions in the park. Feeling that it
would be easier to teach climbers to be rangers than rangers to
be climbers, they advertised the job to elite climbers as a chance
to be paid to spend time in the mountains.

Since its inception in 1948, the team has been considered
the best in the business, the crew that sets the standard for
mountain rescue throughout the country. In 2003, Renny Jackson was their leader.

A world-renowned climber who began his career as a Jenny
Lake ranger before Erica Summers, the unresponsive woman
on the top of Friction Pitch, was born, climbing is the only real
job Renny has ever had. Born in 1952 outside Salt Lake City,
Reynold Jackson grew up hiking and exploring in the mountains of Utah with his parents. On picnics with his family at Big

Cottonwood Canyon southeast of Salt Lake City, he became fascinated watching climbers maneuvering around on quartzite. He particularly found it interesting, as he says, to "get on top of something" and began climbing as a teenager, taking a beginner's course through the Wasatch Mountain Club in 1969.

The Wasatch Club was fairly serious about new climbers learning the basics, and there was nothing theoretical about its classes. The students dropped weights out of trees, for example, to tests the limits of what they could hold with a standard hip belay. Rather than reading about how to climb, they got outside and practiced—team arrests, boot-axe belay, body rappels, self-arrests from every imaginable position. The lessons in self-arrest involved the novice climbers dressing in the slickest ski suits they could find and sliding as fast as possible headfirst down a hill. Occasionally, the instructors would mix in some safety protocols and put the students on belay during those sessions.

The Wasatch Club brought Renny to the Tetons, where he summited the Grand for the first time at age 19. His primary skills as a climber were limitless tenacity and an uncanny ability, even as a beginner, to cling to the rock. His willingness to spend all of his time climbing didn't hurt, either, paying off in a phenomenally quick learning curve. While other climbers took the winters off, he trained year-round.

After attending the University of Utah, Renny accepted a seasonal position on a trail crew at Park West (now called the Canyons Ski Resort) near Park City so he could spend the summer climbing in the Tetons. His foot in the door to becoming a ranger at Jenny Lake was working on trail crews there in 1974 and '75. On his days off, he climbed with the rangers and made sure they knew that his goal was to work with them.

At age 24, in 1976, he became a Jenny Lake climbing ranger, and he never looked back.

Renny was employed as a seasonal ranger at Grand Teton

National Park until 1989, working ski patrol at nearby resorts in the winter off-seasons. Quickly establishing a reputation as one of the preeminent climbers in the Teton range, he began tackling routes that had never been climbed before. He made the first winter ascent of the South Buttress of Moran, claimed the steep Emotional Rescue route on the north side of the Grand's Enclosure, and was a team member on the first winter Grand Traverse. While most rangers tend to move around the country, working for various national parks, Renny devoted his career, except for a two-year stint in Denali National Park in Alaska, to the Jenny Lake rangers.

Renny is the rare kind of individual who not only identified exactly what he wanted to do at a young age but also success-fully engineered a life around that passion. The freedom that accompanied the ranger position, the relationship with his sur-roundings, the sensation that transcended merely being in the mountains and shifted to a feeling of belonging to the moun-tain's whole both satisfied and sanctioned his yearning to build his life around climbing. None of it was done for glory or fame and certainly not for money. Renny's emotions about the job were akin to the way some professional athletes feel about their sport: he did it simply for the love of the game.

Earlier on in his climbing career, about five years after be-coming a seasonal ranger, Renny spent a summer morning climbing Mount Owen with friends. It wasn't an exceptional climb; there was a lot of ice and snow on the mountain, and it was a gray, cloudy day, but his friends brought along a striking brunette named Catherine Cullinane, who possessed nearly un-paralleled technical climbing skills. Right away, there was an at-traction between Renny and Catherine. According to her, she was totally smitten by his dazzling hazel eyes and slow, dry wit. As for Renny, he fell for her whole package.

Catherine's obsession with mountaineering rivaled even

Renny's. Her dad had been in the 10th Mountain Division in World War II, so climbing was in her blood. She had grown up fly-fishing, backpacking, hiking, taking burro trips in the Sierra Nevada, and she had enrolled in technical rock-climbing courses as a teenager. She bounced between college in Humboldt and climbing in Yosemite, then balanced nursing school in Southern California with working as a climbing guide in the Tetons, becoming Exum's first female guide.

After that first climb together, Catherine ran into Renny at the ranger station, and he asked her out, but he had an off-again, on-again girlfriend at the time. Catherine dated Renny intermittently over the next few years, but the old girlfriend kept resurfacing. By the winter of 1985–86, with Catherine in Jackson working as a nurse at the Teton Village Clinic at the ski area, she and Renny were finally, by all appearances, together as a couple. Still, he wouldn't completely commit to her. It took Catherine telling him that she couldn't handle the relationship anymore and heading to Tibet for three months—where she helped make a film for the BBC on the history of George Mallory and an adventure film for ABC Sports—for Renny to realize how much he missed her. When he knew she was about to head home from the trip, Renny traveled from Wyoming to her parents' house in Montclair, California, and was there waiting for Catherine when she arrived, declaring his love for her and his desire for a future that included her.

They were married on a ranch in Jackson on September 11, 1988, the year of the Yellowstone fires. The whole area had been hazy from the smoke all summer, but on their wedding day, it snowed, which, in a metaphorical sort of fresh start, cleared the air and started putting the fires out.

Renny and Catherine were the ultimate climbing power couple, celebrities in the climbing world, traveling the globe and summiting the most challenging peaks, especially in Asia.

Renny had found one of the few women in the world who wouldn't hold him up on a mountainside. Catherine understood Renny's inability to wear his wedding ring in the traditional manner—so as not to lose part of his finger in a mountain crack—and supported his decision instead to wear his ring on a cord around his neck (along with a medallion of Saint Bernard, the patron saint of alpinists). They were extraordinarily well matched as climbing partners—she arguably possessed stronger technical skills, but he was braver on lead. Every July on Catherine's birthday, they climbed the Grand together.

The year after their marriage, 1989, was a tough one for Renny. There was no opening for a permanent ranger in the park, so he and Catherine left their beloved Tetons to move to Alaska, where Renny had been offered a year-round ranger job at Denali National Park. In 1989, Renny was planning a third summit attempt of Everest, but his father died, and he called it off. Renny had climbed Mount Everest twice in the past—once in the early '80s, he had ascended close enough to see the top of the world before accepting that he had to turn back; then, in 1987, he had tried again, but a jet stream moved in toward the end of the climb, and no one in his group summited. Shortly after Renny's father's death, Catherine was diagnosed with type 1 diabetes.

In the midst of his grief, disappointment, and fear for his wife, Renny met the challenge, organizing a climb with Catherine to the top of Denali (also known as Mount McKinley), the highest mountain in North America. To pull it off, he designed a fleece and neoprene patch for her insulin vials so they wouldn't freeze.

By 1991, a position had opened in the Grand Teton National Park, so Renny and Catherine returned home, and Renny became a full-time, year-round Jenny Lake climbing ranger. In February 1991, they bought a house in Kelly with a geodesic dome and a view of Indian Head and Sheep Mountain. Renny wasn't wild about the dome initially, but he came around. In August of that year, their daughter, Jane, was born.

Renny was always a very involved father, attending Jane's school activities when she was little, helping her assemble a butterfly collection, taking her swimming in the river, and, inevitably, teaching her how to climb. Every one of Jane's spring breaks and school vacations was a climbing trip. Renny's daughter was privy to a side of him beyond the effortlessly competent leader showcased to climbers throughout the world. Her experience was of a dad who took his family on adventures that she calls, in typical climber lingo, epics.

With Jane, Renny occasionally miscalculated the time of a hike or lost the trail. She was benighted (spent an unplanned and unexpected overnight stay in the mountains) with her dad in a wilderness area in southern Utah when she was eight, rappelled (essentially walking backward, facing the rock, down the side of a mountain) from a slot canyon in Zion with him long after dark when she was 10. While these exploits have not affected her love of climbing, they have taught her always to pack a headlamp.

As time went by, Renny eased up a slight bit, agreeing now and then to take a family trip that wasn't centered around climbing, as long as it was active, and every five years or so, consenting to take a three-day trip to see family in California. For the Jackson family, a vacation was never going to involve lying around on a beach.

Once he became a permanent ranger, Renny even began to take the occasional day off that did not involve climbing, although this "rest day" usually encompassed some sort of long hike or backcountry patrol. Every so often, he would work on the yard or various projects around the house, but he was so fixated, such a perfectionist, that he would usually start full-on, get sidetracked, and end up leaving tasks unfinished. He did sit still long enough to read and study history, however, and managed to parlay this interest into a climbing angle, too, literally writing the book on climbing in the Tetons, a classic guidebook with topographical maps entitled *A Climber's Guide to the Teton Range* (now in its third edition) with Leigh N. Ortenburger (who perished in the Oakland, California, firestorms in 1991).

All of Renny's time as a ranger in Grand Teton National Park has been in the Jenny Lake subdistrict. Every subdistrict in the park has rangers, but some work as road-patrol or lake-patrol law-enforcement rangers. The park rangers are responsible for a variety of tasks, from making visitor contact in ranger stations to resource management dealing with, for example, bears. There are also biotechs who conduct, among other duties, campsite inventories.

In the Jenny Lake subdistrict of the park in 2003, during peak season—June to August—the Jenny Lake team was made up of 16 rangers, four of whom were permanent, year-round park employees. Although most of the rangers were seasonal employees ("seasonals"), because of the enormous level of responsibility involved in the position, no one ever thought of it as a summer job.

All of the Jenny Lake rangers spend their time educating, helping, and rescuing climbers and hikers in the mountains, but the permanent employees, and sometimes a few of the seasonals, are also law-enforcement rangers with extra training and law-enforcement commissions. In addition, several of the rangers (two in 2003, now three) have specialized emergency medical skills.

The application to become a climbing ranger (as opposed to a park ranger) contains an additional, objective set of standards relating to climbing experience and expertise, but the job is so highly competitive that all of the Jenny Lakers radically ex-

ceed the minimums. Applications are so plentiful that Jenny
Lake can demand the full package—a candidate who is experienced, a world-class climber on both rock and ice, incredibly
physically fit (a given once they have secured the climbing ré-
sumé), and ideally conversant with basic EMS skills.

Of the 16 rangers in 2003, all but two—who focused on
backcountry patrols—climbed as a routine part of their job.
Those 14 were hired with a screen-out factor requiring them to
have climbed and led climbs at a certain technical level. It was
those rangers alone, the ones with the climbing prerequisite
contained in their job descriptions, who were permitted to call
themselves Jenny Lake climbing rangers.

There is no confusion about the lure of the job to climbers,
with the concentration on climbing not merely a perk of the
position but a requirement. The rangers rotate shifts at the rescue cache in Lupine Meadows and put in time at the ranger hut
on the Grand's Lower Saddle, but three times a pay period,
meaning three times in ten days, they set off on mountain patrols. These are paid climbing days, in which the rangers are
free to roam anywhere and climb whatever routes they want,
as long as they stay in the park. The idea is to give them as much
direct experience as possible so that they have ultimate credibility to dispense pertinent information about climbing routes to
park visitors. Since they are climbing constantly, they can also
provide up-to-date details about the conditions on various parts
of the mountains. The rangers consider the climbing patrols to
be preventive rescue. To the extent possible, when climbers
visit the ranger station, the rangers try to match skill levels with
appropriate routes and climbs.

There are other benefits to the paid climbing days, too. The
rangers obviously need to maintain their climbing skills and,
moreover, as hard-core climbers say, to "feed the rat," satisfying
their insatiable need to climb. In addition, it is a huge advantage

for the rangers to be intimately familiar with complicated and perilous terrain where a rescue could occur on a moment's notice. To this end, they are also out in the mountains on their days off, gaining firsthand knowledge of the geology and climate of the Tetons and the myriad crevices where hikers and climbers could become lost.

The climbing rangers smugly refer to the position as a job in which they are paid to climb, but it is not necessarily the right fit for all climbers. Climbers have traditionally held themselves out as fairly rebellious, and not all of them want to work for the government. As a year-round Jenny Lake ranger, Renny certainly found the law-enforcement component his least favorite part of the job. In addition, as chief ranger, part of Renny's duty was to insulate the other rangers from bureaucracy, despite his own weakness regarding all things administrative. His strengths, however—a quiet, calm management style, poise under pressure, the skill to band individuals together as a team—more than compensated.

While not into self-promotion, and despite making it clear that he was a climber before he was a ranger, Renny was nevertheless an instinctive leader. More essential than his considerable climbing skills, the vaguely indefinable quality of mountain judgment was his biggest asset as a ranger. The higher the stakes in a rescue, the more composed Renny became.

Renny was focused, no doubt, but his intensity tilted toward the taciturn. Although his style was what could only be considered the low-key side of laid-back, the rangers under Renny's command listened to him unswervingly. With his low, measured voice, he dispensed compliments to each of them based on their own specific talents. He was constantly striving to achieve in all aspects of his life—to climb more difficult routes, to improve his supervisory skills—and the rangers working under him didn't miss that. As a climber, Renny was steady and safe but also visionary, not satisfied with standard routes, always looking beyond them to discover new lines. As a leader of men, he operated the same way.

As head ranger, Renny was exhaustively, maddeningly, all about the details. He took his time, thought things out. He did not rush, and he did not get rattled. He rarely lost his temper. When he did become angry, either with Catherine or with a situation at work, Renny expressed it with fierce calmness. As a boss and as a father, he was strict, believing in consequences and valuing efficiency, responsibility, and, above all, honesty. On the flip side, his sense of humor was so cynical, so irreverent, and his delivery so deadpan that it sometimes required a double-take to determine whether he was joking. He has always been, Catherine admits, "a little complicated."

Adding to Renny's impenetrable and fairly enigmatic nature, decades of summers have been marked and measured for him in terms of tragedy. The first fatality in the Teton range was in 1925, when Theodore Teepe died after tumbling down the glacier that now bears his name. The rangers currently average about 100 rescues a year, spanning a range from twisted ankles to fatalities. Most of the call-outs fall somewhere in between—injuries from rockfall, rappelling accidents, ice- and snow-related slides, tumbles down descent gullies.

Depending on the season, about 20 to 35 of the rescues are considered major, meaning that they cost more than $500. Under that definition, any rescue in which a helicopter's rotors spin is a major one. Even a small technical rescue can often count as major. If there is a sprained knee or a dehydrated hiker in Cascade Canyon, for example, it can require overtime. Every year, approximately three to six people die in the Tetons.

The rangers generally use the helicopter about 10 times a summer, with approximately five of those times involving a short-haul procedure. Since short-hauling is used more frequently to extract patients than to insert rangers, aside from endless training exercises, in an average season, there are usually only one or two occasions for a pilot to short-haul a ranger to a scene.

On the evening of July 26, 2003, the short-haul maneuver was used a total of 13 times—to extract seven patients and to insert six rescuers.

The Jenny Lake climbing rangers are real-life rescue heroes, men whose office supplies are stashes of ropes, ice axes, and helmets. They are team members of the most elite and experienced climbing search-and-rescue team in the country, trained not just in technical climbing but also in altitude rescue—emergency medical care, setting anchors, raising systems, patient packaging, and high-risk helicopter operations.

The rangers certainly don't receive much monetary compensation, and the seasonals receive no benefits in the traditional sense of that word. There is hazard pay and holiday pay and overtime, but the permanent rangers fall into the GS 7–9 levels of the government pay scale, with base yearly compensation just north of $30,000 a year. Seasonal employees work only from the end of May until September, and pay at a GS 5 level, where many park employees start out, is $12 an hour. Park garbage collectors, compensated according to a different pay schedule, are paid more.

In any event, the climbing rangers know that they are ultimately paid not so much for what they do as for what they have the potential of having to do.

The commonality of experience keeps the rangers intensely linked—to the mountains, to the job, to one another. The solidarity is also secured with the shared bonds of confronting trauma together on a near-daily basis. In terms of physical gore, it doesn't get much more revolting. All of the rangers have had to collect body parts strewn about the mountain and wrap them up together as neatly as possible.

Many rangers have been faced with the daunting task of scraping brain matter off the mountain and, if unable to push the material back into the skull, packing it separately (in sandwich bags in the early days) rather than tossing it loose into the body bag. In the scope of emotional trauma, the dead victims whom the rangers are forced to package are almost never sick or old. The fatalities are overwhelmingly vibrant and athletic individuals—hikers struck down while on vacation, climbers killed while pursuing their passion.

Despite the cost to them psychologically, the rangers always do what they can for the victims, small, respectful acts of kindness and compassion, to try to facilitate the healing for those left behind. On one occasion, rangers loading the body of a married man into a bag realized that his wife would need to see him one last time, would want to hold his hand again. On the side of the mountain, they removed saline, gauze, and paper towels from their packs and painstakingly washed the blood off his fingers.

Every ranger copes with the trauma differently. Some abuse alcohol, some turn inward, a few quit. But there is extremely low turnover among the Jenny Lake rangers, leading to a level of experience and maturity virtually unparalleled in other search-and-rescue teams.

Returning seasonal rangers are fairly rare in other national parks. There is more upheaval, for example, at Denali and Mount Rainier. It is extremely draining—on finances, on relationships—for most rescue personnel to maintain long-term summer employment. As the job only provides income for five months, the seasonals have to find other work to support themselves for the rest of the year, and structuring a career that accommodates an extended summer break every year is generally not an option. By necessity, the rangers end up taking any job that enables them to protect their Jenny Lake schedule. They are forever crashing with friends or living in their cars during the shoulder seasons between summer ranger duties and whatever job—frequently ski patrol—they can find to pay the bills that winter.

Longevity at Jenny Lake comes from loyalty, history, knowledge. There is a place, a community, a sense of belonging to a collection that is greater than its separate components, its individual rangers. Their link is immune to divergent backgrounds, personalities, education, social class, age, or geographic roots. These tough mountain men are sensitive, compassionate, and occasionally moved to tears when describing what it means to them to be Jenny Lake climbing rangers.

The rangers throw the word "brotherhood" around frequently but not casually. It is spoken with reverence. Central to their outlook is their core belief that at Jenny Lake, they are truly accepted for who they are and respected for what they do. Their various skills and strengths are appreciated, their weaknesses acknowledged. All points of view are entertained. Everyone has a voice, and each of them knows that he is heard.

Just as in the pursuit they worship, the climbing rangers need not be connected by a thick rope. Their lives revolve around, and depend upon, a thin strand of triumph and tragedy. Very few people in their adult lives have experienced a bond like that, but these men have seen it, felt it. The reason all of these alpha dogs are able to work cooperatively is that they are all climbers at heart, sharing a love of any label containing the word "vertical," participants in a vertical ballet, players in the same vertical chess game. Some are cockier than others, and they are all relatively antiestablishment, but for the most part, they defy the type A assertive stereotype and instead just sort of keep to themselves.

If lone-wolf climbers can ever be described as a team, it is during lifesaving mode in the midst of chaos. Aside from the danger—and the rangers have to compartmentalize the danger—a rescue is an endeavor involving practically all of their climbing buddies. They get to hang out with their friends, try out the coolest toys. They have a ton of fun, but they never lose sight of the reality that it is a very serious game they are playing. In the end, as much as they all love to climb, they do what they do to save lives. The personalities just more or less sort themselves out.

These are men who understand each other implicitly, who know that their shared passion for the job flows well beyond the traditionally recognized and socially ordained "acceptance of risk" to something much more profound: the seeking of risk.

In 2003, the team hadn't had any turnover for three years, with most rangers averaging 10 to 15 years on the job. Several rangers involved in the Friction Pitch rescue—Renny, Leo, Dan— had been working together for more than a quarter-century.

The physical conditioning, plus the stress, involved in the duties of a climbing ranger would seem to make it a young man's game, but that wasn't necessarily the case with the 2003 Jenny Lake rangers. Many of them were in their 40s and 50s, and although stories of climbers sharing girlfriends are legendary within the climbing community, most of these guys had long settled down with wives and children. All of the rangers' children tended to be pretty amazing climbers and skiers, whether they wanted to be or not. Jim Springer took his kids on canyon patrols; Dan Burgette brought his kids along on certain rescues.

By 2003, decades of training and executing hundreds of rescues side-by-side unquestionably provoked the rangers' seamless execution, their highly polished, nearly choreographed moves. They often finished one another's sentences, both literally and in a figurative sense. When one of them required a certain tool, another ranger often already had it out and was handing it over. They didn't all socialize after working hours, and there were definitely cliques within the team. To say that a few of them didn't like one another outside of the job was certainly an understatement, yet, interpersonal dynamics aside, they all quite readily trusted one another with their lives.

Although Catherine's life has ultimately revolved around Renny's work as a ranger, often a source of frustration if not outright fear for her, she has never forgotten what drew her to him in the first place. "He's very funny, you know? So funny, that's what got me, totally worked on me. He made me laugh until I was rolling on the ground. I always remember the quality I *had* to marry him for." While she didn't dwell on the danger Renny faced with each rescue, pleas for help came at all hours, and she was not unaffected by Renny's need to drop plans in his personal life for the sake of his job.

When the call came in about the accident on Friction Pitch, Renny was home watching Jane while Catherine was working a 12-hour shift as a labor-and-delivery nurse. Ironically, not realizing the enormity of the incident, it was a rare time that Catherine not only didn't bail Renny out, but she didn't even have sympathy for his predicament. She was furious at him for having to respond to a rescue on, as she says, "the one day" he was supposed to be watching Jane. When Renny called her, she hung up on him. "You figure it out," she said. "I'm at work."

Renny called in a favor with a neighbor who agreed to look after Jane, threw some chocolate bars and Mountain Dew into a pack, dropped Jane off, and headed to work. The drive from his home in Kelly to the rescue cache in Lupine Meadows takes 25 minutes. He made it there—flashing lights and sirens in his police vehicle—in 12 minutes flat.

THREE

"When lightning hits a Pecky Cypress, it
continues to live, but it no longer grows."

—

Nolan Trosclair, tour guide, Honey Island Swamp, Louisiana

"Lightning strike on the Grand."

—

Heather Voster, dispatch operator

After the alert tone cleared, every ranger could hear the tension
in Heather Voster's normally steady voice. At 3:45 P.M. on July
26, 2003, the Teton Interagency Dispatch Center received a 911
cell-phone call from a frantic climber on the Grand Teton and
immediately forwarded the call to the ranger station. By 3:46,
Heather had disseminated the message to ranger Brandon Torres via the radio.

The full message she conveyed was: "431, Teton Dispatch, respond to a report of a lightning strike on the Grand
Teton. Five people down. I'm trying to get a better location
for you. . . . The party appears to be on Friction Pitch on the

Grand. One person not breathing, one person hanging upside-down and not breathing, three people missing and not responding to verbal."

While it conjures up images as comic as jagged yellow bolts and as innocent as a little kid counting the seconds between seeing lightning and hearing thunder, in reality, lightning is weather's version of an absolute sucker punch. Synonymous with a random strike with virtually no warning, electricity from the sky is one of the least understood and most unpredictable forces of nature. Unlike other forms of weather, this powerful and mysterious spectacle genuinely conducts its devastation before those it hits know what struck them. Also, unlike other extreme weather occurrences, lightning seems somehow purposeful, pointed, aimed, almost designed to pick off distinct individuals.

Lightning is an extremely lethal phenomenon and yet also an exceptionally rare one in terms of how few deaths it causes given how frequently it strikes. In the last decade, thousands of Americans have been injured by lightning and hundreds have been killed. It is the second-leading cause of fatalities in the United States related to violent weather, responsible for more deaths than earthquakes, tornadoes, or hurricanes. Only floods kill more people. According to the National Weather Service, lightning kills an average of 58 people in the United States every year, although scientists suspect that the reported number is likely much lower than the actual number, as some lightning deaths are not recorded as such.

Still, this is an incredibly small number of victims given the intense amount of lightning activity. Approximately 20 million cloud-to-ground flashes are detected every year in the United States, and since about half of all flashes strike the ground at more than one place, that means that lightning hits the ground about 30 million times each year in the country. Nearly 8 million lightning flashes occur every day worldwide, which translates to a flash somewhere on the planet about 100 times every second. Lightning is a phenomenon that extends well beyond the planet, also occurring on Venus, Jupiter, and Saturn.

Despite the incredible number of lightning strikes in the United States each year, the odds of lightning striking a person (as opposed to the ground, a tree, etc.) are only about one in 750,000. The chances of a lightning strike actually killing a person are significantly smaller than that—strikes are only fatal about 10 percent of the time.

Contrary to images in cartoons, it is not true that a person who is struck will burst into flames or be instantaneously reduced to ashes. While most people assume that death from a lightning strike results from burns, in fact, the only cause of immediate death is cardiac arrest.

In cloud-to-ground lightning, the energy seeks the shortest route to earth, which could be through a person's shoulder, down the side of the body, through the leg, and to the ground. If the lightning does not pass through the heart or the spinal column, the victim will often survive. Lightning current can pass through tissue and not cause harm, as long as it is tracking an uninterrupted route and doesn't get slowed down. If a bolt gets caught inside a body and spends time there, however, it can burn and cook from the inside out.

While lightning is generally thought of as descending and hitting one target, it can actually jump around. The degree of lightning injury may vary considerably with the mechanism of injury—direct strike, side flash (also known as a splash), or ground current. Cloud-to-ground lightning can kill or injure people by direct or indirect means. Objects that are directly struck may result in an explosion, a burn, or total destruction. When a person is directly hit, the current ripping through the nervous system can kill the victim instantly by shutting down the heart.

Direct strikes cause maximum injury, as the entire charge of lightning passes through or over the victim's body. Since the duration of contact during a lightning strike is so short, there is often not enough voltage transferred to break the insulating effect of the skin. In these cases, the charge simply passes along the surface of the body in a process known as flashover. When lightning flashes over the outside of a victim's body, less damage occurs, but it may vaporize moisture on the skin and blast apart clothes and shoes, leaving the victim nearly naked.

Direct current—the DC in AC/DC—is similar to the charge in a defibrillator, but as lightning strikes are usually more diffuse than that of high-voltage electrical currents, the injuries present differently. Lightning usually does not cause significant tissue destruction along the path of the grounding of the current; instead, blunt physical injury can occasionally occur as a result of a lightning strike.

Side flashes occur when lightning hits an object and then travels partly down that object before a portion jumps from the primary strike area to a nearby victim. They can also take place from person to person, if, for example, people are standing close together.

A ground strike occurs when the charge hits the ground in close proximity to a victim or travels through the ground after connecting with a nearby tree or other tall object. Being struck by a flow of conductive current from the ground is unlikely to result in death, although multiple victims are not uncommon in this situation. The extent of injury depends on a number of variables, including amperage, voltage, current pathway, length of contact, and the resistance of the body to discharging electrical fields.

The brutality of a lightning strike is as capricious as its location, varying based on the character of the strike, the severity of the dose, the duration of the strike, even the split-second timing of the bolt, whether, for example, it strikes a victim during a more vulnerable part of the cardiac cycle. While 90 percent of lightning-strike victims survive, even a partial strike often renders a victim temporarily unconscious, and survivors can suffer devastating internal injuries. Serious lightning injuries can result in cardiac and neurological damage. Since the injuries resulting from lightning strikes are so variable, most medical personnel characterize them as severe, moderate, or mild.

Severe lightning injury usually presents as cardiopulmonary arrest, caused by sudden cardiac dysrhythmia, meaning abnormal electrical activity in the heart. The situation is often complicated if there is a prolonged period in which the victim does not receive cardiopulmonary resuscitation (CPR). Sudden death is common, with or without CPR, and survival is rare with this level of injury.

Neurological complications can range from severe to mild, depending on whether the current passes directly to the brain stem. They include comas, seizures, intraventricular hemorrhage (bleeding into the brain), permanent paralysis, aphasia (a language disorder caused by brain damage), retrograde amnesia, loss of consciousness, and confusion.

Moderate lightning injury can cause seizures, respiratory arrest, or cardiac standstill, all of which may spontaneously resolve with the resumption of normal cardiac activity. Keraunoparalysis, the specific name for temporary lightning-induced paralysis, can occur as a result of a discharge of calcium in the musculature. If paralysis of the extremities is prolonged, it can indicate a spinal-cord injury.

Mild lightning injury is associated with loss of consciousness, amnesia, confusion, tingling, and numerous other nonspecific symptoms.

Lightning-strike victims at all levels of injury will commonly have burns, both those that appear initially and ones that are delayed. Lichtenberg figures, also known as ferning patterns or lightning flowers, frequently remain on the skin of victims for hours or even days afterward. This diffuse skin mottling looks almost like reddish feathers. It is caused by the rupture of small capillaries under the skin and the inflammation of lymphatic muscles caused by the passage of the lightning current flashing over the skin. The condition is so specific to lightning strikes that its appearance is often used by medical examiners when determining cause of death. A lightning bolt can also create large Lichtenberg figures in the grass surrounding the strike; these have been located on golf courses and grassy meadows.

When lightning strikes a person's body, a portion of the current usually enters cranial orifices—eyes, ears, nose, mouth—resulting in numerous problems. The most common of these injuries is the rupture of the tympanic membranes. Temporary hearing loss can be caused by the shock wave created by the accompanying thunder. Eye injuries and cataract formation resulting from lightning injury can occur within days of the strike, but victims have also reported these symptoms appearing as long as two years later.

Another common physical symptom, one that appears to last a lifetime, is chronic paresthesias, a sensation of tingling, pricking, or numbness of the skin, similar to the feeling of "pins and needles" or of a limb "falling asleep."

Although a lightning flash generally does not stick around long enough to cause tissue breakdown in the classic burn sense, lightning goes into one place on a body and comes out another, so victims do bear permanent entry and exit wounds. Aside from these burn imprints, there are often few other external signs of a lightning strike. Sometimes a lightning victim can look almost unscathed, and medical personnel cannot properly evaluate the severity of injury until they have removed all of the patient's clothing.

More disturbing than the permanent marks that lightning brands on its survivors are the neurological symptoms it inflicts on them. Certainly, the psychological ramifications present the biggest challenge recovery-wise. Victims often describe mysterious, long-lasting symptoms that develop afterward with no clear explanation. The most frequent consequences are memory loss (short-term and long-term) and attention-deficit problems, although issues with aggression—even uncontrolled rage—and dramatically altered personalities have also been reported. Other inexplicable and debilitating symptoms—including sleep apnea, chronically interrupted sleep cycles, irritability, numbness, dizziness, stiffness in joints, fatigue, weakness, muscle spasms, depression, and an inability to sit still for long periods of time—only add to the mystique of the phenomenon.

Inspiring fear and fascination for thousands of years, in early times, lightning was magic fire from the sky, heavily involved in superstitions, folklore, and early religions. A lightning bolt has been a powerful symbol throughout history and is the focus of many mythologies, often as a divine manifestation or as the weapon of a sky god or a storm god. The gods who possess it in ancient stories are the ones quick to rage, and as a means of dramatic instantaneous retributive destruction, lightning is unrivaled.

Lightning is Herman Melville's "God's burning finger," the phenomenon feared by Romans as the wrath of God. In Greek mythology, the Cyclops gave Zeus, king of the gods and the god of sky and weather, the weapon of lightning. Zeus is often depicted brandishing a thunderbolt over his head like a javelin. The Greeks regarded any spot struck by lightning as sacred, often erecting temples at those sites to worship the gods and attempt to appease them.

Similarly, in Hindu mythology, Indra is the god of lightning, and he also used it as his weapon of choice. In Scandinavian mythology, Thor, the thunderer, was the foe of all demons and tossed lightning bolts at his enemies.

In the 21st century, a somewhat more scientific understanding of lightning has evolved, although there continues to remain a blend of natural and supernatural, science and superstition, meteorological science and random coincidence. Lightning-strike survivors often seem less interested in the medical science behind their injuries than in existential questions about life and death, destiny, and divine retribution. Despite leaps in information, many modern storm chasers admit that they still find lightning the most baffling and frightening form of severe weather.

The often hazardous field of lightning research, known as fulminology, has been in existence for more than 250 years. In the 18th century, Benjamin Franklin allegedly concocted two experiments to prove that lightning was naturally occurring electricity. As the story—or myth—goes, Franklin flew a kite in a thunderstorm in 1752, drawing sparks to his hand from a key tied to the kite string. At the first sign of the key receiving an electrical charge from the air, Franklin proved his theory. The other test, involving a lightning rod and a bell tower, resulted in the electrocution of a German scientist in St. Petersburg the following year.

After these experiments, there was little improvement in the theoretical understanding of how lightning was generated for close to 150 years. The impetus for new research came from the field of engineering; as telephone poles and power-transmission lines became widely used, engineers needed to learn more about lightning to protect lines and equipment.

In the 1890s, Nikola Tesla generated artificial lightning by using a large Tesla coil, enabling generations of future scientists to experiment with voltages enormous enough to create lightning. In the 1930s, Basil Schonland made significant contributions to the study of atmospheric electricity in the South African high veld, capturing lightning with fast-film photography and proving that each flash of lightning is actually a complex series of events.

Beginning in the 1960s, the study of lightning took on a new urgency, particularly in the United States. On December 8, 1963, Pan Am Flight 214, a Boeing 707 flying from Baltimore to Philadelphia, was in a holding pattern because of high winds when a lightning strike ignited fuel vapors in the left reserve tank. The wing blew apart, and the plane crashed, killing all 81 people onboard.

Eight years later, on Christmas Eve, 1971, LANSA Flight 508 crashed in a thunderstorm en route from Lima to Pucallpa, Peru, killing all of its six crew members and 85 of its 86 passengers. Lightning had ignited one of the fuel tanks on this aircraft, too, causing it to explode in midair. As the plane disintegrated, a 17-year-old German girl plummeted into the Amazon rain forest two miles below, still strapped to her seat. Despite sustaining a broken collar bone and a concussion, she was able to trek through the dense Amazon jungle for 10 days until she was rescued by local lumbermen.

More significant in terms of funding for lightning research, between the dates of those two doomed plane flights, Apollo 12 was struck by lightning twice during takeoff on its way to the moon. On November 14, 1969, the spacecraft was hit first at 36.5 seconds into its flight by cloud-to-ground lightning, then again 52 seconds in by intracloud lightning. The strike caused the fuel cells in the service module to falsely detect overloads and knocked all three of them offline. The loss of all three fuel cells put Apollo 12 entirely on batteries, and the power-supply problem lit nearly every warning light on the control panel and caused much of the instrumentation to malfunction.

The astronauts were able to execute a fairly obscure switch to a backup power supply and ultimately saved the mission. The launch continued successfully, becoming the second manned flight in the Apollo program to land on the moon. In a lengthy NASA report entitled "Analysis of Apollo 12 Lightning Incident," scientists concluded that "atmospheric electrical hazards must be considered in greater depth for future Apollo flights."

The result was a wave of research, much of it funded by NASA, in which scientists ascertained many of lightning's physical characteristics: speed, temperature, and current. In various tests, lightning was triggered in an effort to increase the safety of aircraft parts, runways, houses, and power lines. Lightning strikes were observed and recorded by various detection systems around the world.

As a result of all of this monitoring, it is known that a flash usually measures anywhere from several hundred yards in mountainous areas where clouds are low to about four miles long in flat terrain where clouds are higher. The most common length is about a mile. The longest bolts start at the front of a squall line and travel horizontally back into the clouds. The longest recorded streak of lightning stretched 118 miles over Dallas, Texas. The stroke channel is only about half an inch in diameter, but it is surrounded by a glowing sheath that can be 10 to 20 feet wide.

A bolt of lightning travels at about 224,000 mph, or 3,700 miles per second, but the visible light from the lightning moves at the speed of light, which is roughly 670 million mph, or 186,000 miles per second. Lightning can burn at up to 54,000 degrees Fahrenheit, about six times hotter than the surface of the sun. Within a few milliseconds, that temperature decreases significantly, dropping to the heat of a normal high-voltage electric arc.

Technically, lightning is an electrostatic discharge accompanied by the emission of visible light and other forms of electro-magnetic radiation. In short, it is an atmospheric discharge of electricity; lightning storms are also commonly referred to as electrical storms. Lightning is caused by the buildup of electric charge in storms—when the charges become too great, the air breaks down and conducts electricity between them.

Lightning strikes both from the sky down to the ground and from the ground up, although the majority of lightning flashes (about five to 10 times as many) actually occur from cloud to cloud. In a typical cloud-to-ground flash, a channel of negative electricity, invisible to the naked eye, descends from the sky. In less time than it takes to blink, this path, known as a stepped leader, zigzags down in several rapid steps or spurts. As it snakes down to the ground, this stepped leader may branch into several paths in a forked pattern. This phase involves a relatively small electric current.

Objects on the ground generally have a positive charge, and opposites attract. As the negatively charged stepped leader nears the ground, a channel of positive charge, called a streamer, reaches up from the object about to be struck (usually something tall, such as a tree, a house, or a telephone pole). When these two paths connect, a much more powerful electrical current, the return stroke, is released, and it zips back up into the sky in about one-millionth of a second.

While lightning is generally perceived as traveling from the clouds to the earth, the vast majority of energy is actually dissipated in the opposite direction with the tremendous speed of the return stroke. The return stroke is the visible, luminous part of the lightning discharge. Each lightning flash contains anywhere from one to 20 return strokes. When the process rapidly repeats itself several times along the same path, the lightning looks as if it is flickering.

During the return stroke, the expansion of the heated air

compressed by the surrounding air produces a supersonic shock wave that decays to an ordinary sound wave. This is heard as thunder. It is not possible to have lightning without thunder, although the thunder is often too far away to be heard.

A spate of lightning research in the last 10 years has led scientists to determine that lightning emits radiation, despite having no obvious physical means to do so, and is also capable of blasting huge quantities of gamma rays, more often associated with collapsing stars.

Despite the recent focus on the science behind lightning, it seems to remains nature's most confounding, and perhaps feared, phenomenon. Not only are atmospheric scientists unclear about exactly how lightning is initiated, but they also do not understand precisely why it is able to promulgate over great distances or even where it will strike.

Recently, the U.S. government has renewed its interest in understanding, if not controlling, the underlying properties of lightning. In 2009, the Defense Advanced Research Projects Agency (DARPA), the research-and-development arm of the Pentagon, has embarked on a project called NIMBUS. In an agency announcement, DARPA stated that "fundamental questions remain unanswered," and "The mechanism of lightning initiation inside thunderstorms is one of the major unsolved mysteries in the atmospheric sciences."

The stated goal of the NIMBUS project is the protection of people and assets, specifically the "more than $1 billion a year in direct damages to property in addition to the loss of lives, disruption of activities (for example, postponement of satellite launches) and their corresponding costs." The initiative hopes to ascertain "optimal strategies to reduce the probability of lightning strikes in a given area in the presence of a thunderstorm" and includes plans to direct where lightning strikes, in part by attempting to trigger flashes using rockets.

Skeptics claim that the project may, in fact, be an attempt by the government to tame lightning for use, as in Greek mythology, as a weapon of war. NIMBUS is certainly not the U.S. government's first foray into lightning research. In the mid-1960s and again in 1993, the military explored the concept of weaponizing ball lightning (an enigmatic phenomenon associated with lightning that manifests as luminous, energetic spheres during storms), but the projects, including one called Magnetically Accelerated Ring to Achieve Ultrahigh Directed Energy and Radiation, or MARAUDER, have been classified.

In the past, the U.S. Defense Department has also funded the possibility of creating a "lightning gun," a weapon that shoots bolts of electricity. As recently as 2009, the U.S. Army signed a multi-million-dollar contract with an Arizona company called Applied Energetics (formerly Ionatron) to develop a lightning weapon that uses ultrashort laser pulses to channel electrostatic discharges. The technology in question involves using a laser beam to create a plasma tunnel through the atmosphere to allow a powerful electric spark discharge—an artificial lightning bolt—to be directed onto a target with, ideally, some level of precision.

One area in which scientists do seem to have gained more knowledge relates to the weather patterns within which lightning is likely to occur. It is generally agreed that the primary ingredient for natural lightning formation is a significant amount of moisture in the lower and middle levels of the atmosphere. The other necessary element is a mechanism to lift the moisture. Thunderstorm clouds, known as cumulonimbus clouds, are formed wherever there is enough upward motion, turbulence, and moisture to reach a temperature below freezing. These conditions most often intersect in the summer. The highest frequency of cloud-to-ground lighting in the United States and the greatest number of lightning deaths occur in Florida,

especially along Lightning Alley, between Tampa Bay and Ti-
tusville, where a large moisture content in the atmosphere
meets high surface temperatures and strong sea breezes.

The western mountains of the United States, however, also
produce strong upward motions that contribute to frequent
cloud-to-ground lightning. Along the mountain slopes in the
Tetons during the summer months, especially late July and August, updrafts are produced almost daily. These wind currents are
strongest in the afternoon, when the ground surface temperatures are the highest and the warm air rises, causing vertical instability among the charges in the clouds. The majority of lightning
storms in the Teton range occur between 3 P.M. and 6 P.M.

These storms don't last long, especially in terms of precipi-
tation. Sometimes the rain falls on and off, but a more typical
pattern within what is known as the monsoon flow is a 15-min-
ute bout of heavy, sometimes even violent, rain. It is extremely
common for lightning to illuminate the afternoon sky in the
Teton range, and as Leo Larson says, "The Grand is not a place
you want to be in a lightning storm." (All of the Jenny Lake
rangers seem to share the gifts of understatement and deadpan
delivery.) Leo still vividly recalls an intense electrical storm on
an icy east route of the Grand in the '80s. He and a couple of
other rangers had to hunker down as best they could, then get
up and over the route as fast as they could to get away from the
lightning. The terrifying feeling of loss of control over the elements in a life-threatening situation has never left him.

Often, the weather can be seen coming, building up in the distance over Idaho as it streams in. Other times, day thundershow-
ers can come on from the west without warning, so fast that
climbers can't see them until they are virtually on top of them.

The morning of July 26, 2003, dawned cool, with temperatures in the high 40s. The weather forecasts and observations
indicated that thunderstorms were likely to develop that after-

noon. The Teton Interagency Dispatch Center issued a morning report stating that sunrise was at 6:05 A.M. and sunset would be at 8:53 P.M. In the weather section, the report predicted, "Partly cloudy with scattered showers and thunderstorms. Highs 65 to 75. Chance of rain 40%."

The heat built as the day progressed on July 26. By late morning, it was 73 degrees at low elevations, and warm air was rising. There were still blue skies at noon, but thunderstorms had moved in over the Tetons during the previous two afternoons.

Lightning fatalities in the United States are less rare than in the past—likely because of the increasing number of golfers, boaters, hikers, and climbers—but still, the probability of someone being struck by lightning is fairly minuscule. The chance of one single bolt dancing down rope and rock on a late-July afternoon in the Tetons to batter six individuals domino-style is, quite simply, infinitesimal.

FOUR

"I need their *names!*"

–

Brandon Torres, Incident Commander

Once the situation was sorted out a bit, it became apparent that the reality was even a little worse than the first dispatch account. There were actually seven people injured, rather than the five originally reported.

Brandon Torres was the ranger on call for the 24-hour SAR (search-and-rescue) coordinator rotation. The rangers used a military Incident Command System, with the four permanent rangers (Renny, Brandon, Dan Burgette, and Scott Guenther) and five seasonals taking turns as coordinator. Each potential coordinating ranger was on call for two rotations every pay period. Aside from overtime, they worked five eight-hour days a week, then took two days off. Someone was on call at all times. The learning curve for the position was generally considered to be about four years.

According to the random rotation schedule, Brandon, at age 31, was automatically the incident commander for the rescue, in charge of overseeing the entire operation. Upon receiving the initial report, he requested that the Dispatch Center perform a Jenny Lake group page and contact the closest contract helicopter to respond.

As he drove to the SAR team's rescue-operations base in Lupine Meadows, seven miles from the Grand, Brandon had the 911 call transferred to his cell phone and spoke to Bob Thomas, the climber at the top of Friction Pitch who had called for help. As Brandon's first priority was preventing further injuries, he initially instructed Bob to make sure that everyone was watching one another and tied into anchors. Bob responded that he was still trying to account for all members of his group on the Motorola radios that many of them had been carrying. Brandon assured Bob that help was on the way but that it would take some time for rescuers to reach them.

At that point, Brandon asked about the victim who had been described on the 911 call as hanging upside-down from a rope. He was concerned about the condition of the rope following both a lightning strike and a fall of unknown distance. He feared that the rope might shred, plunging the man to his death before they even had a chance to try to save him.

Brandon asked Bob point-blank whether he or anyone on-scene had the ability to rappel down to that victim, attach another rope with a different anchor, and then ascend the rope after rappelling. Without hesitation, Bob replied in the negative. Brandon did not ask follow-up questions. He did not know if the issue was that the climbers did not have the ability to tie in another rope, or they lacked the proper equipment, or they were too severely injured from the lightning strike to climb, or they were simply too emotionally exhausted from the entire situation. In any case, Brandon appreciated the honesty, and he was relieved to know that there would be no further injuries from the climbers attempting a maneuver that was too risky for them given the circumstances.

By that point in the conversation, Brandon had arrived at

the rescue cache in Lupine Meadows. He told Bob that he had to hang up so that he could brief the rescue team and get the operation moving. By the time Brandon called him back, less than 10 minutes later, Bob's cell phone was out of batteries.

A little shy of the four years expected to master the incident commander role fully, this was just Brandon's second year as a permanent employee in Grand Teton National Park. Born in western Washington, he had grown up climbing in the Cascades. He first came to Jenny Lake as a seasonal in 2000, then worked in Olympia and Lake Powell before returning to the Tetons as a permanent employee in 2002. Young, brash, and just a bit haughty, Brandon had a logistically oriented bent that was a perfect fit for the organizational challenge of this operation.

In response to the high-level Jenny Lake page, essentially an alert tone, that Brandon had sent out before he even reached the rescue headquarters, the rangers began streaming into the rescue cache. Several of them happened to be close by, hanging out in the adjacent park-assigned cabins that the seasonals lived in all summer.

Veteran Jim Springer, age 48, a tall, mustached, exceptionally relaxed native of Washington, was in his cabin at the time, grateful for the far-off thunder he heard. The sound signaled another afternoon rainstorm that would cool down the valley from the sweltering midday heat. Within seconds of hearing the page, Jim ran down to the rescue cache to check in, then hurried back to his cabin to pack.

Dan Burgette, a steady and grandfatherly ranger just a few days away from his 56th birthday, was nearby in the fire cache in Moose finishing up an 8:00-to-4:30 P.M. shift when the call went out. Dan, who grew up in Indiana, received both his undergraduate and master's degrees in conservation at Purdue. Within two years of receiving his graduate degree, Dan became a Jenny Lake seasonal climbing ranger in 1977. He knew right away that he wanted a permanent ranger position, so he went to a park in Indiana for three years and was then able to transfer back in the fall of 1981 as a permanent member of the staff.

Some of the rangers, seemingly affectionately, referred to Dan as Breakaway Dan as a result of a ride he took in a rescue litter (a foldable supportive cot) at a spring snow rescue training one year. Sled riding had been a recreational activity at snow SAR training for years but was almost exclusively conducted in areas where there was a smooth, flat runout to stop the litter. At the time, Dan was acting as the patient in the sled, and when the instruction wound up, Dan and the ranger hauling him on the sled rope were in steep terrain with a fairly gentle slope below. Dan asked the ranger to release the rope so he could go sledding, and the ranger obliged. As it turned out, the slope smoothed out up to a small rise, beyond which was a sheer vertical slope. Unfortunately for Dan, he wasn't riding in the battered old litter with the rough bottom he thought he was in but in a new litter with a smooth underside. Somewhere in the course of his rapidly accelerating pace, he realized that his momentum would take him over the hill ahead and then off to the valley. He shoved his feet over the sides to slow himself as much as possible, then, when he hit the rise, grabbed a rock sticking out of the snow. Despite bruising an arm with the rock, he was able to save himself (and the sled) by successfully executing a crash landing.

Dan's trip to the rescue headquarters was as streamlined as it gets. As one of the rangers with a law-enforcement commission, he immediately flipped on his overhead lights to breeze through the park entrance station, heading straight for Lupine Meadows. Once he arrived, he called his wife to bring his camera and some cookies up to the rescue cache.

Even when off duty, the rangers tended to remain in fairly close proximity to the rescue headquarters. On their days off or when on a backcountry patrol, they were notorious for lying about their location in relation to the SAR headquarters when responding to a page. Unlike a dynamic that might occur in other jobs, the rangers weren't being deceptive to get *out* of work but, rather, fabricating their whereabouts in order to get *in* on the rescue.

The moment a ranger was paged and asked where he was, he generally turned around and started jogging toward the rescue cache. Instead of revealing his actual location, the ranger began doing math in his head to figure out how quickly he could make it back to Lupine Meadows. If, for example, a ranger was hiking about an hour away from the headquarters, he would calculate the time it would take him to return at a full-on run, then radio in his position as a half-hour away and begin sprinting toward the rescue cache. There were plenty of rescues to go around in a season, but none of the rangers wanted to be left out of any one of them if he could help it. They often deluded themselves that half the reason they stayed as fit as they did was because they didn't want to pass up anything.

In addition to the rangers' physical conditioning, the Jenny Lake ranger training schedule is notoriously grueling. The rangers themselves control the level of safety and come up with tests for pilots. As head of the Jenny Lake rangers, Renny was in charge of training and scheduling both rangers and pilots. Two or three times a year, Renny led scenario-based training. He made it as realistic as possible, starting from the initial call, making himself the patient, requiring the rangers to perform a reconnaissance mission.

For the seasonal rangers in the Jenny Lake subdistrict, most of the training happened during three weeks and three days in May. There was emergency medical training for all rangers, including a three-day basic refresher, and advanced training for two or three wilderness medics. Day one was payroll and review systems day, half of which was spent outdoors, followed by four days of search-and-rescue training in the field. In addition, there were snow training, scenario days, and eight short-haul training protocols run by Renny throughout the summer, including a peer review of the short-haul program from representatives of visiting parks. Five of the climbing rangers also had a mandatory 40-hour law-enforcement refresher course.

Beyond the standard training, Renny also liked to deconstruct every accident, whether he was on the scene or not, in an attempt to learn how to avoid or escape from a similar incident in the future. Each summer week, he gathered his staff to review past rescues, pore over pictures, scrutinize rock angles.

The rangers debated each operation after the fact and obviously analyzed rescue plans before they acted, but in the thick of the action, once the missions unfolded, they had learned to move in sync with very little need for discussion. The only way this worked was for every ranger to complete the individual job he had been assigned while also adapting to the changing situation, seeing needs and filling them, having one another's back in a very extreme sense.

As a consequence of the intensive training program, the rangers were able to evaluate the relative urgency of a call with ease, and it was obvious to all of them right from the start that this rescue was going to be immense. Leo and ranger Craig Holm happened to be inside the rescue cache writing reports when the call came in. Chilled by the audio, Craig referred to it as a show stopper.

Given the location of the accident, nearly at the top of the highest peak in the park, with difficult access, it was bound to be a massive undertaking even if it had involved only one injured climber. In this case, combining the elements of multiple patients and stormy weather, it was a rescue that no one wanted to miss.

Before receiving the dispatch, Brandon had been on the phone with a mother who had lost her 12-year-old son in the park. After years as a rescuer, Brandon had developed a familiarity with the flow and tempo of emergencies, and while he was treating this one with the utmost seriousness, he knew that these situations virtually always resolved themselves within a few minutes. Missing-child cases in the park were often solved as simply as a ranger, with the straightest of faces, asking the parent, "Have you checked the car?" In addition, Brandon had a strong suspicion based on the facts that this child had not strayed far from the family. He was straining to get off the phone to focus his attention on what was happening with the Friction Pitch rescue. He was just about to assign Marty Vidak, 45, a ranger whose eager-to-please attitude and boyish good looks caused him to appear about 10 years younger, to search for the boy. Fortunately, a member of the local fire crew who had been monitoring the frequency offered to handle the situation to free up all possible rangers for the accident on the Grand. (The situation with the lost boy was quickly settled—he had ducked into the woods near String Lake to pee—and mother and son were safely reunited.)

Relieved that he would be able to take part in a rare multi-victim rescue after all, Marty headed straight to the rescue cache. While MCIs (mass casualty incidents) occasionally occur in Grand Teton National Park, they almost always involve a motor-vehicle accident, a boating or rafting accident, or a horse-drawn hayride gone terribly wrong. When MCIs do happen in the mountains, they are inevitably weather-related. The significance of this fact is that in the most complex, resource-draining rescues, the rangers' response is also complicated by weather—wet rock, a continuing lightning storm, and so on.

After confirming that all available rangers were heading in, the first action Brandon took at the rescue cache was to tear outside and look up. The weather appeared to be rapidly deteriorating. The sky was pelting rain, there was a swirling mass of clouds and winds, and the Grand was nearly obscured. "We're screwed," he thought to himself, then muttered other, more colorful obscenities under his breath.

Brandon believed, correctly, that this rescue was hugely weather-contingent, and he knew, also correctly, that under the current weather conditions, there was no way for rangers to be short-hauled to the scene. Running a hand over his face to clear away the raindrops, he headed back into the building to discuss rescue strategies and hand out assignments.

Brandon would spend every minute of the next six hours coordinating air support, medical help, ambulances, and all other outside support necessary for the rescue to succeed. Throughout the night, his voice on the phone (held to his ear with one hand) and the radio (cradled in his other hand) would be calm, steady, and authoritative. Only those in the rescue cache with him that night would glimpse any of the tension he was feeling. His inner anxiety would be released only through his body language—in the midst of juggling those calls, he would be running his hands through his cropped blond hair, rubbing his hands over his chin, raising his eyebrows to the sky, sticking his tongue out in relief.

When the distress call first came in, the vast majority of rescue resources were at the Lupine Meadows rescue cache on the valley floor at 6,700 feet. The priority was to get the rescuers and the gear to at least the Lower Saddle, which has an elevation of 11,600 feet, if not directly to the stranded climbers at 13,000 feet. To save the climbers, the rangers needed to fly.

The conditions at that point, however, were hardly flyable. If the storm cells remained suspended over the Tetons, the rangers would not even be able to land helicopters at the Lower Saddle, much less at Friction Pitch. The Lower Saddle is a broad area formed where the Middle Teton meets the Grand Teton. At several thousand feet above timberline, the area is cold and windswept. The landscape consists of several climbers' campsites protected by stone walls, two Exum guide huts, an out-door toilet on the west side of the ridge, and part of Middle Teton Glacier (the running glacier melt to the left of the trail is the last reliable water source before the summit). The view to the west is into Idaho and the south fork of Cascade Canyon, a popular hiking route with a developed trail, and the southern view is dominated by the Middle Teton. To the north, the trail proceeds up in a northeastern direction to the crest of the wide ridge toward the mass of the Grand Teton.

The rangers maintained a rudimentary helipad on the Lower Saddle, which they could theoretically use as a base to fly rangers to higher elevations. Short-hauling rangers up to the scene on Friction Pitch, however, would require near-perfect flying conditions and, even so, would be incredibly dangerous given the extreme altitude. Still, weather patterns in the Tetons were infamous for changing scary fast, moving in a matter of hours, even minutes, from sunbathing conditions to a wild win-ter storm and back again. Brandon chose to act on the chance that the weather could clear.

In most national parks or recreational areas in the United States, there is no helicopter available to swoop in and rescue victims on a moment's notice. The Grand Teton National Park is unusual in this respect. During the summer of 2003, the park shared an exclusive-use contract for two helicopters with the Bridger-Teton National Forest. The helicopters were based out of Jackson Hole Airport near Lupine Meadows, and each of them came with a five-person helitack crew. The contract ex-isted as a result of the need for helicopters to spot and fight fires across the millions of acres of national forest in the area, and during most days, at least one of the helicopters was away on a fire-suppression job. The two pilots worked on a rotation to de-termine who was "up" for the rangers' use on each day.

It was clear from the beginning that both helicopters were

going to be required for the Friction Pitch rescue, but helicopters and pilots were much less likely than the rangers to be nearby and available. Like the weather, this was an area of the rescue over which the rangers had no control. If one or both of the helicopters were out on other far-flung missions, it could have delayed the rescue for so many hours that executing it before nightfall would have been impossible. As it turned out, on July 26, 2003, both helicopters just happened to be working close to home.

At 3:46, Laurence Perry was shuttling equipment in helicopter 2LM to the East Table fire in Hoback Junction, about 10 miles south of Jackson, when he heard that there was "some big flap up on the mountain." He didn't ask for the specifics of the rescue call until he arrived. The information could be wrong or confusing, and he wanted to wait and hear the details directly from one of the rangers. He responded instantaneously, firing up the helicopter and flying toward Lupine Meadows, but there was so much lightning in the air that flying regulations forced him to land en route.

Laurence waited on the ground in a large open field for, in his opinion, a fairly arbitrary 15 minutes before continuing in the storm to the rescue cache. The sky was still full of electricity when he took off—"big clouds here, lightning over there"—compelling him to rely on "the hairy-eyeball method of weather predicting." He arrived at the rescue cache less than 45 minutes after the initial call for help.

The other helicopter, N604HP, piloted by Rick Harmon, was on a firefighting assignment for the Sublette County Sheriff's Office in the Wind River Range east of the Tetons. That helicopter cleared its operation and responded to Lupine Meadows within two hours. There was also a third helicopter used in the rescue: Air Idaho Rescue, an Agusta A 109-K2 air ambulance based at the Eastern Idaho Regional Medical Center in Idaho Falls, responded to wait on standby. The aircraft had been handling another emergency but arrived within 90 minutes of being called. As the trauma center was a two-hour drive or a 25-minute flight away, Brandon's intent was to cut down on that time by having the air ambulance ready to fly patients directly there if necessary.

Brandon raced through a mental checklist over and over again, anticipating every possible rescue requirement, ordering resources to meet those needs, delegating responsibilities, safely managing the helicopter base. From an outsider's perspective, it likely resembled some sort of manic beehive with people moving about in all directions, but for those on the inside, the preparations were actually quite deliberative. Brandon's plan was to make the Lower Saddle a second staging area for the rescue if at all possible. Ideally, he wanted to use Laurence to insert rangers from the Saddle directly onto Friction Pitch as well as to transfer the injured climbers from Friction Pitch back to the Saddle. Then he intended to use the second helicopter to shuttle the patients down from the Saddle to the main rescue base in Lupine Meadows.

In leading the rescue, Brandon had to evaluate his pile of tools methodically, in this case meaning which rangers were available and what abilities they possessed, and tailor the operation based on that set of variables. He decided that rather than trying to insert a ranger into the scene right away, the first priority was to conduct a fly-by to assess the situation on the mountain and determine what, and who, would be needed for the rescue. He assigned Leo Larson as operations chief for the on-scene matters and Dan Burgette as spotter in the helicopter on the recon flight.

The very instant Laurence landed, the rangers began hot-loading helicopter 2LM. This is an extremely rare maneuver, only used in aircrafts fitted with the specialized ability to keep the rotors running while passengers board the aircraft. Laurence lifted off with Leo and Dan onboard at 4:31, less than three minutes after his arrival in the meadow.

Meanwhile, in the event that short-hauling would be an option following the fly-by, the other rangers began changing into their helicopter clothes. Renny, who had arrived earlier, changed from his shorts and T-shirt into green Nomex pants and a couple of outer layers, including a yellow and black Flamestop fleece pullover. Cotton, worthless in the event of a fire, had long been replaced by Nomex, fire-retardant and fire-resistant clothing required on helicopters to protect the rangers in the event of a crash. The fabric was designed to protect the skin for a short period of time. There were two options for the rangers to wear. The first choice was a two-piece Nomex outfit: a jean-weight pair of olive-drab pants and a yellow button-down shirt (the wardrobe of choice for wildland firefighters). The other was a one-piece Nomex flight suit, in olive or international orange, also worn by the pilots.

The rangers wore Nomex flight gloves and carried Nomex balaclavas to protect their heads and necks. The material didn't keep the rangers especially warm, but most of them stripped off their flight suits after they landed on the mountain and wore regular climbing clothes underneath the Nomex. The underlayer they chose was generally stretchier and easier to move in than the Nomex and also often more wind-resistant and warmer.

After they finished dressing, the rangers began packing up their equipment in anticipation of being flown to the scene: rescue sit-harnesses with extra gear, ropes, belay devices, headlamps, climbing helmets, climbing pants, warm clothes, rescue kits, food and water for one night.

Despite their status as some of the fittest human beings in the country, the rangers did not tend to bring healthy snacks or commercial energy bars on a rescue. For quick sustenance on the mountain, Renny, who despised PowerBars, instead hoarded Caramello and Milky Way bars in his pack. He was not, however, a ready-pack person, so he gathered the combination of snacks and soda he had snatched on his way out the door at home plus junk food he scrounged from the stashes of other rangers. Most of the rangers had a favorite candy bar, and all of them ate various combinations of thrown-together gorp. Veteran George Montopoli, whose first job as a ranger was in 1977, prior to receiving his PhD in statistics, favored pepperoni and jerky for fast calories.

Dan Burgette loved cookies, and over the years of trial and error, he perfected his own cookie recipe that he baked himself and shared with the team. According to Dan, they lasted for years.

Here is Dan's recipe:

LARGE TRAIL COOKIES

1½ cups brown sugar

1 cup white sugar

2 sticks margarine

3 large eggs

2 teaspoons lemon flavoring (or vanilla or maple)

3 teaspoons vanilla

1 cup white flour

2 cups whole wheat flour

½ cup bread flour

1 teaspoon baking soda

1 tablespoon baking powder

½ teaspoon salt

2 cups oats

4 cups any combination of vanilla chips, butterscotch chips, peanut butter chips, chocolate chips, nuts, raisins, M&M's, dates, brittle bits, or Craisins

The only instructions are to mix the ingredients together, then put baseball-sized lumps of dough on an ungreased cookie sheet and bake at 350 degrees for 24 minutes. The recipe yields approximately 18 (large) cookies.

*   *   *

While Laurence was in the air, Brandon and the other rangers in the rescue cache flipped a sign on the door reading "Rescue in Progress" and continued coordinating their options, floating potential routes and strategies, monitoring the weather constantly. They used a white board to map out routes, with Jim Springer taking the lead on this, both because he was talented at it and because Brandon's drawings always tended to turn inadvertently phallic.

Almost every ranger involved in the strategy session (and in the air) had held leadership positions on rescues in the past, and every one of them was qualified to make quick, sound decisions regarding patient care and rescue operations. Laurence, the master of understatement, repetitively used the word "competent" to describe this particular assortment of rangers.

The group dynamic in the rescue cache was fluently efficient, with more listening than talking—everyone threw out his own opinions yet carefully weighed opposing points of view. In coming up with a plan, each ranger had the opportunity to be heard while the others listened intently. The crucial difference from, say, a board meeting was that the whole process spun out in rapid fire.

Wind, altitude, angle of terrain—all of these aspects fed into the enormously complicated decisions they had to calculate as a group. In rescue scenarios, there is frequently an elevated level of what the rangers refer to as objective hazards. In this situation, for example, by putting themselves at the top of the Grand on a summer afternoon with storm cells swirling, there was the very real risk of additional lightning strikes.

On occasion, the rangers themselves have been shocked by ground currents that run through the rock after the mountain is struck. Both Renny and ranger Jack McConnell have been blown off rocks on the Grand by ground current. It's considered an objective danger for them, and one of the reasons they ideally get an early climbing start is so they are off the mountain when things get, as they say, "sparky" (or, more irreverently, "zappy"). The rangers obviously don't choose the timing of their rescues, however, a reality that puts them at risk in weather situations they would otherwise avoid.

In hashing out a plan, the rangers raised and evaluated small details, lifesaving minutiae: it's been warm lately, so watch for rockfall; yesterday there was ice on that pitch. The rangers' divergent backgrounds were all tossed into the analysis of the mission in varying degrees, sort of like a backcountry think tank, culminating in a finely tuned collective mind-set.

In the midst of this, Brandon was also simultaneously anticipating potential needs about five steps ahead, ordering resources—ambulances, for example—that even in the best case wouldn't be used for hours.

While they waited for the feedback from the aerial view of the scene, the rangers were in further cell-phone contact with the climbers trapped on the Grand. The husband of the woman who was directly hit by the lightning had a cell phone in his pack, and Bob Thomas called back on that line. The rangers learned that the climbing party was a group of 13 people from Idaho, an extended family and some work buddies from the IT department of a health-care company in Idaho Falls. They had been ascending the Upper Exum Ridge of the Grand around the 13,000-foot elevation when clouds and wind moved in and rain began to fall, and they had abandoned their summit quest less than 800 feet from the top. Members of the group who had summited the Grand in the past were experienced enough to realize that the fastest way down from that point was actually to climb a bit higher, up and around Friction Pitch.

In North America, climbs are assigned difficulty ratings using the Yosemite Decimal System (YDS) (different countries use different rating systems). The goal is to help climbers identify routes that fall within their skill level or that represent the next level of challenge. Climbs are typically rated based on the hardest move, or the crux, of the route, although modern ratings may also take into consideration the overall length and difficulty of a climb. In addition, climbing guidebooks often add an unrelated star ranking to the YDS rating, to indicate a climb's overall "quality" (meaning how fun or worthwhile the climb is). Although there is an attempt at precision with the YDS rating, climbing standards evolve, and changes in the rock occur over time, so the scale is considered a bit subjective.

The YDS was initially developed by the Sierra Club in the 1930s to classify hikes and climbs for mountaineers in the Sierra Nevada. Before that time, climbs were described only relative to other climbs, and this primitive system was difficult to learn for those who did not yet have experience. The Sierra Club established a numerical system of classification that was easy to learn and seemed practical in its application.

The grading system now divides all hikes and climbs into five classes. The Class 5 portion of the scale is the serious rock-climbing classification. The exact definitions of the classes are somewhat controversial, but in general, Class 1 is categorized by walking on an established trail with a low chance of injury. Class 2 refers to hiking or simple scrambling up a steep incline, with the possibility of occasional use of the hands for balance, with little potential danger encountered. Class 3 refers to scrambling with increased exposure up a steep hillside. A rope can be carried but is usually not required. Falls are not always fatal. Class 4 is simple climbing with increased exposure. A rope is often used. Natural protection can easily be found. Falls may well be fatal. Class 5 is technical free climbing involving rope, belaying, and other protection gear for safety. Unroped falls can result in severe injury or death.

Class 5 was subdivided decimally in the 1950s. The system was developed by members of the rock-climbing section of the Angeles Chapter of the Sierra Club, and it was initially based on 10 climbs of Tahquitz Rock in Idyllwild, California. The climbs ranged from the Trough at 5.0, a relatively modest technical climb, to the Open Book at 5.9, considered at the time the most difficult unaided climb humanly possible.

By the 1960s, however, increased standards and improved equipment meant that Class 5.9 climbs had become only moderately difficulty for some climbers. Rather than reclassify all climbs each time standards improved, it soon became apparent that an open-ended system was needed, and as a result, further decimal classes of 5.10, 5.11, and higher were added.

To add to the confusion, it was later determined that a 5.11 climb was exceptionally harder than a 5.10, and consequently, many climbs of drastically varying difficulty were bunched up at 5.10. To solve this problem, the scale has been further subdivided above the 5.9 mark with suffixes from a to d.

Current grades for climbing routes vary between 5.0 (very easy) to 5.15 (extremely hard). Further designations of plus and minus are sometimes used to create even more exact ratings.

A breakdown of the Class 5 YDS scale is as follows.

5.0 to 5.4: Very easy climbing with good holds.

5.5 to 5.7: Steeper climbing with good holds. Ropes generally required. This is the upper end of climbs considered suitable for beginning climbers.

5.8: Vertical climbing with smaller holds.

5.9: Route may be slightly overhung with smaller holds.

5.10: Far more technically challenging, possibly more overhung with small holds.

5.11: Steep and difficult routes that require exceptional technique and a high level of strength.

5.12: Very difficult, often professional-grade climbs.

5.13 to 5.15: Extremely difficult climbs considered among
   the hardest in the world.

The YDS scale rates the Upper Exum Ridge route up the Grand Teton at 5.5. This route, on the south ridge of the Grand, is the most popular way up the mountain.

The Direct Exum Ridge route, which includes the Lower Exum Ridge route, a difficult 13-pitch exposed route, is considered one of the most classic and enduring climbs in North America. The route has long been split into the Lower and Upper Exum Ridge routes. It is common for climbing parties to bypass the more technically challenging lower section and climb exclusively the upper section.

The first ascent of the Grand via the Exum Ridge route was on July 15, 1931, by Glenn Exum, climbing solo, on a day when his mentor, Paul Petzoldt, was busy guiding a couple up the original Owen-Spalding route. The second ascent of the Exum Ridge route was made by Petzoldt, later the same day. Exum and Petzoldt went on to open Exum Mountain Guides that year. Fifty years later, Exum made a final climb of the Exum Ridge route on the anniversary of his first ascent.

Renny Jackson's guidebook makes the following observation about the route: "There are so many variations available on this ridge that it is possible to make two or three ascents and scarcely touch the same rock twice." Depending on conditions and the strength (and confidence) of the climbing party, the difficulty level of the climb can vary considerably. More experienced climbers can safely climb most of the ridge with very little belaying, while other climbers may want to belay the whole route.

Other climbing guidebooks generally describe the route with some variant of comments that the rock itself is generally considered excellent and that the sweeping views from the top are magnificent. Reviews and descriptions warn that climbing parties should not expect, especially on a Saturday in the middle of the summer, to have this route to themselves. They also note that a problem with the route is that if climbers become too tired to summit or the weather turns bad, there is no easy way to escape.

To reach the Exum Ridge route from the Lupine Meadows trailhead, where the rangers' rescue cache is located, climbers hike the trail up Garnet Canyon to the Lower Saddle. There is a fixed rope in the final section to help with the scramble up to the Saddle.

From the Lower Saddle, climbers follow a path north up a gully, where they pass to the left of a smooth pinnacle known as the Needle, a tower most easily reached via a switchback route that involves crawling under a boulder. Ideally, climbers then pass through a tunnel called the Eye of the Needle, but if they miss the Eye, there are other ways through the maze. From here, the ledge of Wall Street can be seen on the wall above.

Above this point, climbers must traverse right, crossing a broad and relatively easy couloir to the start of Wall Street. The beginning of the Upper Exum Ridge route is marked by the giant ascending ledge of Wall Street leading from the gully to the crest of the south ridge. The Wall Street ledge is a wide, slanted ramp that angles up the west face of the Exum Ridge. It slowly narrows as climbers ascend it until it disappears just before the ridge crest. At the very end, the last 10 feet suddenly become very narrow and extremely open to the elements.

Climbers can fall several hundred feet from this point before hitting anything flat. The step-around is the most exposed, intimidating move on the entire route. To get past this corner, climbers have to execute a wide straddle across a gap with 2,000 feet of air between their legs. All but the most experienced climbers rope up in this section.

After that is the Golden Staircase, the second roped pitch,

which ascends directly up the ridge crest to a steep, knobby face. It has cracks and lots of knobs for holds, so it isn't especially arduous climbing, although it is quite steep. Climbers then follow a horizontal section near the ridge crest, bearing right up and under (often icy) rocks to a chute known as the Wind Tunnel. After proceeding through the Wind Tunnel gully and following the ridge up for several pitches, climbers are then led straight to the base of Friction Pitch.

Just 770 feet short of the peak, Friction Pitch is known as the crux, or most difficult part, of the climb. It consists of 120 feet of unprotected sheer, slick granite that is considerably more slippery when wet. The rock is generally smooth and unbroken, and the few cracks for handholds and footholds are particularly thin. The pitch (meaning any distance climbed carrying a standard rope) is so named because in order to scale it, climbers must depend on the friction of their feet against the mountain.

Once a climber has scaled Friction Pitch, summiting the Grand at that point only entails scrambling for two more pitches. Directly above is the V Pitch, one of the most exposed areas of the route, where climbers have to ascend a southwest-facing dihedral (a vertical right-angled corner on the cliff). At that point, climbers continue following the ridge on the Petzoldt Lie-back Pitch, which can be challenging if, as is the case nearly year-round, it is covered in ice. From there, a small 10-foot tower can be climbed directly via a crack, and another 100 feet above that, the ridge becomes broad and nearly level. Then there is just a scramble to the east of the crest to the summit of the Grand Teton.

Once the climbing party from Idaho made the decision not to summit, they began to retreat from their location by scaling Friction Pitch with the intent to rappel down the V Pitch. The first two rope teams (groups of three and four) climbed the pitch and traversed a rubble-covered ledge system to position themselves, after one long rappel, at the start of the Owen-Spalding route down the mountain.

The third three-person rope team was in the process of climbing Friction Pitch, and the fourth three-person team was waiting its turn on the ridge below, when, at about 3:35, a single, colossal lightning bolt struck the Grand.

The strike hit a 25-year-old female member of the climbing party directly, causing her immediately to go into cardiac arrest. The same bolt then fingered out, traveling down the rope and the ridge, pounding through the bodies and convulsing the muscles of the other five climbers on and below Friction Pitch.

Within what seemed a freakishly short time after flying Leo and Dan past the scene on Friction Pitch, Laurence was back with the digital photos Leo had snapped at the scene. On his way down the Grand, Laurence had landed at the Lower Saddle to let the rangers off, then took to the air again to ferry the pictures down to the rescue cache. Brandon displayed the photos on a computer screen for the rangers to view. This was an invaluable extension of the initial size-up by Leo and Dan. Rescuers not yet on-scene could actually see for themselves what they were up against and gain a more complete understanding of the needs at the site.

The visual of the Folded Man dangling in the middle of the rock face, his body bowed grotesquely backward to an extreme angle, sharply illustrated the desperation of his situation to every ranger scrutinizing the photos. He was hanging from his harness on the vertical face on the right side of the ridge just above the crux. It looked as if his back was broken. The rangers were uneasy about how extensively his ability to breathe must have been compromised. The climber obviously had to be critically hurt to remain in that pose without trying to do something to right himself. The photographic evidence of his existence galvanized the priority of getting to this man, of attempting to save him before they ran out of time.

The location of the three climbers who had disappeared off a ledge below Friction Pitch and hadn't been heard from since remained uncertain. Bob, the climber who made the cell-phone call for help, thought that the three men had fallen down to the area of the Golden Staircase, just above Wall Street. One of the missing men was Bob's son.

The rangers were not yet able to pinpoint the exact locations of all 13 climbers. It still wasn't completely clear from the recon flight where the three climbers who fell off the bottom of Friction Pitch had ended up. The rangers had spied three climbers above the Golden Staircase at the base of the Jern Crack, but the Idaho group was a large climbing party, the numbers seemed confusing, and it was possible that other climbers in their contingent had fallen and landed someplace else entirely. Either way, these three climbers were in dire need of rescuing.

The Jern Crack is a slit that goes up a vertical face of rock, named after Ken Jern, an Exum guide, after he fell from it. It ranges from just wide enough for a climber to grasp with fingertips to expansive enough to jam in a foot. It is considered a relatively easy section of the route because climbers can generally find some sort of a handhold or foothold there. The Jern Crack is a nasty place to fall, as the climber either lands on pointy rocks that stop his descent, or he doesn't and bounces down another 70 feet until reaching a shelf. Jern had slipped on verglas (a thin coating of ice that is very difficult to see) and tumbled down to the pitch below him, breaking several ribs.

From the air, it had appeared that the three climbers near the Jern Crack—presumably the three missing climbers—were still tied together, about 100 feet below their original location. Two of them were stacked in a split in the rock face, and the third had landed on a tiny ledge. Inexplicably, in the process of hurtling off the Grand Teton to their deaths, their ropes appeared to have somehow wrapped around rock horns and bunched up in cracks, snagging them on the side of the mountain. They were quite definitively trapped where they had landed, tenuously clinging to the side of the mountain with no way to move.

As helpful as the photos were, the next step was to get a ranger on-scene to evaluate the situation firsthand. The storm cells seemed to have shifted away from the Grand a bit, enough that Brandon determined that they should attempt a short-haul insertion. The rangers began rigging helicopter 2LM for short-haul operations, putting their rigging-for-rescue training to work, popping the doors off the Bell and hooking a 100-foot short-haul rope to its belly.

Given the 200-foot distance separating the top of Friction Pitch and the area where the three fallen climbers had landed, Brandon decided to split the rescue into two distinct sites: an upper scene (which included the Folded Man) and a lower scene. He assigned Jim Springer to be in charge of the lower scene.

The rangers rolled with this shift in plans, quickly sifting through their gear and dividing it into separate packs for the two scenes. The rescue cache was stocked with a bunch of pre-packaged rescue kits, known as blitz kits, that enabled the rangers efficiently to grab whatever combinations of specialized bags they needed. There were several climbing-gear kits that included supplies to build anchors, plus EMS kits containing oxygen and airway-maintenance equipment. Another series of bags held a set of specific tools needed to raise and lower litters.

Knowing from experience that the victims would be wet from the rain and already hypothermic, several of the rangers also packed warm clothes and sleeping bags to transport to them. With the uncertain weather conditions, the late hour of the day, the large number of patients, and the extreme elevation involved in the rescue, it seemed apparent that emergency

medical care and rescue operations would extend into the
night, with evacuations continuing the following morning. The
rangers conveyed this information to Bob on the cell phone, explaining that the convergence of these factors might force the
climbers to spend the night on the mountain.

As Brandon scrawled on a scratch pad, reworking the logistics, crossing things out, he was becoming increasingly frustrated
trying to keep the various bits of information straight. In sorting
out where everyone was, he knew that if the climbers who fell
off the mountain out of sight were not the three men stuck in the
area of the Jern Crack, the mission would entail a search in addition to a rescue. Plus, the innovative decision to treat the mission
as two separate rescue scenes added an extra layer of complexity.
The rangers' use of labels such as "the three patients at the lower
scene" or "Victims 1 and 2" to describe various groupings of the
Idaho climbers was not helping matters. In response to nearly
overwhelming confusion about who was where in the multiple
sites, Brandon finally expressed his mounting tension in a terse
demand for the victims' actual names.

Names were quickly provided. The 25-year-old mother of
two at the top of Friction Pitch next to her husband, the woman
who was struck by a lightning bolt that entered the top of her
head and exited her right thigh, was Erica Summers. Erica took
the brunt of the strike for her husband, Clint, age 27, who was
sitting to her right on the ledge. Voltage smashed into Clint's
left leg and knocked him unconscious, then snaked down his
belay rope to strike four other members of the climbing party:
Rod, Jake, Justin, and Reagan.

The name of the Folded Man was Rodrigo Liberal. Clint
had been belaying Rod up Friction Pitch when the shock
knocked Clint unconscious. Clint dropped the rope, and Rod
was blasted off the granite. He had been in free fall for dozens
of feet before his rope snapped taut, discarding his twisted body

at the end of his belay line, where he swung like a pendulum, motionless in his harness.

Below Rod, the three climbers waiting their turn to ascend Friction Pitch were Jake, Justin, and Reagan. It would soon become clear to the rangers that they were, in fact, the three men who had fallen out of sight below Friction Pitch, cartwheeling 100 feet down the cliff until their ropes snarled in the rocks. There were later, somewhat jumbled cell-phone reports from Bob about the potential severity of their injuries—one or more of them shocked into unconsciousness, one initially blinded and made deaf by the electrical charge with his limbs temporarily paralyzed, another bleeding severely from his leg.

As the rangers readied themselves for short-haul insertions, there was a delicate balance at play to determine the exact number of them, and which ones, who could be short-hauled given the extreme altitude of the accident. In order for the helicopter to achieve momentum and lift in the storm, there was a strict weight limit. A load manifest had to be completed at takeoff time that took into account the weight of the aircraft, fuel and oil (which could be 400 pounds by itself, although Laurence never filled it up completely), cargo and baggage, passengers and crew members and, after factoring in a variety of mission-specific calculations, computed the maximum allowable weight.

In determining the passenger manifest, it was an obvious principle that 400 to 500 pounds of people would eat up the maximum amount of fuel. Laurence had to fill out a form specifying the weight of the passengers and the weight of the fuel at a particular altitude, and he had an abundance of charts, books, and graphs to aid him in balancing precise weight and altitude factors. After calculating the amount of weight at the specific altitude of a rescue, Laurence could ascertain the amount of time his helicopter would be cleared to fly. The calculations never considered absolute maximum performance;

200 pounds was always subtracted as a built-in fail-safe. Depending on passenger weight, a helicopter can fly for two and a half hours if filled with gas, but Laurence always flew with partial loads of gas to conserve weight (in this situation, he settled on 275 pounds of fuel). Given the weight of the passengers and the extensive amount of gear in this situation, Laurence was looking at approximately 30 to 40 minutes of flying time before he would need to refuel.

On top of these computations, Laurence also used mathematical formulas and performance charts to establish load capacity at 13,000 feet and 83 degrees. The rule of thumb to consider in these situations is high, hot, and heavy. Temperature was not a consideration in this circumstance, but the high was just about as high as possible in the Teton range. The pressure at that extreme altitude is a factor, and the lower the temperature, the thinner the air, so the higher a pilot flies, the less he can lift. Laurence also had to take into account the amount of fuel that would be burned off during the flight, allowing the helicopter to take on more cargo weight—here, injured parties.

The bottom line was that Laurence would give Brandon a number that would allow him to choose exactly which rangers could be short-hauled and in what order. Even accounting for a cushion, the calculations were sensitive enough to make the individual body weight of every ranger relevant. To aid in the decision, each ranger in the rescue cache began slapping up his flight weight—body weight plus gear—onto the white board.

FIVE

"For a ranger to be really needed, a visitor has
to have a bad day."

—

Leo Larson, Jenny Lake ranger

As soon as the short-haul rope was rigged, Leo Larson clipped himself into the 100-foot line attached to 2LM and began the 1,400-foot journey from the lee side of the Lower Saddle to the top of Friction Pitch. Clouds continued to blow in and cover the ridge, but enough of them seemed to be gusting by to create visibility at the top of the peak. Laurence Perry lifted off at 5:21, about an hour and a half after the lightning strike, and headed for the highest summit in Grand Teton National Park.

In northwestern Wyoming, only 10 miles south of Yellowstone National Park, Grand Teton National Park receives more than 3.5 million visitors a year. The park consists of approximately 310,000 acres, including the Teton range, about 40 miles long by seven to nine miles wide, as well as most of the northern sections of the valley known as Jackson Hole (technically, the name Jackson Hole refers to the valley, but it is often used interchangeably with Jackson to refer to the town). The Tetons, which began forming between 6 million and 9 million years ago from a fault block that rose up from the ground as a result of massive earthquakes, are the youngest mountain range in the Rocky Mountains.

The town of Jackson at the foot of the mountains was bustling in the fur trade days of the early 1800s, then remained mostly unpopulated until the 20th century, when Indians used it as a summer camping ground. In the 1860s, an Englishman named Richard Leigh settled in the region with his Shoshone wife, Jenny, where he made his living trapping and guiding. He brought Jenny along when he led the Hayden Geological Surveys of 1871 and 1872. F. V. Hayden explored Yellowstone (established as the country's first national park in 1872), while a smaller group under James Stevenson conducted a scientific exploration of the Teton area and took the first photographs of the mountain range. The expedition is credited with naming several of the mountains and lakes in the region, including Jenny Lake after Leigh's wife.

Jenny Lake, approximately 260 feet deep at its deepest point, is in the heart of Grand Teton National Park, nestled at the base of Teewinot Mountain. Mount Moran is a bit more than six miles north of the lake, and Buck Mountain is more than six miles to the south. The lake, along with the five main canyons in the park—Moran, Leigh, Cascade, Avalanche, and Death—was formed by melting glaciers about 60,000 years ago. Jenny Lake is the starting point for some of the most popular hikes in the park, including Inspiration Point and Hidden Falls, and it is ringed by an incredibly scenic trail, almost seven miles long, that winds around the entire lake. A shuttle boat travels across the lake to the Cascade Canyon trailhead.

South of Jenny Lake, between the base of Teewinot Mountain and Cottonwood Creek, is a large open field known as Lupine Meadows, named for the tall, spiky, purple flowers that proliferate in the area every summer. The log cabins where the seasonal Jenny Lake rangers live in the summer are in a grove of trees between the creek and the meadow.

The park is obviously named after the Grand Teton, the tallest mountain in the range and the centerpiece of the Teton skyline. Early on, the Grand and its neighboring Middle and South Tetons were referred to as "Hoary Headed Fathers" by Shoshone tribal members. By 1931, the name Grand Teton Peak was used so frequently that it was recognized by the USGS Board on Geographic Names, and another usage shift led the board to shorten the name on maps to Grand Teton in 1970.

The origin of the current name is somewhat divisive. Some historians claim that the mountain received its designation from the Teton Sioux tribe, but the most common explanation is that the peak is named after a part of the female anatomy, a translation of "large teat" in French, coined by either French-Canadian or Iroquois adventurers. Many early explorers failed to see a resemblance, but the moniker is more descriptive from the Idaho side, where the mountains appear more gently rounded. Viewed from Wyoming, the distinctive way that the Grand juts straight up to the sky from a relatively flat valley makes it appear very much like the prototypical upturned V that schoolchildren produce when drawing a mountain.

There is a bit of controversy surrounding the first person to summit the iconic Grand. James Stevenson and Nathaniel Langford claim to have reached the top on July 29, 1872, but were later essentially discredited when it appeared that their description and sketches matched the summit of the Enclosure, a side peak of the Grand Teton. It is generally held that the first ascent was in 1898 by William Owen, Franklin Spalding, Frank Petersen, and John Shive. In the next 26 years, the Grand was summited on only eight more occasions, including four times by Paul Petzoldt in 1924.

Well into the 1940s, only 325 people had reached the top of the Grand. The mountains in the Teton range have since become some of the most visited in the world. The Grand alone receives approximately 4,000 summit attempts every year, with about 50 percent of the climbers making it to the top.

Approximately half of the climbers attempting to summit the Grand use a guide. The top guiding companies in Jackson use a ratio of three clients to every guide. Two to three guides will escort a group of up to seven people; climbing parties larger than that are generally considered unwieldy. The climbing guides and their clients all camp close together in huts the night before their summit bid. The guides wake their charges up early, meaning the middle of the night, and leave the Lower Saddle by 4:00 in the morning. Under way long before first light, the guides assure that a high percentage of clients summit by 9:00 or 9:30 A.M.

About half of the people climbing the Grand—unfortunately, not necessarily the same group as the guided half—are beginning climbers. Longtime climbers have a term for inexperienced climbers whose primary motivation in climbing the Grand is to be able to say that they have climbed the Grand: trophy hunters going on safari.

Despite their profound familiarity with all of the Teton nooks and crannies, until relatively recently, it may have taken the rangers days to rescue even one person (trophy hunter or otherwise) injured on the Grand or elsewhere in the mountain range. Just a little more than two decades before the Friction Pitch accident, when Leo Larson broke his femur in the Black Ice Couloir, it took 36 hours after he radioed for help for him to reach the hospital.

In the summer of 1979, during his second year as a Jenny Lake ranger, Leo and two other climbing rangers were on an extended mountain patrol on the backside of the Grand. The Black Ice Couloir is a remote, spooky place that melts out into a pile of rubble. The rangers began the preparations for their climb at 3:00 A.M., but they hadn't gotten far when they reached a base of ice at around 7:00 A.M. After a short discussion about whether they needed to rope up, they opted for the cautious approach.

Leo, age 23 at the time, and likely also the other rangers, wouldn't have lived through the climb if they had made the other choice. At that early stage of his climbing career, Leo believed that if he ever got into trouble in the mountains, he would be able to wiggle out of it on his own. By turning that assumption inside out, the events of that morning forever changed him, humbled him.

Leo heard the rocks plummeting down the cliff before he felt them pound his body. The rangers were just beginning their ascent of the couloir (a steep, narrow mountain gully usually filled with snow and ice) when a truckload of boulders poured down from above. At that point, Leo's left foot, along with a crampon (a metal framework with spikes attached to the bottoms of boots to increase safety on snow and ice), happened to be awkwardly pointed in the wrong direction as he climbed. He was caught on a 15-foot-wide gully of ice with no room to wander. He tried his best to bury himself into the ice as debris crashed around him. In the end, the rocks smashed Leo's femur, as well as the patella of one of the other rangers, leaving them stranded in one of the most isolated sections of the Teton range.

Tom Kimbrough, another longtime Jenny Lake climbing ranger, was running the Grand that day, valley floor to valley floor, and he knew that Leo and the other rangers were climbing the couloir. While Leo was hanging from his rope, his leg shattered, he heard Tom, out of sight and far away on the other side of the ridge, chanting, "Leo, Leo." Having no idea that Leo and the other rangers were hurt, Tom just meant to call out a greeting. In his pain and delirium, Leo thought the voice was the Lord calling his name and sought confirmation by asking one of his climbing partners if he had heard it.

The rangers were unable to communicate with Tom, but Leo had a radio with him since he was on duty. His nearly instantaneous ability to communicate his location definitively ended up saving his life. In response to his call for help, fellow rangers Renny, George Montopoli, and six others were flown to the Saddle. They traversed around the mountain on foot to reach Leo. He was lying on a ledge, still roped up, when they arrived.

This was before the short-haul era, but the rangers were able to locate a military CH-47 Chinook helicopter with a winch system to pluck their colleague off the mountain. The rangers managed to lower Leo several hundred feet down Valhalla Canyon to a ledge at the base of the Enclosure buttress before nightfall, but to their disbelief, the military pilot was unable—or, more precisely, unwilling—to extract him. The rangers knew that there was enough clearance for a landing, but it was getting dusky enough that someone was lighting off flares, and the pilot had never seen a high alpine cirque like that before. As soon as he came up Cascade Canyon into Valhalla and saw their location, he did an abrupt 180-degree turn in the air. Intimidated by the enormous rock walls surrounding him, he refused even to attempt a landing.

The rangers spent the night keeping Leo alive, although most of them later admitted that they were surprised that he was still breathing in the morning. He had almost bled out in the night, losing more than two liters of blood from his leg. The rescuers spent the day executing another series of lowerings, descending nearly 1,000 feet of dense and hazardous alpine terrain with Leo in a litter until they finally reached a promontory ledge that the pilot deemed safe enough for pickup.

Leo was hoisted off the mountain that afternoon and flown

to Jackson, home of some of the world's best orthopedic surgeons, thanks to lots of practice from all of the skiing and climbing accidents in the area. His systems were shutting down by that point, his body crashing. While inserting a rod into his femur and generally putting him back together again, the doctors told him that had he remained on the mountain, he would have survived only a couple of hours more at most.

Leo's girlfriend Helen was at his bedside at the hospital. They had met while he was a student at Humboldt State and she was an instructor there teaching in a technical writing program. He was introduced to her by his roommate, who assured Leo that although she was not a climber, she was at least outdoorsy, a fact borne out by the pile of *Outside* and *Backpacker* magazines that Leo saw stacked up at her place.

It was while Helen was emptying Leo's pee jars and brushing his hair in the hospital that she declared that the level of caretaking had reached a point where they might as well get married. Leo's accident happened in August; they were married in December of that year.

Within the realm of climbing, Leo had witnessed tragedy, including watching a friend die in front of him. Intellectually, he knew that everything might be going along just fine and that the mountains could then take someone in a heartbeat. Even so, Leo's own accident was life-altering for him.

He had imagined himself invincible, but this crisis forced him both to shift that perspective and to realize that he was responsible for putting himself in danger's way. Most climbers assign a fairly high percentage of climbing ability to nonphysical aspects; Leo's opinion is that the pursuit is 95 percent mental.

The stakes are infinitely high if a climber lacks confidence in himself and is out on the mountain without the right mindset. When Leo first returned to Jenny Lake, he underwent plenty of physical rehabilitation, but he continued to endure emotional trauma that often prevented him from feeling that he was present. It took him most of the next season to get back into shape, physically and psychologically. For most of that time, when he would hear rockfall—or jets, which sound like rockfall—he would run for cover. Even a decade later, while Leo was helping to chip a dead climber out of the frozen snow in the Black Ice Couloir, he suffered a flashback when someone yelled, "Rock!"

Growing up in Hesperia in the upper Mojave Desert, Leo had long identified with the outdoors and mountaineering, and he had quickly found that alpine climbing took him to the places he wanted to go. He began climbing in a gym, then quickly transitioned to climbing in Joshua Tree in Southern California, belaying off the bumper of his car. That type of controlled environment, where he didn't necessarily have to commit to the route, actually allowed him to gain more experience. He got out on the mountains even in unsettled weather, knowing that if rain or wind moved in, he could simply rappel one or two pitches and safely return to his car.

While in college, Leo applied for a summer job with the National Park System, filling out a blanket application that did not specify a particular type of employment. In the summer of 1977, at age 19, Leo was hired to work on a trail crew, and by the end of the season, he was offered a job climbing the following summer. Initially, he saw the opportunity as a way to make his college friends jealous by meshing a hobby he was crazy about with his need for summer employment.

Leo graduated from college with a degree in resource management and interpretation and went on to get a master's degree in environmental education, neither of which, he freely admits, was essential to his climbing-ranger career. He did teach a rescue class at Humboldt, however, with practical instruction on issues such as raising systems and how to construct a litter with rope.

Despite consistently maintaining the belief that the seasonal ranger position is designed for the stage in life when a person is working summers while in college, Leo nonetheless ended up working as a seasonal Jenny Lake climbing ranger for decades.

While climbing had been of crucial importance to Leo in his early 20s, it became less so after his accident. Although he no longer necessarily possessed the same fervent climbing drive as some of the other Jenny Lakers, he did regain his self-motivation, his belief in himself. He thrived on high-risk missions when called upon to do rescue work, but he also believed that it was his duty to become a well-rounded ranger. To that end, he revisited his educational pursuits, focusing on resource work such as mapping out trails, monitoring erosion patterns, and exploring all of the lakes and canyons in the backcountry.

Leo managed to parlay this interest into outside employment by starting (with his wife, Helen) Earthwalk Press, a printing company that produces mostly topographical maps. The epicenter of the business was Jackson, where Leo and Helen crammed a 15-by-25-foot locker full of publications. The company was seasonally cyclical, with projects in the winter, sales in summer months, marketing and shipping in the shoulder seasons.

Despite the success of his nonranger job, Leo's position at Jenny Lake was paramount, and he never failed to approach it by embracing his own personal perspective. Having faced rescue firsthand as a patient, he held a deeper understanding of the experience as well as a profound appreciation of lifesaving heroics. He was fully aware that every other national park was envious of the rescue program at Jenny Lake, and he firmly believed that he would not be alive if his accident had occurred elsewhere.

Since the time of Leo's accident, the search-and-rescue principles of locate, access, stabilize, and transport have evolved rapidly. If Leo's calamity in the Black Ice Couloir had happened in 2003, the rescue would have taken a couple of hours instead of two days. Less than a quarter-century after Leo's accident, a dedicated helicopter was more or less at the Jenny Lake rangers' beck and call, flown by an expert pilot familiar with mountain terrain and altitude. By employing advances in technology, chief among them cell phones and helicopters, the Jenny Lake climbing rangers have seriously revolutionized and refined mountain rescue.

There are other tales of Teton rescues, ones less close to home than several rangers saving one of their own in the Black Ice Couloir. Three in particular, all on the North Face of the Grand, all of which resulted in the rangers receiving Department of Interior Valor Awards for their bravery, demonstrate just how far mountain rescues have progressed.

The North Face of the Grand has long been considered a huge and punishing climb, with a 2,500-foot icy glacier, many technical sections, snowy ledges, and a hazardous route at the top. The face is easily recognizable to climbers as the logo of the American Alpine Club. Dick Emerson, one of the original Jenny Lake rangers, led the first pendulum pitch of the Direct North Face in 1953. In those days, the climb, viewed as both mysterious and devastating, was a true test of mountaineering skills, one only attempted by bold and experienced climbers. The early rangers knew that an elaborate rescue on the inaccessible face was inevitable, as bad weather or even a minor injury on that route would likely be catastrophic.

The first climbing disaster on the North Face occurred in 1967, about two-thirds of the way up, when a climber being belayed by his girlfriend was struck by rockfall that crushed his leg. Although both climbers were technically skilled, they were nonetheless trapped in unfamiliar and remote terrain with no easy way off.

The reporting of the accident alone took close to half a day, from the afternoon when it happened until after 1:00 A.M., when other climbers who had heard the couple's screams for help alerted the rangers. As it turned out, that delay paled in comparison with the incredibly time-consuming ordeal of extricating the wounded climber.

In the 1967 operation, the rangers were ferried to the Lower Saddle, then climbed up the back side, carrying all of their rescue equipment on their backs. Seven rangers were involved in the rescue, a dream team of 1960s climbing rangers. Ted Wilson, Ralph Tingey, Rick Reese, Pete Sinclair, and Mike Ermath traversed the entire mountain to reach the scene, meeting up with Leigh Ortenburger and Bob Irvine, who had ascended from the south side. All seven of them had climbed the North Face previously, and Ortenburger in particular (author, with Renny Jackson, of *A Climber's Guide to the Teton Range*) had a meticulous knowledge of the topography.

The exhausted female climber was roped up and brought off the mountain with the assistance of four rangers the day after the accident, but the rescuers knew that an attempt to carry the injured male climber, with his smashed, bleeding leg, on one of their backs would kill him or all of them. They provided basic medical care—an inflatable splint—for the climber's protruding broken bone and radioed for morphine, a litter, more ropes, and a 325-foot steel cable with a lowering drum that they could anchor to the mountain.

Pain management consisted of a ranger flying overhead in a helicopter the next morning, nearly two days after the accident, to toss a packet of morphine down to the scene. The victim's location did not allow the rangers to hoist him up the mountain, so instead, they had to lower his litter laboriously 1,600 feet straight down, an inch at a time, a perilous undertaking that involved repeatedly ducking rock showers as they worked. Several rangers ended up spending two nights, with little food or rest, tied to various points on the cliff with the injured climber. Ultimately, the climber was saved, but between the delayed notification and the lengthy rescue efforts, it took four days for him to travel from accident to hospital.

Rescue techniques had advanced by the time of a second significant rescue on the North Face during a late-August storm in 1980, when excessive snowfall had caused the face to ice up. The rangers initially received a report of an overdue climbing party and headed up to investigate. At the first ledge, the rangers were able to make voice contact and determined that some members of the climbing party had retreated, but two of them had continued their ascent.

At that time, there was no exclusive-use contract with a helicopter, so the rangers were forced to call on the nearest helicopter service for help. They were stuck with whatever pilot was available, without having worked with him, without knowing if he even had any mountain experience. The helicopter that was sent to them was an Alouette, a light-utility aircraft most commonly used in military operations overseas.

The rangers realized the level of danger they were asking the pilot to accept by carrying three of them with gear into the snowstorm. The pilot hovered near the sheer face, bailing once but then returning, gathering the courage needed to hold the helicopter steady enough to allow the rangers to step out onto the mountain. Once on-scene, the rangers spent the rest of the night on the face, tucked into a cave, to wait out the squall. The next morning, they decided on a place to lower the patient for aerial pickup. The helicopter used a painstaking winch system to extract the climber, which involved spinning him in midair over treacherous terrain for several agonizing minutes. Still, the rangers completed the actual extraction process of the rescue, an endeavor that likely would have taken several days in the past, in less than six hours.

A third classic operation shows the extent to which mountain rescues had advanced by the turn of the century. In 2002, rangers were inserted on the North Face to respond to an unconscious climber who had been hit by a rock and suffered a head injury. They had received a cell-phone call for help from his partner, so they were aware of the accident almost immediately. At 16 years into the short-haul program, the rangers had both a contract with a helicopter company and an established relationship with a pilot. The pilot happened to be Laurence Perry, a man whom the rangers had trained and worked with extensively and trusted implicitly. The insertion was especially tricky given the continual amount of rockfall, and it required an immense amount of cooperation between rangers and pilot, but in the end, an event that was nothing short of dazzling came off as almost routine. Laurence found a landing spot on Teton Glacier, and the short-haul was completed quickly and cleanly.

Before the use of cell phones, if a climber was injured in the mountains, the only way for his or her partner to summon help was by yelling (an option with a low probability of success) or by climbing or running back down the slope (often quite a protracted process). It usually took hours for the rangers to hear about an accident.

Initially, only a few climbers brought cell phones into the backcountry, as service wasn't reliable and early cell phones were heavy. The first phone call from a mountain in the Tetons was placed in the summer of 1994 to report a fall on the Exum Ridge of the Grand. Within five years or so of that incident, climbers began carrying cell phones fairly regularly.

From the rangers' perspective, the downside of a proliferation of cell phones on the mountain is that they can create a false sense of security. The concern is that climbers may rely less on basic mountaineering skills and judgment if they have a cell phone with them as backup. Most rangers will admit that the widespread use of cell phones cuts both ways, and they sometimes wish that certain climbers and hikers didn't have the means to ask the rangers nonurgent questions at 3:00 A.M. Still, it is clear that cell phones in the backcountry have become a major lifesaving tool.

In the past, by the time rangers arrived at an accident scene, the injured person had usually either already died or was unlikely to do so. That dynamic has been nearly obliterated with the combination of cell phones and helicopters. Once rangers began to reach victims while medical aid was still critical, it was much more possible for patients to die on them after their arrival on-scene—or, to look at it another way, the rangers had a much greater chance to actually save lives.

As a result of the increased need for emergency medical training, every climbing ranger began to achieve the equivalent of first-responder status, enabling all of them to provide basic medical care in the backcountry. In addition, some of the Jenny Lake rangers became advance-life responders, meaning that they could set up IVs, administer medication, and provide oxygen to patients.

As comprehensive as it was, the advanced medical training did not envision a scenario in which a ranger would be forced to dispense medical care while suspended from the end of a rope, and therefore, the classes did not offer anything in the way of practical guidance or instruction in how to handle such a scenario. Without classroom preparation or in-field experience to fall back on, on July 26, 2003, the rangers simply had to improvise on the fly.

SIX

"I like the pilot to know that I'm Jane's dad."

—

Renny Jackson, head Jenny Lake ranger

As Laurence Perry ascended with Leo swaying underneath, the wind began to reach a howling sort of crescendo. Between the swirling current and the necessity of flying in tight proximity to the mountain face, Laurence was concerned about a sudden massive updraft. The problem with wind, from a helicopter pilot's perspective, was that a pilot couldn't react to it until he was actually getting hammered by it. Laurence didn't want to deposit Leo on the landing site and have him halfway unclipped only to smash him into the side of the mountain.

Even more significant weather-wise, a cloud seemed to be forming on the western edge of the mountain and wrapping its way over the Exum Ridge, posing a potential threat to Laurence's visibility.

For an injured victim in Grand Teton National Park, there can be no sound more visceral than that of rotor blades slicing the air. The first time a helicopter was used in a Tetons rescue was in 1960, for the body recovery of the only ranger fatality in the history of the park. Helicopters were first operated in mountain rescues in the 1960s, initially just as reconnaissance missions—locating victims and helping rangers asses the extent of their injuries—then, several years later, actually landing at sites on the mountain and picking up injured climbers.

Still, in the first decade or so that mountain operations used helicopters, rangers continued to have to use valuable rescue hours climbing or hiking to accident scenes, severely cutting into the victims' chances of survival. In order to reach someone on the Exum Ridge, for example, nearly a dozen rangers would first spend time climbing to the victim, then take additional hours to lower the patient to a site where a helicopter could safely land. In addition, for decades, Grand Teton National Park did not have a full-time helicopter dedicated to rescues, and the rangers often had to scramble around to borrow an aircraft from local scenic-tour operators.

In time, more powerful helicopters, summoned from Air Force bases in neighboring states, as well as techniques copied from the military and the logging industry, led to long-line lifting and load dropping and rescuers rappelling from the open doors of the helicopters. Beginning in the mid-1970s, in situations where there was no safe place to land a helicopter near an accident site, pilots began inserting rangers (and their gear, including litters) and extracting patients directly into and out of a scene. Initially, the three most commonly used techniques—hoist operations, fast-rope insertion, and heli-rappel—dramatically altered rescue missions in the Tetons.

The most recognizable method is a hoist operation, as depicted in the movie *The Perfect Storm*, when passengers jumped off a sailboat, climbed into a rescue basket, and were raised into a helicopter. In 1983, Jenny Lake rangers summoned a huge Air

Force Chinook chopper to rescue an injured Exum guide who had fallen more than 80 feet on the Jensen Ridge route on Symmetry Spire. Rangers lowered a cable to him from the helicopter and winched him up into the aircraft, saving his legs and likely his life.

The fast-rope insertion technique was shown in the movie *Black Hawk Down*, when the rescuers exited the helicopter by sliding down a thick braided rope that almost looks like a pole, using their hands and legs to slow their descent. Fast-roping is primarily used by the military and law-enforcement tactical teams, although some civilian rescue crews use the procedure for rescuer insertion and then a hoist operation or short-haul to extract patients and rescuers.

In heli-rappel, used mostly in wildland firefighting and law enforcement, rescuers employ a friction device to rappel down a rope anchored inside a helicopter. The major disadvantage is that, like fast-rope, it is an insertion-only technique. Even when rangers reach accident victims quickly with these procedures, it can still take two days to move them to a helicopter landing site for extraction, and many wounded climbers can't survive that long.

The rangers knew that deaths from serious injuries, hypothermia, shock, or loss of blood could ideally be reduced if they not only accessed the victims quickly but then were also able to whisk them off the mountainside to be flown directly to a hospital. The first makeshift short-haul, in which a victim was moved off the mountain while hanging on a rope suspended under a helicopter, occurred in the Tetons in September 1981, when a man from Pocatello, Idaho, plummeted 100 feet while descending the north side of Nez Perce. Rangers climbed to him and treated his head and femur wounds, but they believed he would die in the time it would take them to carry him off the mountain. In desperation, they hooked the climber's litter to a line hanging from a helicopter, taped the back opening of the chopper shut, and flew him to safety, a maneuver that the Forest Service had not yet approved for its helicopters.

In 1985, Pete Armington (who held Renny's job before him) joined the Jenny Lake rangers after serving 13 years in Rocky Mountain National Park. Armington was focused on the safety risks involved in mountain rescue, particularly after an especially dicey mission on the Grand's Petzoldt Ridge in July 1985. In that circumstance, a 28-year-old trail crew member from Yellowstone National Park slipped off a hold and swung about six feet through the air before smashing into the rock face. The rangers traversed the bottom of the route to Glencoe Col, the nook between the spire and the mountain, and several of them climbed about 300 feet up the ridge to reach the injured climber. They packed the patient in a litter and lowered him with ropes to the col. As the pilot flew into the gap, parking the left skid on a boulder and the right skid on air, the rangers cautiously slid the stretcher partially into the opening of the helicopter, where the rear doors had been removed, leaving the litter sticking out the back.

Convinced that there was a way to improve aerial maneuvers, Armington pushed the boundaries of mountain flight. All that summer, he routinely asked the pilots to undertake extreme risks by sidling the helicopter up as close to accident scenes as possible, with rotor blades narrowly missing rocks and white-bark pines, to enable them to perform delicate toe-ins—where just the front tips of the helicopter's skids touch down—and one-skid landings. Rangers would then bolt out of the helicopter as it hovered, knowing that one ill-timed gust of wind while they were exiting the aircraft could lead to disaster for everyone. The procedure obviously put the rangers and injured climbers in jeopardy, but it was especially perilous for the pilots who were required to fly while pressed against ridges and mountain faces. In addition, toe-ins and one-skid landings were impossible on the Exum Ridge on the Grand Teton and in other places in the Teton range.

Armington spent the next year investigating ways to make mountain rescue faster and safer, focusing on the short-haul techniques that had been developed in Switzerland in 1966 and adopted by Parks Canada for use in search and rescue in 1970.

Once Armington received approval and funding from the National Park Service to pioneer a short-haul program in the United States, he still needed a pilot willing to experiment with mountain air rescues. He found that pilot in Ken Johnson, a retired Army warrant officer who had spent his last duty as part of the 54th Medical Detachment at Fort Lewis, Washington, where he flew military helicopters for air ambulance and rescue work. Johnson gained the immediate respect of the rangers on an operation where he toed in on top of the 12,804-foot Middle Teton and allowed a ranger to step first out onto the helicopter skid and then directly onto the mountain, shaving hours off the rescue. From there, it was only a matter of degree for him to agree to fly human cargo beneath his ship.

The objective in short-haul rescue is to transport rangers or survivors (or sometimes both simultaneously) a short distance as they dangle from a long, static, fixed-length rope or cable, usually 0.4 inch thick, beneath the helicopter. The huge benefit of the procedure is that it severely cuts down on the time a pilot is compelled to remain in a precarious position. On the downside, however, the technique demands a tremendous amount of training for both pilots and rangers and can generally only be attempted in idyllic weather.

Unlike fast-rope and heli-rappel, where rescuers can only be inserted into an accident scene, short-hauling allows rangers and victims (and equipment) to also be extracted from the site. Depending on the gravity of their injuries, patients are either extracted from the scene while clipped into a protective harness known affectionately as a "screamer suit" or are packaged into a litter.

In the Tetons, a 100-foot line is the standard, but depending on the rotor clearance needed from cliffs and trees on each specific rescue, a 150-foot or 200-foot rope can be used instead. It generally becomes more difficult for a pilot to judge depth perception with the longer ropes. In certain circumstances, however, such as a rock wall jutting out at exactly 100 feet above the accident site preventing the helicopter from getting close enough to the mountain at that elevation, the spotter and the pilot will request a longer line.

In a short-haul procedure, as in other rescue techniques involving a rope suspended from a helicopter, the helicopter never lands. As opposed to a winch-and-hoist operation, however, in a short-haul rescue, the bottom, or hook, end of the rope is unable to be raised or lowered. With short-hauling, neither the rescuer nor the patient ever enters the helicopter. This is a disadvantage of the technique in that if the weather suddenly takes a nasty turn while a ranger is hanging under the helicopter, that ranger cannot be pulled up into the aircraft. In that case, either the ranger continues to dangle on the end of the line while the pilot orbits and waits for the weather to clear, or he remains on the rope while the pilot returns to the location where the aircraft took off and places him back on the ground.

In exchange for their participation in these incredibly dangerous rescue techniques, the rangers must endure being referred to around the park as "the dopes on the ropes." In more discreet parlance, the rangers, as well as the injured parties extracted from a scene, are considered "jettisonable human external cargo."

The Jenny Lake rangers first officially experimented with the short-haul system during training exercises in the summer of 1986, learning how to package a patient in a stretcher for exposed flight and how to connect a stretcher to a fixed line below the airship. In July of that summer, they put their preparations to use in the first sanctioned short-haul rescue in the Tetons.

Nicola Rotberg, 21, of Lexington, Massachusetts, was working in Yellowstone National Park that summer and came to the Tetons with five friends to climb Mount Moran via the Skillet Glacier route. One of the more identifiable peaks in the range, at 12,605 feet, the monolithic Mount Moran is on the west shore of Jackson Lake.

Only four members of the group, including Nicola, reached the peak. While the climbers were descending the glacier's snowfield, Nicola tumbled down the steep slope and darted out of sight. A few minutes later, one of her friends also slid out of control down the mountainside. Both women soared over a 200-foot rock island, but Nicola's friend was killed when she fell into a deep crevasse, while Nicola randomly landed on a snow ledge, badly bruised and bleeding internally. When her friends reached her and realized that she was still breathing, they carried her broken body down the mountain a couple of thousand feet, then climbed down to the shore of Jackson Lake to bring a rescue team back for her.

Pete Armington got the call at about 8:30 in the evening and knew that the rangers were going to be racing daylight. Ken Johnson flew to Lupine Meadows, keeping the helicopter running as he tore off the doors, and three rangers, including Renny Jackson and Dan Burgette, scrambled onboard.

Dan acted as spotter while Renny and the other ranger heli-rappelled from the helicopter, landing just a few feet away from Nicola, who was severely hypothermic. In the dusk, the pilot couldn't see the hand signals he had practiced with the rangers in training, so Renny extemporized by guiding Ken via radio.

Renny packaged their patient into the litter, then clipped

the litter into the rope. As the helicopter flew away with Nicola swinging far beneath it, he stood back to witness the first official short-haul operation in the park's history.

Nicola was successfully resuscitated at the hospital. Her core temperature was 82 degrees when she arrived, however, making it clear that she would not have survived a night on the mountain had the rangers not short-hauled her to safety.

For the next few years, the rangers conducted rescues using that same combination of heli-rappel and short-haul. In heli-rappel, however, the pilot was forced to spend minutes hovering while the rangers climbed down the rope and disconnected the friction gear, a situation referred to as loitering in the dead man's zone. In contrast to heli-rappel, short-hauling keeps the helicopter's hover time to an absolute minimum—mere seconds sometimes—a critical consideration given the often erratic wind conditions that exist along the high Teton peaks. The rangers pushed the point that it was quicker and arguably safer for them to arrive on the scene at the end of the rope than to slide down it, and they began using short-haul for insertions, too.

There are only seven programs within the National Park Service that use short-hauling, and only three—Grand Teton, Grand Canyon, and Yosemite— that use it with any frequency. A few companies in the private sector in the Tetons and California employ the technique as well.

Every summer, representatives from other national parks come to Jenny Lake to rate the short-haul program, observing both proficiency tests with a set of expectations outlined in writing, as well as rescue scenarios involving "typical" terrain. The bulk of short-haul training at Jenny Lake occurs in May, at the beginning of the summer season, but in the rare instance when a 28-day period goes by in which a short-haul hasn't occurred in the field, the government exclusive-use helicopter contract sets a requirement of additional training.

No rangers or patients have been killed or hurt during short-hauling in Grand Teton National Park, but there was a fatality while using the procedure in Yosemite, in which a rescuer and an injured climber in a litter hit a tree, killing the patient.

The worst short-haul accident in American history happened on July 21, 1995, on the Hawaiian island of Oahu. A Honolulu Fire Department McDonnell Douglas 369D helicopter searching for a missing hiker in the Koolau Mountains crashed, killing the pilot and two rescuers suspended in a net 50 feet below the aircraft. The National Transportation Safety Board determined that the probable cause of the accident was loss of aircraft control resulting from the pilot's inexperience and poor judgment in flying into adverse weather conditions in mountainous terrain with an external load and no spotter.

At elite programs like the one at Jenny Lake, the risk management is fastidiously calculated to reduce the chance of failure. There is no such thing as a small mistake in the short-haul technique. If any one thing, or series of things, goes awry, the potential for the entire process to go fatally, catastrophically wrong is essentially 100 percent.

While research efforts have been made to address the inherent risks in the procedure, the technique remains vulnerable to tragedy on a grand scale. Richard Sugden, a pilot of fixed-wing and rotary-winged aircraft, developed a parachute system that can be incorporated into the short-haul system to give the rescuer a chance to survive an emergency situation such as mechanical failure of the helicopter. Sugden presented his idea of a short-haul escape emergency parachute system, known as SHAPE (for Short-Haul escAPE), at an interagency short-haul conference. While the helicopter pilots at Jenny Lake were uncomfortable with the idea of flying with a parachute that might open inadvertently and cause a crash by effectively putting brakes on the helicopter, the state of California purchased the system, as did the federal Department of the Interior for use in transporting law-enforcement officers.

There is no doubt about the level of intricacy involved in mountain flight and rescue. The weather is a constant wild card. Snowstorms can occur even in summer months. Wind patterns can turn in an instant. If a pilot experiences an onboard emergency or equipment failure while in a hover, there may be no time for him to recover. The combination of the environment at extreme altitude and the scope of the terrain often forces a pilot into unexpectedly complex maneuvers and delicate landings. It is said that mountain pilots are not born, but go through a process of creation. Fortunately for the climbers stranded on Friction Pitch in the summer of 2003, Laurence Perry had gone through that process more spectacularly than most.

Born in 1953 in Kent, England, Laurence left home at age 15 to seek adventure. Never losing the essence of that thrill-seeking boy, Laurence has spent the rest of his life crafting nothing but one exploit after another for himself. In his early 20s, he was a trooper in the Army, then wandered around Australia and North America. He worked at the Swindon Outdoor Center in Devon, teaching courses in rope handling, climbing, exploring underground caves, and sailing. He signed up for the voluntary reserves of the Special Air Service in England (akin to American Special Forces). He was an instructor in both canoeing and kayaking on the L'Ardeche River in France.

He then traveled to Newfoundland and Labrador, finding work as a radio helicopter operator at the Grenfell Mission (a medical and religious mission that helps provide food, clothing, and medical care to poor people), where his duties also included outpost nursing and loading aircraft. After that, he did a stint as an Outward Bound instructor in western Canada. He was a commercial diver. He also dabbled in various positions at a radio control tower and a weather observation center and briefly held a position as a medic in the oil industry. To that point, he had only worked in proximity to the flight industry. He had yet to fly.

Laurence obtained his commercial helicopter license with the aid of some very individualized instruction—he was the only student in a 12-week class. His father had been particularly mechanically inclined, and it became evident in week one of the course that Laurence was phenomenally spatially aware. The confluence of good genes and mad natural talent made for one sensational pilot. Although on a few occasions he would fly other forms of aircraft, mostly borrowed from friends, it was helicopters alone that held Laurence's interest. He was fascinated by everything about them, gripped by the sensation of flying them, at home in the rhythmic deafness created by their rotors.

The main problem with a helicopter-flying obsession is that helicopters can't really be rented and flown as a hobby—a licensed pilot has to either buy one or commit to flying them commercially. Once Laurence found a position as a helicopter pilot, which took eight months, flying helicopters was the only job for him.

Of course, within that seemingly narrow scope, he did manage to work at virtually every job in existence that involved piloting that particular aircraft. He took clients heli-skiing. He flew for an archeology group whose expeditions included musk ox counting, polar bear tagging, and wolf culling. He piloted one of billionaire Paul Allen's private helicopters. He fought forest fires, where he gained his first experience with long-lining. He traversed grids in the high Arctic exploring for uranium, transporting the element in a special rack attached to the outside of the aircraft. Although that project took place in the days before global-positioning systems and navigation is an arena that Laurence does not identify as a strength, he somehow managed, as he says, to "roar up and down."

In Alaska and British Columbia, Laurence flew clients on a search for hard rocks, including lead and zinc. He worked avalanche-control at several ski resorts, transporting ski patrollers over the slopes while they flung bombs down into the snow to set off avalanches. He also flew avalanche-control operations along a 40-mile access road leading to a copper mine. He obtained additional practice with long-line work while flying a logging helicopter in Canada. He flew with a huge diamond drill onboard his aircraft to allow drill crews to secure core samples in their quest for gold. He circled back to long-lining while flying helicopters at several ski resorts, including Blackcomb in Whistler, where he received his initial exposure to mountain rescues and medical evacuations.

Laurence's first job as a pilot had been limited to four months, after which he had the winter off and then moved to another job entirely. Now decades into his career, that pattern of relatively short bursts of intense assignments has never varied. Laurence thrives on the independence, the coming-and-going-as-he-pleases aspect of working as a contract pilot.

Mountain rescue is hands down the most challenging, dangerous, and satisfying area of flying Laurence has ever done. After getting the feel of it for a few months at the Canadian ski resorts, he found himself drawn to what he terms the "magic of the mountains," and he built fast, comfortable friendships within the mountaineering community. These were his kind of people, passionate adventurers whose level of swashbuckling skill and high-functioning expertise matched his own.

It was while heli-skiing in Alaska that Laurence met an old-time Vietnam pilot who raved about the advanced mountain-rescue work being done in the Tetons. Confident that his long-lining talent and experience would be an ideal fit with the Jenny Lake program, Laurence headed to Jackson, where the climbing rangers were having a hell of a time finding a pilot

who was both willing to do the work and able to pass the ridic-
ulously precise proficiency tests.

Many pilots voluntarily knocked themselves out of the running. As a result of split job duties with the national forest, the position was billed to candidates as firefighting work, and the pilots
who applied didn't necessarily take that to mean high-altitude
mountain rescues. In big-relief mountainous terrain at 10,000 or
12,000 feet in elevation, sometimes more, the wind can flare up in
an instant to 60 to 80 knots. Engine failure means a vertical descent of 1,000 feet per minute. Few pilots were equipped to handle those elements, and even fewer had a corresponding interest
in taking on that kind of risk.

In addition, not every pilot liked long-lining when the cargo
on the end of the line was human, and plenty of competent
long-line pilots simply wouldn't agree to short-haul rescue personnel or patients.

Conversely, it seemed that the applicants willing to fly rescue missions in the Tetons did not possess the requisite physical
capability. The enormous, 3,000-foot drop-offs in the range
tended to cause a pilot's depth perception to drop off as well.
When transitioning over a chasm, a pilot had to adapt to a sudden change in closure rate and depth perception. It was a tough
operation to transport a ranger to a rock face—delicate to visualize, complex to compensate for mountain air flow and wind.
On top of that, there was a very real and highly specialized
need for pilots to block out the depth—pretend it's not down
there, pretend it's not scary.

The few pilots both talented and eager enough to take on
the level of peril associated with the position still had to fit in
with the rescue crew. The rangers were searching for a pilot to
whom they would doubtless be trusting their lives, and the connection had to be there, the feel had to be right.

At the stage when Laurence arrived, the rangers had been

churning through pilot after pilot. As Laurence says, "They chewed them up quite well. If their personality was shit, Renny and the boys would eat 'em alive." Starting off, Laurence was buoyed by the realization that within at most one degree of separation, given the tightness of the Canadian, American, and English mountaineering communities, he and the rangers knew the same people, had all the same contacts.

His initial interview more or less took a turn toward hazing. As it turned out, however, he breezed through the getting-to-know-you session, in which he sat in the middle of a group of rangers while they took turns launching multipart, high-speed questions at him. Single-malt Scotch may have been involved.

Within moments, it became clear to the rangers that inter-rogation-style interviews did not faze Laurence; in just a few minutes more, they realized that he was destined to flourish in this environment. At six-foot-one, 190 pounds, with a hard, muscular build, short grayish hair styled high and tight, and un-faltering blue eyes, Laurence certainly looks the part of a dy-namic, daring pilot. When he opens his mouth, British accent still very much preserved, and begins to banter in his offhand, irreverent way, the full force of his charisma nearly shimmers. Exceptionally charming, endearingly self-effacing, and gener-ally awash with competence, Laurence is hard not to like.

Laurence sums up his mutual admiration fest with the rangers this way: "I could tell that they knew what they were on about. They could tell that I knew what I was doing, too."

Personality test roundly passed, Laurence moved on to the dreaded pilot proficiency tests. The Jenny Lake piloting job fo-cuses on long-line work with vertical reference—height above ground or object surface—as well as precision placement. The position requires painstakingly meticulous flying skills, since the pilot operates very close to the terrain while constantly monitoring the proximity of the rotors and the short-haul load

to the cliffs. The pilot needs to be comfortable with slanting terrain and the angular component of the short-haul rope, especially when supporting a patient in a litter, and he must be able
to adapt to erratic and unpredictable air movements.

The pilot also has to be cognizant of the location of the helicopter in relation to the mountain, because in certain circumstances, the aircraft can actually be hit from above by rockfall, a
situation that adds a sheen of complexity to the whole operation. Most helicopter pilots, meaning the overwhelming percentage who do not spend their careers executing high-altitude
rescues, do not confront rocks crashing onto them from the sky.

The proficiency tests are designed to evaluate not just the
actual skills the rangers require in a pilot but also more subjective traits, such as the level of cool the pilot displays under intense pressure. Many of the exercises are scenario-based, with
situations that are generally more worst-case than real-life.
Some of these assessments cover aspects of the job such as aerial victim searches, but the majority of them involve short-hauling skills.

The pilots use 100-foot ropes in most of the tests, although
they are also required to demonstrate command over short-
hauling with 150-foot and 200-foot lines. Shorter ropes, less
than 100 feet, cannot be used because of potential complications arising from the downdraft of the helicopter, but depending on the slope of the mountain, there are situations in which
a longer line becomes a necessity. Most long-line pilots feel that
it is easier to maneuver with the 100-foot rope than the longer
ones, but Laurence actually believes that the loads on longer
ropes can at times swing less freely and move more smoothly
through the air.

The pilots are also expected to perform various accuracy assessments where they have to hit marks on the ground when
setting down items suspended from the short-haul rope, but the

really hard one, the one that separates out the best of the best, is the circle test. This is the test, in Laurence's words, in which a pilot "needs to bring all tricks and goodies to the table."

The test was devised to establish how long and how well a pilot can hold a hover. In other words, it is meant to measure how successfully he can park a helicopter in the sky.

The rangers mark off a circle 10 feet in diameter with stakes all around it. The stakes are six feet high. The 100-foot short-haul rope is attached under the helicopter with a 200-pound load on the end approximating the weight of a body, usually either a log or a tank filled with water. The act of keeping the helicopter still in the air already requires pinpoint intensity and a balancing act of forces, but the tension is ramped up exponentially with a suspended load undulating in the wind currents below.

The exam requires a pilot to hover high in the air above the circle with the log on the end of the long rope directly over the 10-foot circle. The load cannot be more than six feet above the ground (the height of the stakes), and it cannot bump the ground, or the pilot fails.

The pilot has to maintain the log in this position for a total of two minutes in the course of three minutes. There are two rangers standing by timing, one manning a two-minute timer and one clicking a three-minute timer. The load can swing or drift out of the circle briefly, but the pilot has to bring it back in immediately.

There are maybe a handful of helicopter pilots in the world who could pass this test in the three minutes. Laurence passed it in two.

He admitted afterward that it was the longest two minutes of his life, which is significant in that he recognized that it was not the longest three minutes of his life—Laurence seemed to realize even before he took the test that he wouldn't need to take advantage of the extra minute of cushion. Control is the most important aspect of the exam, but overhandlers, known as stick handlers (an old hockey expression), would never be able to hold a stationary hover that long. When Laurence found himself overcontrolling, he made himself break, completely shut down to a stop. He jostled the controls slightly to stabilize the aircraft but didn't shift the helicopter from its relative position in the air. The movement in his wrist was almost imperceptible.

In reality, there was virtually no situation in which a pilot would be required to hold a hover with cargo that static for such a long time, but the rangers' theory was that if a pilot could execute a trick that demanding, he should be able to handle just about anything Teton rescues could throw at him.

Laurence attributes his steady hand in part to time spent emulating the helicopter pilots he worked with in long-line logging. In his early days as a pilot, he admired the way they flew so smoothly that their logs would barely move, and he tried to match their movements. Helicopter pilots don't tend to fly with one another much, but they do watch one another fly. When Laurence was first learning, he felt that there was always someone better than he, and he was competitive enough to say not just "I'll try that" but "I'll try that again," as many times as it took for him to master a particular skill.

One of Laurence's major strengths lies in his ability to split off in his mind all of the emotional aspects of short-hauling. He considers a human on the end of the line as no different from a barrel of fuel or a diesel engine that has to be placed carefully on a landing pad. He compartmentalizes the idea that his cargo happens to be a person who needs to be set down in exactly the right place. The same principles apply—don't drop the load, don't bang it into anything. Unlike inanimate freight, however, the rangers were able to show their appreciation when their pilot avoided bashing them into the mountainside, becoming, as Laurence says, "huggy and unmanly."

Laurence does concede that he couldn't help but feel a visual human connection when he looked down and made eye contact with a ranger hooking into the long-line. Just before takeoff, he often heard some cavalier variant of "I don't want to die, LP," to which his jaunty response was inevitably "I don't, either."

Laurence left his wife at home in Whistler while he worked at Jenny Lake—she visited once or twice during the summer, but, as he explains rhetorically, "People are different when they are working, aren't they?" The sacrifice of eliminating family distractions for the sake of his focus at work did not go unnoticed, leading Renny to refer to Laurence as both an exceptional pilot and a complex character. In the category of supreme compliment, the head ranger also asserted that in the cockpit, Laurence was "always in total control."

Those episodes of control were extremely sporadic—during the summer, there could sometimes be two or three short-hauls a week, then nothing for several weeks. Laurence received a daily rate for a 9:00 A.M. to 6:00 P.M. shift from June though October, whether he was flying or not. He was on call for 12 days in a row, meaning that he had to be within a one-hour call-out, then got two days off. The firefighting aspect of the position in conjunction with the national forest took up a lot of his work hours, but he still had a large amount of downtime, and the on-call system was set up fairly loosely. Laurence was basically instructed to go about his business within a one-hour distance parameter, and the park just sort of seemed to hope that the situation would work itself out. Luckily, Laurence, despite partaking in the occasional glass of Scotch, the drink of choice among the Jenny Lake rangers, was not a heavy drinker. In the evenings, he could almost always be found taking a mountain-bike ride.

When he wasn't cycling or performing death-defying maneuvers in the sky, Laurence was welcomed into the rangers' inner circle on and off duty. His comic sensibilities meshed well with the rest of the team, running to the bawdy but not to black humor. Joking in the face of death simply wasn't Laurence's style, and the Jenny Lake rangers didn't seem to find dark comedy so funny, either, despite its prevalence on most rescue crews.

The affable, playful side of Laurence was the one most often on display with the rangers. He was notorious for initiating grab-ass games even while flying and for ramping up silly challenges just after takeoff. "Oh, you think that was funny? Watch this!" He and the rangers onboard would volley back and forth about who could be goofier on the way to a scene, with Laurence occasionally getting caught cursing on the radio as a result.

It was only when he was about a minute away from an accident that Laurence revealed the impassive, contained piece of himself. When this persona came out, it came out quickly. Once Laurence determined that "the show was on," his transition was total. Often flippantly describing him as a different person when he was on-scene, those closest to him knew that the sudden ruthlessness of his intensity was merely the other side of the same coin.

Laurence's first major rescue with the Jenny Lake team was on the oppressive North Face of the Grand. He inserted two rangers on the sheer rock face, and as soon as they unclipped from the short-haul rope, pieces of the mountain began to crash down from above. The rangers were forced to spend the night on the side of the mountain, with rocks intermittently rattling down on them. Once the victim had been evacuated the following morning, the rangers wanted to climb down (they preferred to "walk out," is how they said it), but it was far too dangerous for them to move around on the mountain in the midst of all the instability. In evaluating the risk of the helicopter flying directly into a rockfall zone, Laurence contemplated how precisely he could time the extraction, weighing how much time he might have to do it versus how long it might take. In the end, he went blasting in, the rangers clipped into the rope in two seconds, and they all escaped unharmed. The whole escapade was sort of like one big trust-building exercise.

Another time, the Jenny Lake rangers brought their short-haul operation to Sun Valley in a desperate attempt to save a father and son. The victims had already been stranded on a mountain for 36 hours when Laurence flew in with Renny. Given the location of the accident, there was virtually no place for Laurence to put Renny down, so he dangled him up against the cliff while Renny grabbed onto a crevice with one hand and unclipped with the other.

It was during the CIDs (critical incident debriefings), where the rangers and pilot got together in the aftermath of the rescues to reevaluate them over Scotch or a few beers, that their immense respect for one another was revealed, Laurence announcing that he couldn't believe how brave the rangers were, the rangers responding that they couldn't imagine how Laurence could act so casually about what he did in the air. Laurence's stock reply was generally that it was hard enough flying the copter without hanging underneath it. In truth, he was grateful that he didn't have to interact with battered and disconnected limbs and that he wasn't responsible for gathering and packaging body parts the way the rangers were.

One body recovery that made an irrevocable impression on Laurence occurred on the north end of the range. He had been flying pass-bys searching for a climber for hours, only finally to find him draped on the mountainside like a rag doll, dead beyond all doubt. As much as the sight disturbed Laurence, he was overcome by knowing that the trauma must have run so much deeper for the rangers who actually had to cut the man free and load him into a body bag.

The vast majority of Laurence's rescue missions with the Jenny Lake climbing rangers occurred during daylight hours. His workday generally ended at 6:00 P.M. because the contract helicopters were not equipped, or permitted, to fly at night. On July 26, 2003, Laurence was unable even to insert the first ranger on-scene until after 6:00 P.M.

At dusk, a helicopter pilot has less feeling for movement and speed and approach. He thinks that high might be low or vice versa, and he may confuse slowing down with speeding up. His depth perception shifts, virtually disappears. With night flying, as thrilling as it is for a pilot, everything about the environment changes, and much of it slips away. There are far fewer visual cues. And in the words of Laurence Perry, "When things go sideways in the dark, they tend to go sideways fairly quickly."

SEVEN

"Jack is a mutant. I asked him and Jim to run
up to the base of Friction Pitch. To haul ass,
basically."

—

Renny Jackson, head Jenny Lake ranger

By the time of Leo's second insertion attempt, Renny Jackson was onboard the helicopter as the spotter. Dan Burgette had started out in that position on the recon flight, but once Renny reached the rescue cache, given the complexities of the incident and the scope of the operation, it made sense for him to take over as spotter.

Renny lost count of his rescues long ago, but he does recall his first significant one, just after he was hired, when he spent the night with a man who fell down a gully on Baxter's Pinnacle. Mass-casualty incidents (MCIs) are easier for him to remember, both for their rarity and for the fact that they overwhelm resources. In the vast majority of climbing accidents, only one climber, not several, falls off a ridge or gets struck by a rock.

A two-patient rescue on the daunting North Face of the Grand in 1980 is an operation that Renny recollects vividly. A helicopter flew him and other rangers to 13,000 feet to the East Face snowfield near the summit, where they spent the night. In the morning, the other rangers lowered Renny down to two stranded climbers to assess their injuries. When he had the wounded climbers ready to be raised, he ended up trapped and swinging on the mountainside with them, as vicious winds and a lightning storm forced the rangers above them to seek cover. Five hours later, they were all successfully raised to safety.

In another MCI, in September 1985, Renny and a second ranger left the valley in pelting rain to save five climbers trapped in a snowstorm on the Exum Ridge of the Grand Teton. The snowdrifts were more than three feet deep, and the wind was gusting at 80 mph by the time they reached 10,000 feet. Nearly crawling through the snow, Renny managed to follow a blinking headlamp to the victims' location in a gully. Three members of the climbing party had already died, but Renny spent the night with the two survivors and at sunup began the laborious process of extricating them.

The skills associated with the spotter position on a mission of this magnitude—most notably, split-second timing under the crush of manifold life-and-death decisions—rivaled whatever stone-cold self-possession was required of Renny in any of his prior rescues. The spotter acts as a go-between for the pilot and the ranger on the end of the rope, therefore orchestrating the mission on the mountain to a certain degree. The ranger in this position controls the pace of the operation—ensuring that the timeline is not unspooling too quickly, watching for warning signs such as communications becoming too terse, slowing the tempo down a bit if necessary.

The pilot does not know exactly what is going on in the spotter's head in terms of judging conditions, and conversely, the spotter can't know exactly what the pilot is thinking. The situational awareness in each of the two positions is a little skewed in this circumstance. The key to the whole dynamic flowing seamlessly is the quality of pilot-spotter communication.

In addition to interacting with the pilot, the spotter is in constant radio contact with the ranger hanging from the line. He also simultaneously assists the pilot with rotor clearance, tail and main, and manages the backup short-haul lines. There is a tremendous amount of multitasking involved in the position, much of it performed while leaning out of a doorless helicopter in strong winds at high altitude. It is an ultra-high-stress job, and it cannot be winged on the spot. It is not a place for ad-libbing, or for being instructed in the moment about the pilot's expectations. The ranger must already know exactly what to do or, more accurately, precisely what the pilot wants him to do.

Fewer than half of the Jenny Lake rangers had been specifically trained for the spotter role, and Renny had by far the most experience. In addition, the spotter position was the right place for Renny on a rescue that would require an intricately choreographed air show. Renny had managed the short-haul program for more than a dozen years, he devised and ran the pilot proficiency tests, and he knew the program and the pilots more intimately than any of the other rangers. He had been present at the inception of the program, initially working with pilot Ken Johnson for five years. Perhaps most important, as a result of a connection forged and intertwined in the course of the previous two years, Renny was particularly in sync with Laurence. Beyond being effortlessly comfortable together, they also had utter confidence in each other.

Laurence had so much faith in, as he calls them, "Renny and the boys," that during the short-haul rigging, when the area around his helicopter was buzzing with excitement, with peo-

ple running back and forth, piling in gear and equipment, loading the line, he simply tipped his head back and closed his eyes.

Despite the exactitude required to rig the helicopter for
short-hauling, Laurence found that there was no point for him
to check the rangers' work. He did, of course, inspect it, but he
knew that it wasn't necessary, and his conviction was vital in a
process where the players didn't get a second chance to fix an
error. He believed with absolute certainty that the rangers were
true professionals, and in an effort to distinguish them from
what he terms "the REI crowd," Laurence describes them, almost worshipfully, as "capable." That word comes up a lot in
Laurence's parlance concerning the Jenny Lake rangers, occasionally preceded by "just very" or "super" and always delivered
in a tone indicating that it was the highest praise he could be-
stow on another man.

Laurence knew from experience that these rescuers could
rig a helicopter blindfolded if the situation called for it, and he
was confident that they wouldn't bump their heads on the rotor
or put an arm up into a twirling blade. Rather than get worked
up worrying needlessly, Laurence merely waited, his eyes shut,
calming himself for what was to come.

While the spotter acts as a backup voice to the ranger and
the pilot, Laurence actually had a strong preference for nonver-
bal communication, and Renny was happy to accommodate.
The two of them could have entire conversations, regarding,
for example, the helicopter's proximity to the mountain face, all
in hand signals. For the most part, what Renny could see, Laurence could see. Laurence was not, for example, wild about a
countdown on his distance to the landing spot. "Seventy-five
feet, 10 feet, it's just numbers, it doesn't mean much," he says.
"You can say 75 if you want. It's not necessary."

Fluid communication between pilot and spotter becomes
especially crucial when the spotter conveys the signals of the

rangers as they are detaching themselves from the short-haul rope or clipping patients onto it. Rather than in a stream of chatter—this looks good, this looks bad, this is a disaster—Renny could accomplish the same message wordlessly. Even when he did speak, he still used hand signals, in case the radio failed or somehow couldn't be heard.

There were, of course, occasions when Laurence and Renny would actually talk on the radio. When Laurence was landing the helicopter on the mountain, the conversations tended to go something like this:

Laurence: "See that gray chunk there on the left? Is it flat? I can't tell if it's flat."

Renny: "No, go to the left."

Or, more tersely, when Laurence was sidling up beside a mountain face, pressed against it as close as he possibly could get, he would simply ask Renny, "Got the reference?" By this, he actually meant: "Are you registering our distance from the mountain, how close are we getting to it, are we going to smash into it, are you going to warn me if we are?" But all Laurence asked Renny was if he had the reference, and he knew, and Renny knew, that was all it took, all the communication they needed. It was trust in action.

All things being equal, Laurence preferred to pull up to a mountain on the rock-face side so as to gauge proximity visually for himself. Depending on the angle and the location of the rescue, however, he couldn't always have it that way. Few pilots would consider approaching the off side of the mountain and allowing someone else to be their eyes, but Renny was on a very select list that Laurence trusted in that position.

Laurence explains, in his almost comically understated way, the importance of not crashing into the mountain in that situation: "You have to be really careful with this one. There are no curb feelers on the ship. Once it taps on things, blade on rock, things tend to go pear-shaped. I try to avoid that as much as possible."

There is a certain amount of mandatory communication on the part of the ranger being short-hauled to a scene. About six feet above the end of the short-haul line, slack and hooked in with a prusik loop, is an orange bag made of Kevlar-based material containing 10 pounds of lead shot. It is meant to hold the line down, although the bag still sails out below in big arcs. (Longer lines require more weights, and two weight bags are used.) When the ranger lands at the insertion site, he is trained simultaneously to announce "Down and comfortable," place the bag on the ground in front of him, and signal with his hands. Then, almost instantaneously, he unclips from the line.

Sometimes when Laurence deposited a ranger on a rock face and he unclipped while clinging to a crack, the ranger couldn't always immediately release his hands to signal to Laurence. If Laurence couldn't see the ranger's hands, he had to guess that he had detached from the short-haul line and safely snapped into a carabiner just by feeling the line go a little bit light. There was obviously a huge risk of Laurence pulling the ranger back off the mountain when he flew away. The communication at this point was supposed to be "Clear to lift" from the ranger and "Lifting" from Laurence in response. Still, Laurence made an extreme point of withdrawing slowly, both looking and operating by a sense of feel for whether a hand or a glove had caught or hooked on something.

The rangers were so ready to clip back into the short-haul rope during extraction that the process took a few seconds at most. Sometimes when they were ready to leave the scene, they would deviate from standard radio protocol to summon their ride extra-casually, using Laurence's nickname: "Come on in, LP, we're ready." Once they had reattached to the line, the standard phrase was "Hooked and ready," to which Laurence would again respond, "OK, lifting."

It was essential for Laurence to be directly above the ranger at this point, or he was in danger of jerking him off the face. Laurence proceeded excruciatingly cautiously as he ascertained that the ranger was free from all encumbrances. If he had left his harness attached to the mountain or if his safety gear was still connected to both him and the rock, it would likely have ended tragically for him as well as everyone onboard. Once Laurence was convinced that he was clear, he would ease off his grip on the machine and slowly move out into the abyss.

One of the most high-pressure aspects of Renny's spotter responsibilities was the obligation to signal to Laurence to "Drop the load" if necessary. If the helicopter suffered a mechanical failure or the short-haul line became entangled with a tree or a rock or other obstacle, the line had to be cut to prevent the helicopter from going down. The ranger outside had to be sacrificed to save the pilot and the people inside the helicopter.

The decision to jettison the load—the load in this case being Leo Larson—would ultimately be Laurence's, but the execution would partially be up to Renny. Once Renny slashed the backup lines, the pilot could disengage the short-haul rope simply by triggering the release mechanism. Based on the shape of the switch, the rangers whimsically referred to this act as a pilot "pickling the switch" to kick loose the extended load and drop the ranger to his death. Renny therefore had a knife, blade extended out, stuck upright in a plastic holder inches in front of him, poised, if need be, to sever the lifeline suspending Leo.

As Renny leaned out of the helicopter to check on Leo swinging far below him, a lone cloud cloaked that part of the mountain, obscuring the landing area. By the time Laurence had fully ascended to the correct elevation, the clouds had thickened around the ridge.

Laurence kept the helicopter hovering in the area of Friction Pitch, allowing Leo to orbit on the end of the rope, hoping for the clouds to clear. The gap he had just passed through was especially windy, gusting at maybe 45 mph, and it was a supreme challenge for him to remain suspended at that altitude, so close to the very top of the mountain.

The three men were barely able to restrain their urgency to reach the Folded Man to fix—or at least attempt to fix—his airway. Leo was longing to get on-scene to size up the entire situation and then, if it wasn't already too late, to focus on saving the suspended climber who was bent backward nearly in two. Laurence was trying to count the people at the scene and calculate, assuming that they could even land, how many minutes it would take to extract each one of them before nightfall. As he waited, he monitored the engine parameters, the engine temperature, and the torque setting, transmitting them all to a radio operator who logged the information.

A few minutes went by, with clouds continuing to slide over and past the insertion site, and still Laurence held the hover.

A helicopter can fly in any direction—forward, backward, upward, or sideways—and can make sharper turns than airplanes. It can also, depending on the skill of the pilot, hover over a single spot. It has two sets of propellers—a larger one at the front, above the cabin, and a smaller one at the tail.

The blades on a helicopter's main rotor (the large horizontal propeller that spins on top of its body) are essentially moving wings. The rotor blades create a strong wind as they slice through the air, and that current creates a lifting force enabling a helicopter to go straight up. Each blade produces an equal share of the lifting force. Unlike an airplane, a helicopter does not have to move forward in order to achieve lift.

The tail rotor prevents the helicopter from spinning around when the main rotor blades are turning. When a helicopter's main rotor turns in one direction, the body of the helicopter tends to rotate in the opposite direction. This is known as torque reaction. A tail rotor produces thrust in the opposite direction of the torque reaction and holds the helicopter straight.

By changing the angle of the main rotor blades slightly, the pilot controls where the helicopter goes. To increase or decrease overall lift, he alters the angle of all of the blades by equal amounts at the same time. To tip forward and back (pitch) or tilt sideways (roll), a pilot alters the angle of the main rotor blades cyclically during rotation, creating differing amounts of lift at different points in the cycle. If he wants to go forward, go backward, or turn completely around sideways, tilting the spinning rotor will cause the helicopter to fly in the direction of the tilt.

A helicopter pilot manipulates four separate flight controls to achieve flight: the cyclic stick, the collective lever, the antitorque pedals, and the manual throttle. The changes he makes to the flight controls are transmitted mechanically to the rotor, producing aerodynamic effects on the blades.

The cyclic control, also called the cyclic stick or just the cyclic, looks like a joystick and is usually located between the pilot's legs. To make a helicopter fly in a certain direction, the pilot maneuvers the cyclic stick to tilt the rotor disc. This alters the pitch of the rotor blades cyclically, meaning that the feathering angle of the blades changes depending on their position as they rotate around the hub, with all blades changing their angle the same amount at the same point in the cycle. If the pilot pushes the cyclic forward, the rotor disc tilts forward, and the helicopter produces thrust in that direction. If the pilot pushes the cyclic to the right, the rotor disc tilts to the right, causing the helicopter to move sideways or to roll into a right turn.

The collective pitch control, or collective lever, is on the left side of the pilot's seat and is responsible for changing the pitch angle of all of the main rotor blades at the same time and independent of their position. When this flight control is used, all of the blades change equally, and the helicopter increases or decreases its total lift derived from the rotor, causing it to climb or descend.

The antitorque pedals control the direction in which the nose of the aircraft is pointed by changing the pitch of the tail rotor blades. The manual throttle is also generally considered a flight control because it is needed to maintain rotor speed and keep the rotor producing enough lift for flight.

Forward flight and hovering are the two basic flight conditions for a helicopter, with hovering clearly the most exacting aspect of helicopter flying. A helicopter generates its own wind while in a hover, and that acts contrary to the flight controls. When a pilot keeps the rotor disc completely flat, the helicopter hovers because all of the lift force is straight up, keeping the helicopter in the air. If one side of the rotor disc has more lift than the other, the disc will tilt, and the helicopter will move in the direction it is pushed into. The pilot is therefore required to make constant control inputs to keep the helicopter standing still in the air.

The cyclic eliminates drift in the horizontal plane, controlling forward and back, right and left. The collective maintains altitude. The pedals control nose direction. The interaction of these controls is what makes hovering so incredibly complicated, since an adjustment in any one control requires an adjustment of the other two, creating a cycle of endless corrections. To complicate the flying process further, in any rotor system, there is a delay between the time a change in pitch is introduced by the flight controls and when that change is manifest in the rotor blade's flight, forcing the pilot to calculate this lag continually.

While Laurence was looking down at Leo, contemplating making a move to get in close to the face, a wispy cloud slithered in directly beneath him, scaring, as he says, the "bejesus" out of him (and this is not a man who gets the bejesus scared out of him easily). The ground was indistinct to Laurence, and Leo was in fog. Laurence's level of disorientation was much like that of a skier racing into a sudden whiteout. He later confessed that the abrupt appearance of the cloud below him had freaked him out, not that anyone could read that in his face at the time, much less in his voice. His unease centered around the idea that there could be more swiftly moving clouds, and the process needed to be completely visual for him at that point. If he fully committed to take Leo to the face and another cloud darted in under them, he would lose all reference with the ground and have no idea where he was in space.

Although the pilot is in command in a short-haul procedure, either the spotter or the ranger on the end of the rope can also call off an insertion. Laurence, Renny, and Leo each had an independent angle on the situation, and each of them trusted the ability of the other two to go right up to the edge of the risk. If any one of them felt that it wasn't right, that the safety threat was too great, that person could decide for all of them.

In this case, there was a completely unanimous decision to abandon the attempt. Laurence knew what he could and could not do. When he communicated to the rangers that he was not going to be able to work it out, they knew one another and the mountain well enough that both of them already understood and agreed. The only option at that point was for Laurence to fly them back down the mountain.

Laurence brought Leo back to the Lower Saddle and set him gently down on the ground—a landing, as Laurence says, like "angel's breath." They were all plainly frustrated at their inability to get straight to the scene, and an image of the Folded Man being alive and in need of profound help was on everyone's mind, but they separated out those emotions and systematically began strategizing the next steps.

There was a ranger hut on the Saddle containing a weather port and backup rescue and climbing equipment, which the rangers used to supplement the gear they had gathered from the cache. Laurence immediately got back in the air, flying down to Lupine Meadows to ferry more rangers up to the Lower Saddle. On the next flights, George Montopoli, Marty Vidak, Jack McConnell, Chris Harder, and a couple of other rangers arrived at the staging area.

This was a day that the rangers had trained for, a rescue that, quite simply, they lived for. While they all participated in the same training, they clearly brought different skill sets to the rescue, and Brandon assigned them diverse responsibilities depending on their abilities. He considered various scenarios, how much time they had, how many people were available, who was the most experienced at short-haul, who were the most proficient medics, who was the best at setting anchors, who was the fastest and strongest to hike up to the scene. By the time he had finished delegating tasks, he had all of the right people in place, including the support personnel in Lupine Meadows. He designated Dan Burgette as medic for the lower scene. For the upper scene, including the Folded Man, Brandon tagged ranger Craig Holm, who had turned 35 just days earlier, as medic.

Extremely sweet and a little shy, with a self-deprecating streak that does little to mask deep reserves of both poise and self-awareness, Craig at the time was only in his fourth season as a ranger. His career motivation pendulum had come full swing, from an unfocused seven and a half years playing on the beach in college in Santa Barbara to watching a short-haul procedure in a Teton meadow in 1999 and deciding that he had to get a job as a climbing ranger, whatever it took. When Renny called him the following summer, stating that they had an opening for an emergency hire and asking if Craig could be there in a week, what it took for Craig to get the job was to rent out his apartment in Boulder, quit two jobs, and drop out of grad school. He made it to Jenny Lake within the week.

The first rescue Craig took part in, a couple of days after he arrived, was on a falling ice glacier on Mount Moran, where he again watched a short-haul operation, this time as a Jenny Lake climbing ranger. The helicopter was heavily weighted, and to achieve forward airspeed, the pilot had to use gravity to point downhill, which caused the aircraft to drop like an elevator, and the doors were off, and the whole experience was so over-whelming that Craig couldn't believe it was his job. There was no looking back for him at that point.

Once Leo's short-haul attempt was aborted, it was unclear when or if the weather would clear long enough for Leo or Dan or Craig or any of the rangers to be inserted into the scene through the air. Most of the clouds had begun to drift away, ex-cept for a thick band that had unequivocally settled itself in the vicinity of Friction Pitch. The summit was basically cloudless, the area below the pitch was relatively clear, but a turmoil of clouds was clustered right at the elevation where the rangers needed to be. In the event that the weather prevented short-haul insertions entirely, Renny made the call that they needed ground support.

Jim Springer, whom Brandon had assigned to lead the lower of the two rescue scenes and who had been gunning to climb up the mountain the moment it looked as if they might not be able to short-haul, was quick to volunteer to go. Every-one realized that it was imperative for someone to get on-scene to make contact with the climbers as soon as possible, and even as the initial decisions were being made and Leo was first gear-ing up, Jim had been pushing his agenda to climb.

"Why don't I just go?" he asked Renny. "I'll just go."

Once the first insertion attempt failed, with Renny's bless-ing, Jim took off alone, assuming that another ranger would be coming up behind him. With about 40 pounds of climbing gear and rescue equipment—a first-aid kit, some technical apparatus, rope, some of his own personal gear, warm clothes, rain gear—on his back, he proceeded up the mountain at a steady jog.

Jim had begun climbing as a kid, summiting Mount Rainier at age 16, then moving on to technical climbing in Yosemite. He hadn't been to the Tetons before he applied as a Jenny Lake ranger in 1984, but he was hired right away, and he came to the area knowing which specific climbs he wanted to do in the Teton range. His fondness for the job flows from the freedom it gives him to hike and climb without taking other people (other nonrangers) with him. As he says, in a voice so slow it is almost a drawl, "rangers don't have clients."

Jim came to consider himself less of a tech climber and more of a backcountry adventurer, with a preference for hiking and clambering around the mountains. He also became interested in backcountry resource management, rehabilitation, repair, and maintaining the park service for future generations. The only real downsides of the ranger position, from his perspective, are the intensive training and the required shifts in the ranger station. While Jim doesn't necessarily elaborate on his thought processes verbally, he can be relied on to make and implement quick, efficient decisions. It seems clear that if he was your dad, or the ranger instructing you in how he was saving your life, you would do what you were told. His penchant for pink Crocs does nothing to diminish his influence.

About 20 minutes after Jim started up the Grand, ranger Jack McConnell, age 42, arrived on the scene, and Renny asked him to catch up with Jim. Later, Jim expressed his gratitude for the head start. As a result of his unparalleled aerobic skill in scrambling up a mountain, Jack has a reputation as an animal, a beast, a machine. He does not have the compact, wiry body of a climber—at six-foot-two, 195 pounds, he is dense and thick, with legs like tree trunks—but still, Renny deems him Alex Lowe material.

Lowe, known as "the Lung with Legs" and considered one of the greatest American mountaineers of all time, was a frequent climbing partner of Renny's before Lowe's death in 1999 at age 40 in a massive avalanche on Shisha Pangma in Tibet. In Renny's opinion, Jack's cardiovascular system would have given Lowe's a run for its money. "If you are gonna go running up the Grand with Jack," Renny says, "you're gonna get your ass kicked."

From his own perspective, Jack's strong point is an ability to "move quickly in the mountains." His modesty might seem affected if it was not so clear that it is an integral part of his excessively sincere, almost solemn outlook. He also seems somehow legitimately oblivious to his appearance, a mash-up of naturally wholesome innocence and rugged good looks.

Jack grew up in Rhode Island, primarily outdoors, cragging and bouldering, exploring rock-climbing routes in Lincoln Woods. Two events in his childhood helped influence his professional path. When he was four years old, he took a tram ride with his parents up Cannon Mountain. While drinking hot chocolate at the top, he encountered a bearded man with a red hat and knickers, a climbing rope slung over his shoulder, and young Jack determined prekindergarten that he wanted to be like that climber. Then, at age 13, at the Summit Shop in Providence, the owner who sold Jack a pair of hiking boots spoke passionately about the Tetons, instilling what was to become Jack's lifelong fascination with the mountain range.

At that point, New Hampshire set the stage for more serious climbing—granite cliff bands, ice climbs. Jack climbed with friends and read plenty of how-to books, but he never took any formal instruction. After high school in Pawtucket, Rhode Is-

land, and college at the University of Rhode Island, he headed to
Yellowstone, where a high-school friend was working. He hung
out with a community of climbers at a Climber's Ranch in Yellowstone and worked at the Old Faithful Inn, where he determined that six years of bellman duties—hauling luggage up four
floors with no elevator—was ideal training for climbing.

The first time Jack glimpsed the Tetons, hitchhiking into
Jackson, he had the feeling that something was waiting there
for him. He knew instantly that it was where he belonged, but
even so, it took him some time to join the Jenny Lake climbing
rangers. He instead began spending his winters in Jackson, becoming the ski patrol director and running the race program at
Snow King Resort for a decade.

He retained, always, his love for climbing, running, skiing,
moving in the mountains, covering ground, seeing what was
there. The mountains truly drew him in—he considered them
a mystery he wanted to uncover, a problem he yearned to solve.
He understood the tradition of the Jenny Lake climbing rangers, had a tremendous amount of respect for them, but didn't
think he was skilled enough to join them. In 1998, he finally put
his application in anyway.

Feeling that anyone could become a rescue tech with
enough training, Jack knew that Jenny Lake selected for quali-
ties beyond rescue skills and technical climbing expertise. He
believed that the Jenny Lake rangers were specifically looking
for climbers with a passion for being in the mountains, and in
that arena, Jack saw himself as having an advantage in the hiring process.

As predicted by everyone except Jack himself, he was hired
as a Jenny Lake climbing ranger on the spot.

It was abundantly clear that it was the job he was born to
do. On the mandatory mountain patrols every pay period, Jack
always picked the routes with the shortest approaches and the

steepest climbs. He became depressed if he didn't have a chance to cover 5,000 vertical feet in a day. Trying to keep up with him, even for younger rangers in peak physical condition, was extremely painful.

Becoming a member of the Jenny Lake team wasn't simply about the job duties to Jack but rather what he termed the brotherhood of rangers, the ability of the rangers to channel one another's expertise while simultaneously keeping an eye on one another. He realized that there were plenty of sacrifices associated with the job—lack of monetary compensation leading the list—but he knew from the start that the opportunity to be in the mountains would be enough for him. That core belief was what set Jack up for success every time he was called on to help someone. In his sixth year at Jenny Lake in 2003, he still considered himself a rookie.

Jack had spent that Saturday afternoon, a day off for him, taking a seven-mile run around Jenny Lake. He heard a rumble as he was coming across the meadow, but he didn't see the lightning flash. Although he wasn't carrying his radio, he figured something was up when he caught a glimpse of Leo tearing purposefully around the corner of his cabin. Jack raced to his cabin to find out what was happening, flipping on his radio as he simultaneously dialed dispatch. He received the radio page immediately and took off down the dirt road to the rescue cache.

When Jack arrived, activity was blossoming into full swing at the rescue headquarters. He started organizing his gear— flight helmet, suit, rock shoes, approach shoes, rope, light rack (a set of climbing equipment, including cams and carabiners), harness, chalk bag, a handful of candy bars—when Brandon told him that if the weather shut them down, Jack would be climbing to the scene.

By the time Laurence flew Jack to the Saddle, Brandon had already decided to split the scenes and assign separate logistics to the upper and lower sites, an organizational structure that made immediate sense to Jack. He relished the worker role, completing discrete tasks that were assigned to him, as long as doing so put him in the midst of the action. Jack reported to Renny on the ranger hut on the Saddle, who confirmed that his job was to catch Jim and climb with him to the scene.

In preparation for the ascent, Jack tried to dump a bunch of stuff out of his pack, but most of it was essential. His personal gear weighed about 20 pounds, plus he was hauling approximately 20 pounds of rope. He had to keep the ropes, climbing gear, medical equipment, rain gear, insulation and clothing layers, water, some food (energy gel and Milky Way and Snickers bars). There was technical climbing involved in several sections of the route, and moreover, he couldn't imagine that they wouldn't be spending the night on the mountain. He managed to offload a pound or two, but his pack, like Jim's, still weighed more than an average five-year-old child.

Jack then stripped down to running shorts and a T-shirt and, with his 5.10 free-running shoes on, began almost literally running up the mountain. He was in perpetual training, including scrambling and running hills nearly daily. This assignment had him covering about a mile of territory spanning 1,500 feet in elevation. A person can't really increase in altitude like that at a full-out run without dying, but Jack was moving over steep, technical terrain, progressing up the mountain at a pace somewhere between a trot and a dash. He was, quite simply, running as fast as it is possible for a human to run uphill. If he believed that he could have made it alive, he would have considered actually sprinting.

As it was, Jack monitored his pace right on the edge, maintaining an aerobic state, balancing his heart at a threshold of 85 percent of its maximum rate. Straddling a psychological safety line of his own making, he thought of the space he had to cover in small, incremental units in his head—this little pitch, this tiny step—problem solving with every footfall he took.

He caught up to Jim before the end of the Wall Street ledge.

By that point, Jack and Jim saw Laurence back in the air with Leo once again on the end of the rope. Jim stopped to take a picture of the short-haul, with no memory later of having done so. He did recall the desperate feeling of wanting to beat the helicopter to the scene.

Jim, who had been a runner in college, was shuffling-running so fast that he was seeing stars and likely operating at some level of anaerobic shock. Intended for high-intensity, shorter-duration efforts such as diving for the finish line or passing a fellow cyclist, the anaerobic system is not designed to sustain any type of prolonged activity. In this state, without enough oxygen getting to his brain, Jim was producing lactic acid faster than his body could break it down. He was in tremendous discomfort as a result—his breath was very short and rapid, and his muscles were burning. Still, he viewed the climb as a competition, with a singular loop running through his mind: can't stop the pace now, not after all this effort, it wasn't fair for the helicopter to get there before them, they should be the first ones on-scene to see what was going on.

Despite knowing the route cold, Jim and Jack stopped to rope up together at the step across the gap on Wall Street, not wanting the adrenaline of the situation to cause them to slip up and trigger more rescues for the team. Despite the 800- or 900-foot vertical drop if they missed the move, neither Jim nor Jack would normally have bothered to use ropes in that (or any) section of the climb. They were exposed and in high gear, however, needing to force themselves to get their ropes out, decelerate their pace from the race with the helicopter.

Even with that delay, they reached the first victims, on a tiny ledge below Friction Pitch, in just about 45 minutes, covering the same ground that the victims had taken seven hours to climb. (There is a bit of controversy over the timing of this climb, with some records logging it at just less than 70 minutes. It seems likely that Jim left the Lower Saddle and made it to the base of Friction Pitch in something short of 70 minutes, while Jack, who left the Saddle more than 20 minutes later than he did and caught up to him on the ascent, made the climb in approximately 45 minutes. While 45 minutes doesn't set the speed record for climbing the Grand [a mark established by a climber not hauling 40 pounds of gear], it comes damn close.)

As it turned out, Jim and Jack did not vanquish the helicopter after all, but they did, by a split-second or two, beat the other rescuers to the lower scene, pulling themselves over the ledge a moment before the arrival of the rangers who had been short-hauled in and rappelled down.

EIGHT

"Socially, climbers are not that adept."

—

Renny Jackson, head Jenny Lake ranger

On July 23, 2003, Rob Thomas had secured two permits for his climbing group of 13 to camp in Garnet Canyon. The campsites at the Lower Saddle, where the main guiding companies camped with their clients, were already full, so he wasn't able to obtain his first choice of base camp. Instead, Rob got one permit to camp in the Meadows camping zone at just over 9,000 feet in elevation and another one for the Moraine camping area at almost 11,000 feet, and he split his group up between the two locations.

Leo Larson had spoken earlier to a member of the climbing party at the Jenny Lake ranger station, stressing that a group of more than a dozen people needed to get an early start to climb the Grand. The day before the climb, on the trail heading to their base camps, members of the climbing party again ran into Leo and also ranger Marty Vidak. Leo and Marty warned the climbers about recent afternoon storm cycles with the threat of lightning and advised them to get an "alpine start" for their climb in the morning, meaning a predawn approach. Leo suggested that they be on the Lower Saddle ready to go no later than dawn, which was 6:06 A.M., enabling them to look across and see Wall Street by first light.

The purpose of such an incredibly early start is to reduce the dangers that can occur as the day warms up—falling ice and rock and thunderstorms—and to provide a cushion of daylight in case a group is delayed. Based on the rangers' experience, their point was that with a group as large as 13, there must be a time commitment to do a route, or the dynamic can rapidly go downhill.

When asked why they climb, why they love it, why they risk so much of themselves for it, longtime, hard-core climbers will often turn that question on its head. The response of this class of climber lies not in why climbing adds enjoyment to their lives. The answer, in fact, is that climbing is what makes living worth the effort.

If pressed, devoted climbers will admit that the appeal of the entire pursuit is the feeling of membership, of belonging. For a lonely sport, climbers are not alone. By mastering a skill that both is dangerous and defines accomplishment by a precise and measurable standard, a climber is not, after all, an outsider but falls, as it were, quite squarely inside a tightly drawn circle. If a climber is in trouble, other climbers will help him because he is one of them.

Former outcasts are suddenly included, and far beyond merely being part of a group, they are members of a cool community whose password is not money or connections but competence and expertise. It is intoxicating in every aspect, not only the actual climbing, but also just being around other climbers, lingering in a climbing store, fussing with climbing gear. To enter the community, the world, of climbers, to be a part of their aura, is to be embraced in the romance and the glamour of the quest.

The competing allure of the pursuit, of course, is climbing as a drug of self-expression, of calmness, of centering. The idea of pinpoint focus on the struggle toward one solitary goal, breaking down the mountain of a problem into many tiny dilemmas and solving them all, overcoming them, conquering them, one hand-hold, one foothold at a time, is an enticing, powerful draw. As the climber affirms himself through his strength and his resilience, the world falls away and, with it, all of the stress and hassle and monotony of his daily life. Extraneous issues—grief, loss, regret—are not merely obscured or rendered blurry; by necessity, they must vanish completely. The act of climbing is an escape into immediacy, freedom from unrelenting pressure. The climber cannot, at risk of death, focus on, even think about, anything beyond the explicit task at hand. And in that reality, climbing bestows the ultimate gift: it quiets the clutter.

In the post–World War II climbing heyday, cutting-edge climbing dominated the atmosphere in the Tetons, with the range emerging as the cornerstone of American mountaineering. The park supported a dedicated Climber's Camp at that time, where climbing myths and legends were passed down from climbers whose stays overlapped throughout the season.

Back in the day, there was a great tradition of young men at Jenny Lake, along with mountaineers doing high wall work in Yosemite, known as dirtbag climbers. They were recognizable for maintaining an impoverished existence—it was important to them to be perceived as poor, sacrificing for their passion. Showers were in scarce supply. They kept costs way down, wore beat-up clothes (often Army surplus gear), scrounged for their next meal—despite the fact that a fairly high percentage of them were actually trust-fund kids. In the '60s and '70s, as climbers worked out their issues against their parents and society at large, climbing became much less of a seasonal commitment and more of an alternative lifestyle.

Climbers have always been considered fairly rebellious, and while they don't seem to mind the label, in reality, especially as opposed to other types of extreme athletes, they are not overly radical. For the most part, they are tranquil, philosophical, intensely fatalistic, and universally infused with a sort of mournful streak. The quintessence of the climbing community is one long lament.

Although climbers are generally perceived as fearless, most of them actually do get scared from time to time. As former Jenny Lake ranger Ralph Tingey says, "It's what keeps us from falling." Early on in their careers, climbers—the successful ones—adopt a nearly mandatory sense of humility and respect for the mountains.

Any wall can eventually be climbed one way or another, but the spiritual, intuitive core of climbing is to climb the wall the right way. Pete Sinclair, a former Jenny Lake climbing ranger, in his book *We Aspired: The Last Innocent Americans,* captures the essence of that sentiment: "After you've climbed in one area a lot, you have the feeling that the mountains tell you how they ought to be climbed. You climb in a certain way because of the nature of the rock or terrain, the weather, the history and tradition of the place and something of your own, which asks for something more graceful than just surviving. If it works, you feel that you have done something beautiful."

Over time, mountaineering has emerged on a more recreational level, with people climbing as a hobby rather than having it dominating every facet of their lives. While there are lots of names for climbers who take up the sport somewhat casually—wilderness wannabes, for example—the distinction between serious climbers and recreational climbers is not as great as it might seem. All climbers are serious about climbing. Rec climbers generally have jobs outside of the climbing world, however, while the most dedicated climbers tend either to abandon the idea of a career entirely or to find a job where they can get paid to climb. The Jenny Lake rangers could have other, easier jobs in the climbing world—guiding, for instance—but these men choose to be public servants. In the end, there is no climbing job more socially redeeming than one that saves lives.

When most people start out rock climbing, they climb in gyms or engage in what is known as sport climbing. Sport climbing utilizes permanent bolts preattached to the rock. The routes often consist of just a single pitch, and the objective dangers are taken out entirely. As there is no need for a climber to attach climbing aids as he ascends, sport climbing focuses on strength, endurance, and almost acrobatic body control.

In contrast, in traditional climbing, also known as trad climbing, there are no fixed anchors on the rock, and climbers must place their own gear (referred to as protection) as they climb. Climbers must determine both the type and the placement of the equipment. They typically use removable protection, such as cams or nuts, that they can clip back onto themselves and use over and over. Climbers retrieve the gear they wedge or hammer into the mountain not just because of the expense but also because they do not like the idea of excessive bolts marring the mountainside, a condition they refer to as siege climbing. While the routes in traditional climbing can be single-pitch, they more frequently involve longer, multipitch ascents. This type of climbing requires the same physical ability as sport climbing but adds other components such as self-sufficiency, adventure, and risk.

Beginning climbers who learn the sport in a gym or in controlled outdoor environments on smallish, sunny cliffs are not necessarily prepared for true mountain climbing. First of all, it is exceedingly easy to get off route while mountain climbing. Many Teton routes are fractured enough that if a climber moves 10 feet off a climbing line, he could suddenly be climbing a much more difficult pitch. In addition, the elements, such as wind currents, are much more intense, as is the exposure involved in massive drop-offs.

Alpine climbing, generally considered a subset of mountain climbing, adds yet another tier of complexity, as a climber high in the mountains can encounter wet rock or snow or a section where the mountain has iced over. The Tetons are notorious for unpredictable weather and have more ice and snow than, for example, Yosemite. The only places in the country that come close in terms of extreme winter weather are Denali in Alaska and the Cascades in Washington.

The Teton climbing season seems to become more truncated every year. While it used to be three months long, it is currently centered around the end of July and the first two weeks of August. Every day during that season, there are people on the mountain who should have served an apprenticeship first, people who do not realize that things are only fine until the moment when they are not. Excellent sport climbers often end up shocked that their skills do not translate to an alpine environment. People want instant gratification, they want to say that they've climbed the Grand, but the Tetons are not a rock-climbing park. Mountain climbing is a different game entirely, with aspects of altitude and precipices and weather and fear.

Hiking up Garnet Canyon for the first time can be a wake-up call, forcing novices to confront the certainty that they cannot underestimate the Tetons. Yet while the range has humbled climbers attempting routes above their ability, climbers at all ranges of skill have put themselves in situations in which they should not have been. The fatalities in alpine mountaineering occur at all levels of experience—not just the beginners die.

Within the climbing community, Renny is infamous for a few exploits in particular, including a 1984 summit of the north face of Cholatse, a 21,128-foot mountain in the Khumbu region of Nepal that he initially declared "impossible, or at the very least improbable." That trip was one of five he took to the Himalayas in the 1980s. His outlook on the success of major climbing trips was that the "three Ws" have to fall into place: weather, work, and women.

Soon after the turn of the century, his Ws all in sync, Renny turned his attention to climbing the Grand Traverse in winter, a combination of 10 peaks in the Tetons totaling 25,000 vertical feet of climbing and descending. It took him three attempts to do it, and he suffered an extremely close call on the last one. As he was vigilantly downclimbing into a sharp notch between Teewinot and the East Prong, he commented to one of his climbing partners that the cornice buildup appeared to be exceptionally large and overhung on their lee-side route. When the slope gave way, Renny managed to execute a back flip onto the windward side of the ridge as the tons of wind-compacted snow collapsed and triggered a huge avalanche that hit the glacier below.

Part of the draw of climbing is that it appeals to people engaging in it for sport as well as those doing it as a career, and those paths intersect when recreational climbers need to be rescued by professional climbers. Renny's credibility as a climber comes from his decision to turn back with the summit of Everest in sight. That highly developed degree of mountain judgment collided with a group of Idaho climbers who, for a variety of factors, many—including the capriciousness of Mother Nature—out of their control, too late in the day made a decision to call off their summit bid of the Grand.

In the aftermath of the tragedy, when the event was analyzed in newspapers and magazines, the climbing party was always referred to as a group of friends and coworkers from an alternative health-care company called Melaleuca, but in reality, it was primarily a family trip for both Rob Thomas and Clint Summers. Rob had organized the trip for his wife, Sherika; his dad, Bob; his father-in-law, Steve Oler; his brother, Justin; and his step-brother, Reese Jackson.

Clint Summers was in on the trip from the beginning, because when Rob and Clint, best friends for several years, summited the Grand together the previous summer, they called their wives from the peak and made a pact to bring them back to experience the climb with them the next year. The trip grew from there. Dave Jordan was included because he was a strong and longtime climbing partner of Rob's and had summited the Grand many times before. Rob's step-brother, Reese, invited his close friend Kip Merrill.

The last members to join the party were the ones from Melaleuca. Clint, who worked at the company, asked coworkers Rod Liberal, Jake Bancroft, and Reagan Lembke to come along. Rob was initially a little annoyed, since the trip was intended to be "his deal" with his wife and his dad, but he understood that Clint wanted to share the climbing experience with new climbers from his job.

Clint first met Rob just out of college when they were neighbors in Pocatello, Idaho. Rob owned an Internet company at the time, and he hired Clint to work for him as an account representative. Clint was solid and respectful, with a quiet authority that caused people to view him as trustworthy, if not necessarily warm. He would go on professionally to focus on Web development, but not before an incredible outdoor relationship had been forged between the two men. Both Rob, six-foot-two, and Clint, five-foot-eight and more slightly built, were big into snowboarding, mountain biking, and especially rock climbing.

Clint was newly married to Erica when he met Rob, and

Clint once confided to him that when he married Erica, he felt that they wouldn't be together long. The comment was not made from the standpoint of an unhappy marriage. Clint simply had a sort of hazy premonition that Erica would be gone from his life early.

As Rob and Clint developed a friendship, their wives also became close, and the couples ended up either babysitting each other's children or, more frequently, double-dating. Rob, whose passion for climbing was more intense when he shared it with others, had gotten his wife interested, and the two couples occasionally went on expeditions together. On one climbing trip to the City of Rocks in Almo, Idaho, Rob and Clint were the ones experiencing some scary moments on the flake rock, while Erica, belayed by Rob from the top, scrambled up the face like a world-class climber. Although Erica had been climbing for years before she met Clint and could climb like a pro when she felt like turning it on, she sometimes lacked self-assurance.

As it turned out, Erica needed a little convincing to go on the Grand trip. Over dinner in a pizza parlor in Idaho Falls during the planning stages, her brother-in-law, who had climbed the Grand before, attempted to build her confidence by assuring her that she could do it. He explained to her that the climb's long approach and high elevation could wear on someone who wasn't in shape but that she was clearly fit enough to make it to the top.

Erica confided her concerns about the climb to Sherika. Erica realized that just the month before, on June 21, 2003, a 23-year-old woman from Michigan had died after plummeting 800 feet off the crest of the east ridge while hiking up Middle Teton via the Southwest Couloir. In fact, yet another young woman, a 22-year-old from Washington, would die in early July of that summer of massive traumatic injuries after she fell near Baxter's Pinnacle.

After some discussion, it came out that Erica's main reason for hedging against the trip wasn't so much that she was afraid of the climb but that she wanted to have Clint to herself for a romantic getaway to celebrate their fifth wedding anniversary.

In contrast to Clint's more reserved nature, Erica was outgoing and gregarious, but like her husband, she was outdoorsy and heavily involved in camping, skiing, and snowboarding. Erica was a more frequent and more advanced climber than Clint in terms of sport climbing, but Clint was more experienced in big mountain climbs, especially on Teton peaks. Exceptionally proficient on quick top rappels or lead climbs in the cliffs around Pocatello, Erica was ready to cross over to mountaineering. In the summer of 2001, Clint had attempted to summit the Grand but was thwarted by snow; in 2002, he made it to the top of the peak with Rob. The idea of going back and doing it again with Erica, seeing the experience through her eyes, drove Clint's desire to return.

In the end, either Clint's perspective was romantic enough for her or Erica's adventurous side won out. Either way, she agreed to the climb, and Clint and Erica began planning the journey up the Grand as an anniversary celebration.

At Rob's insistence, he and Clint took the three beginners from Melaleuca—Rod, Jake, and Reagan—climbing in Cascade Canyon on a multipitch route a few weeks in advance of the trip to the Grand. From Rob's point of view, it was hilarious to watch how the novices were taking to climbing and eating it up, almost as if they had never been outside before. Rob and Clint kept a watch especially over Jake, who was climbing for the first time, to make sure he trusted the system and wouldn't freeze or freak out on a rappel.

After Rod, Reagan, and Jake jumped on the trip, the total number in the climbing party was 13 (11 men and two women). After his initial reluctance, Rob admitted that they could accommodate as many people as they wanted, as long as they had no more than four on a rope team and the teams were comparable ability-wise. The new additions meant that to keep the climbing groups small, Clint and Rob's brother Justin would also have to lead teams.

Rod, Jake, Reagan, Reese, and Kip camped at the Meadows, about a 4.2-mile hike in from the trailhead, where the climbers were able to replenish their water. From the Meadows, it was another couple of miles up to the Moraine site, where the two married couples plus Justin, Bob, Steve, and Dave were camping. From that point, the Lower Saddle, the real launching-off point, was only about a half-hour away.

Rob and Sherika and Clint and Erica left the Lupine Meadows trailhead the day before their summit bid and hiked nearly seven miles through Garnet Canyon to reach their campsite. Their permit was for an area known as the Moraine, a glacially formed accumulation of soil and rock. With a little advance scouting, the glacial debris in the area, ranging from silt-sized glacier flour to large boulders, made for some fairly comfortable tent sites. Rob later described the pace of the four of them on the way to the Moraine glacier, a trail that wound steeply past rushing waterfalls and hillsides layered in wildflowers, as "not quite lollygagging." Rob and Clint realized that this part of the trip wasn't going to occur at the fast tempo the two of them preferred, so they relaxed, looked around, picked huckleberries from the bushes, and ate them as they walked along. The rest of the climbers camping at the Moraine all hiked at their own rates, too, passing one another at times, pausing for breaks, generally taking it easy in preparation for the big climb and the push to the summit the following morning.

That night, Erica pulled a can of Campbell's Chunky Soup out of her pack for dinner. It was a lot of weight for her to have carried in her backpack on the hike in, but everyone was jealous when she heated it up on Rob's little eight-ounce titanium stove. A self-described gear whore, Rob, age 32, was known always to have the right boots, the ideal pack (selected from his vast collection), the best fabric for every occasion. He realized that what had started out as an interest in ultra-streamlining his packing was turning into a bit of an obsession as he counted just about every gram he hauled.

Shortly before 6:00 A.M. on the 26th, Rob and Sherika emerged from their tent and roused Clint and Erica from the tent next to them. As the two couples sat around the camp stove waiting for the glacier water to boil, there was very little talking. When the other four climbers crawled out of their tents to join them at breakfast, conversation continued to remain at a minimum. At that hour, getting up and moving felt more like a duty than an adventure. Everyone was tired, and Erica in particular, not known as a morning person, alternated between silence and relatively good-natured grumbling. Rob made a point of giving her the first batch of hot water so she could make herself some hot chocolate.

Still, once they all began gathering up their gear—harnesses, 200-foot lengths of red, yellow, and blue nylon rope—and putting on their black fiberglass helmets, the process became much more anticipatory. The climbers' excitement built on itself as they finished off a large breakfast—oatmeal, Pop-Tarts—to consume maximum calories for the exertion ahead.

As they waited for the rest of their group to ascend from the campsite below, the eight climbers piled on the rest of the clothes they planned to wear on the climb. The summit of the Grand is notoriously fickle temperature-wise, often requiring dedicated cold-weather gear. Other times, the peak can be blazing hot. For the past six weeks, the weather had been clear, with temperatures often topping 90 degrees on the windswept plains. (Renny had climbed to the top of the mountain several

times in the previous few weeks wearing only shorts and a
T-shirt.) Afternoon thunderstorms were providing the only relief from the scorching heat.

Erica hedged her bets and dressed for the cold, with full-
length green hiking pants and a relatively heavy, orangeish-red
jacket. In contrast, Clint was, as Rob said, "begging for a beautiful day," in shorts and a sleeveless shirt. There were no signs
of inclement weather, but in keeping with his conscientious
groundwork, Rob was always prepared for the worst in terms
of gear, and that policy extended to his attire. He was dressed
in layers, including a green wind-resistant jacket, and, ever the
Boy Scout, he tucked an extra fleece and a few other warm
items of clothing into his backpack. By late that afternoon, he
would be yanking the clothes out of his pack in an effort to
warm his hypothermic friend.

Once they finished packing for the climb, the group started
off for the Lower Saddle to await the other five climbers.

Meanwhile, down in the Meadows campsite, 2.2 miles and
1,800 feet below, the other members of the climbing party had
begun to stir. Jake, Rod, and Reagan all rolled out of the same
tent and, along with the other two climbers in their party, hiked
up to the Lower Saddle to meet the others. They weren't sure
what time they hit the trail, but the early-morning air was
frigid, and the mountain peaks were still shrouded in darkness.
To Jake in particular, who admitted that he didn't understand
mountaineering, the whole ordeal seemed to be getting off to
an awfully early start.

By 8:00 A.M., the Meadows group had joined the Moraine
group at the fixed rope below the Lower Saddle. Once assembled, they all scrambled up together to the Lower Saddle, the
11,600-foot ridge between the Grand and Middle Tetons, a site
that hours later would be swarming with rescue personnel
and helitack teams. High above them, sunlight glinted off the

granite peaks as they began their ascent up the craggy south side of the peak.

The 13 climbers broke up into four rope teams, distributing the most and least experienced climbers among them. Each team was led by a climber who had previously summited the Grand: Rob, Justin, Dave, and Clint. It was Rob's fourth time climbing the Grand, and "Safety Dave," who had become serious about climbing at Idaho State University and had been hooked ever since, was looking to summit for the 10th time.

Dave led the first rope team of three, followed by Rob leading four climbers. While living in Pocatello, Idaho, Rob had gone climbing in the Tetons four or five times every spring. His familiarity with the Grand as well as his experience on much more technically difficult climbs—for example, Elephant's Perch in the Sawtooth Wilderness, a 5.9 trad climb with a sheer 1,000-foot vertical face—made him the obvious choice as the overall group leader.

In Rob's three previous summits of the Grand, he had begun the ascent as early as 1:00 A.M. and as late as 11:00 A.M. With a group of 13 people, he was shooting to leave the Lower Saddle by 9:00 A.M., and even after waiting for the other members of the climbing party to come up from the lower campsite, they still beat that by an hour.

The team leaders each carried family-frequency Motorola radios to talk to one another, and the group did a last-minute check to make sure that they were operable. Throughout the day, the climbers used them mostly for climbing commands— "On belay," "Climb on," etc.—and occasionally for a more conversational "Hey, Dad, where are you?"

Some members of the group were not just new to climbing but also new to one another. Rod had only met Kip and Reese the evening before, and he was introduced to Erica for the first time that morning. Although everyone was obviously not matched in terms of climbing skill or experience, each member of the party was in great physical shape. As the morning progressed, Rob was especially impressed with the performance of Sherika and Erica, both, according to him, "tough, spirited Idaho girls" (despite the fact that Erica, getting off to a sleepy early-morning start, seemed more shy than sociable at the beginning of the climb). Although neither woman trained year-round for climbing, the consensus among the 11 men was that they were both incredibly athletic. While the climb was strenuous, it was not beyond anyone's ability level, and throughout the day, no one in their group held anyone else back.

The group planned to snack on the way up rather than stop for a whole lunch, because, depending on pace, they expected that it would only take a couple of hours to get to Wall Street. They packed gel packs, string cheese, granola, and beef sticks to devour quickly as they climbed.

As it turned out, they had plenty of time to eat.

The Exum Ridge route is one of America's most famous alpine rock climbs and therefore one of the most crowded. The climbing traffic on the mountain was intensely busy, with the Idaho climbers constantly having to wait as other parties ascended ahead of them. The skies were bright blue, and the weather was sunny and brisk, but people were meandering all over the mountain, and the large group simply couldn't get around them.

By 11:00 A.M., they had made reasonably steady progress to reach the base of the wide, flat ridge of Wall Street that marks the start of the Exum Ridge, but there they came to a complete stop. People were strung out all along the rocky ledge. In front of them, almost a dozen climbers were working their way up the ridge and waiting their turn to rope up and execute the technical move across the open-air chasm at the end of Wall Street. All of the climbers from the morning were backed up at that one funnel point. The whole length of the narrowing ledge was crowded—not only was there a line of people in front of the Idaho group, but there were also climbers coming up behind them.

To pass the time, they ate their snacks. They took pictures of the view and of one another. They talked about how awesome the morning had been, how far they could see, how much rock they had climbed. To this point, some of the footwork on the climb had been tricky, and the holds were not always obvious or generous, but nervous anticipation grew as the group realized that the real technical climbing, the scary part, was about to begin. The sky was clear, and spirits were high. They were restless about the delay but more exhilarated than tired.

As time went by, they began to feel uneasy. After an hour of waiting, they began to get outright anxious. After two hours, the mood had turned somber. And then the clouds moved in.

Erica in particular was having a hard time—without moving around for a couple of hours on the mountainside, she was cold and tired and thinking about turning back. Justin gave her his gloves, and Clint and Sherika cheered her on, encouraging her to eat, telling her how great she was doing, reminding her that they were just 1,500 feet from the summit.

Nerves were likely playing a part as well. Earlier, when they arrived at Wall Street and Erica took her first look at the gaping chasm she would have to cross, she had turned to Clint, saying, "Holy crap, what are we doing?" That was the place, and the time, where the sport climber separates from the mountain climber—the exposure kicks in, the 2,000-foot drop. None of her experience would make that particular maneuver any less intimidating.

In addition, it was getting chillier in the shadows, and the climbers had another lengthy process in front of them. After being delayed more than two hours for their chance to start on Wall Street, the climbers would still have to wait for one another as the 13 of them each roped up and crossed the gap. They realized that after five hours on the mountain, they should have been at or near the summit, and they had yet to move past the first technical section of the route.

Wall Street is considered a point of no return on the ascent of the Grand. After crossing it, it is a complex operation to retreat. Once the climbers cleared the Wall Street gap, they would be committed to climbing to within several hundred feet of the summit before finding the next exit.

Clint asked Erica what she wanted to do. She told him that her legs were hurting her but that after sitting there watching the group above them advance through Wall Street, she had gotten used to the exposure and felt less panicked.

Once Erica said she wanted to keep climbing, Clint decided it might help her to change up their team for the rest of the climb. Clint and Erica had been teamed up with Jake, the greenest climber in the group. Clint asked Rod, who was a stronger climber than Jake, if he would trade with Jake and shift to Clint and Erica's team.

Rod agreed to join the third rope team, leaving Jake, Justin, and Reagan to make up the final team. By the time the climbers all successfully traversed the breach—blood vibrating with adrenaline, hearts hammering wildly—more wispy clouds began to drift across the sky to the east of Exum Ridge.

When the climbers reached the sheer rock face of Friction Pitch, dark thunderclouds were actively building in the northwest. As frequently happens on summer afternoons in the Tetons, the warm, moist air rising over the valley collided with cooler currents flowing in from the southwest, creating a storm cell with a massive electrical charge.

Around 3:00, it started raining lightly. Shortly after that, an icy drizzle drenched the group. The buoyancy of the brilliant sunny day had been swapped for a grim and bleak atmosphere as the climbers waited, once again, for people ahead of them to advance.

At this stage, Justin, who had been studying the overcast sky, was overcome with a sense of foreboding, panic-stricken with the feeling that they shouldn't be waiting so long. The premonition that he was going to die was so acute that he stifled back tears as he pulled his phone out of his pack to call his wife and tell her he loved her.

By this point, the first rope team had ascended the slick, wet granite of Friction Pitch. From his position on the top of the pitch, Dave called Rob on the radio to discuss next steps.

Rob had essentially put the trip together—secured the permits, put the logistics in place—and in that moment, as group leader, he felt the full weight of accountability. He knew that if he ditched the summit bid, certain members of the group would be severely disappointed to have come so far, gotten so close, and not reached the top.

Rob also knew that there was a valid argument to keep going at that point, because in order to go down, they first had to go up. The rainstorm had saturated the rock on Friction Pitch and made it exceptionally slippery, but they had to climb it anyway. Backtracking was not an option. To try to reverse what they had done back down to Wall Street would have taken them hours; it would have meant setting anchors on the mountain and doing some extremely dangerous downclimbing.

Either choice, pressing on or turning back, required the climbers to be at the top of Friction Pitch. It was at the crest of the pitch where climbers could either continue ascending roughly 600 feet to the summit or veer off to the escape route. Even if they abandoned their summit quest, from their location, the only way off the mountain was to climb the most difficult section of the route. And once they had scaled Friction Pitch, the technical section of the climb was essentially over.

Still, neither Rob nor Dave, the most experienced climbers in the group, had a summit-or-die attitude. In the end, Rob, in consultation with Dave, called off the summit attempt. The afternoon had somehow taken on an ominous tone, and both men knew the mountains well enough to trust a sensation that just felt wrong. The group needed to concentrate its energy on getting back to safe territory, and Rob rightly believed that spending extra minutes getting to the peak was contrary to the goal of getting the hell out of there. They had simply been on the mountain much too long, and it was time to get off.

Rob wasn't concerned with his own emotions regarding not reaching the top; he felt as if the issue wasn't about him and the summit but rather his responsibility to get everyone down. Clint was fine with the call, rationalizing that it just gave him an excuse to come back and climb it again. Justin, who had prophesied his own death, and Erica, whose legs were burning, were outwardly relieved at the decision.

Jake, who was, and would remain, blissfully ignorant of the extent of the potential danger the group faced, was mildly disappointed but having a great time either way. Steve, Rob's father-in-law, was nearly furious, cursing at Rob and saying, "Are you kidding me? We are *this close.*" The most frustrated climbers didn't necessarily comprehend the full volatility of Teton weather at that altitude, didn't realize that massive storms could come in above them at any moment.

Even as Rob announced the decision to scrap the idea of the summit, more clouds emerged, and the sky began to darken. There was no thunder or lightning to that point. The group's attitude toward lightning strikes was that they were something that happened on a golf course, not at 13,000 feet. None of the climbers considered lightning as a threat, although Jake and Reagan did joke that the trekking poles Justin and Rob had used during the earlier hiking portions of the trip—folded up and sticking up out of the packs on their backs as they climbed—would make excellent lightning rods.

Once the decision had been made to get off the mountain, the tension level in the group ramped up considerably. Rob and Dave knew how to find the descent rappel by cutting left at the top of Friction Pitch. From that location, they needed to traverse the east ridge, rappel 140 feet down a cliff, then do a quick scramble down a scree slope to land at the Upper Saddle. Dave's team was already at the top of Friction Pitch, and he immediately began to lead them down. After climbing the V Pitch, they headed over to the main rappel. Since they only had one rope, they fixed it there and rappelled down to the Upper Saddle.

At that point, two other climbing parties committed a blatant violation of both climbing etiquette and common courtesy by cutting in front of the Idaho climbers. A team of four and a team of two, unrelated to each other, came between Dave's rope team and Rob's team. Randomly, both teams had meteorologists on them, which was comical in a twisted sort of way, given that they were exposed on the top of a mountain in what was soon to be a lightning storm.

The men on the two-person team, both from New York, were trying to move too quickly on wet rock. One of them would later give Dave, who by that time had reached the Upper Saddle, a rope to use to climb back up the mountain in an attempt to help his friends. The men had climbed maybe 15 feet up when one of them turned around and called down to Rob, "Hey, is it all right if we climb ahead?" The answer was that they were already doing it, and Rob, frustrated and exhausted, merely waved them on.

One of the men alternated between meandering up the mountain and moving too rapidly, as if for an audience. Rob thought the guy might tumble off the face, but as it turned out, both men (and also the party of four) that climbed in between the Idaho climbing party ended up summiting the Grand moments after the lightning struck. Their ice axes hummed like crazy with ground-current voltage steps before they reached the peak.

Immediately after those nonrelated teams moved through their ranks, like a butterfly flapping its wings, forever altering the timing of who would be on which exact rock at 3:35 that afternoon, Rob ascended Friction Pitch first in his group of four. When he reached the top, he set three camming devices (spring-loaded metal anchors) into the rock at the top of the pitch to secure the rope. He first belayed the climbers in his group from above, speeding up their progress on the mountain, then belayed Clint, who clipped into an anchor at the top of the pitch. Once Clint was up, Rob headed toward the traverse to the big rappel down to the Owen-Spalding route to get off the mountain.

Rob's team was spread out above the top of Friction Pitch, climbing unroped in third-class terrain, meaning that three points of contact were potentially required (e.g., a climber might need a handhold on a rocky outcropping). Class 3 is easy climbing—a mountaineer wouldn't do it with his hands in his pockets, but he also probably wouldn't need a rope. Rob's father, Bob, who was on his team, was near the base of the V Pitch. Rob had rounded the corner at the top of Friction Pitch and scrambled upward approximately 15 feet. Sherika was on a ledge a few feet below her husband.

With the switching of the groups, Rod was on the third team with Clint and Erica, the one behind Rob's team. With Clint belaying her from above, Erica began her ascent of Friction Pitch while Rod waited below for his turn to climb. In addition to Rod, the only members of the Idaho group left to climb Friction Pitch were those on the fourth rope team, now made up of Jake, Justin, and Reagan, all tied into a single-point anchor at the base of the pitch.

On any given day, the members of the group could have been at those places at that time in the afternoon and everything would have flowed together the right way. They all were physically capable, and without a storm, they all likely would have summited. Still, in the mountains, in the Tetons, in the summer, there are late-afternoon thunderstorms on many days, and if you were a betting man, you would have been off the Grand hours earlier.

NINE

"This is so beautiful, so breathtaking. It's like
a dream."
—
Clint Summers to Erica Summers, 3:34 P.M., July 26, 2003

Erica climbed up smoothly, solidly, heaving herself onto the
Friction Pitch ledge with a final huge effort. She had a tough
time getting traction on the wet rock, but once she was up and
over, she was visibly elated. Still drenched from the rain and
shivering in the chill wind, she settled into a sitting position on
the ridge and cuddled up against Clint.

At the bottlenecks at various points on the ascent, there had
been other climbing parties both in front of them and behind
them, and they had been climbing all day right next to the other
11 members of their group, but for those few moments on the
top of Friction Pitch, there wasn't anybody else on earth except
Clint and Erica. All of the other teams had gone ahead or long
turned back, and the members of their own group were spread
out above and below them.

The first three climbers in their party were already at the

rappel and on their way to the Lower Saddle. Rob and Sherika and the rest of their group had headed for the V Pitch. Two other unconnected climbing groups had passed the Idaho climbers in their insistence on reaching the summit. Clint had just begun belaying Rod up Friction Pitch, and the last three climbers in their group were waiting their turn on a ledge at the bottom of the pitch.

At that place, at that time, in the mist, it was only the two of them, husband and wife alone on the nearly flat, ten-foot-wide ridge above the pitch, stretching their gazes out over the expansive view of the peaks and glaciers of Teton Valley. As tendrils of fog curled around them, they sat together on the edge, Erica on Clint's left side, hips and thighs pressed close, legs dangling over the top of the world.

Camping in the rocky Moraine in the shadow of the Grand the previous night had been their first night away together since Erica had given birth to their daughter, Adison, just over four years earlier. The week before the climbing trip, the couple had invited Erica's family over for Adison's fourth birthday party, barbecuing in the backyard and celebrating with cake and ice cream. Then, for the first time, they left Adison and her brother, Daxton, overnight with family so they could climb the mountain together. The trip wasn't the way Erica had originally envisioned commemorating their fifth wedding anniversary, but even so, in a tent in the cool mountain air, she got the best night's sleep she had had in years.

Erica and Clint, both from Idaho, first met each other at Idaho State University. Clint was studying accounting, finance, and computer information systems, and Erica was in the nursing program. In keeping with their mutual love of the outdoors, they went snowboarding on their first date. They didn't mess around with their courtship—they were engaged after three months, married after eight, long before finishing college.

Clint took additional college courses in accounting, graduating officially in 2002, by which time he and Erica had had two children. Adison was born in the summer of 1999, and Daxton came along almost exactly two years later. Clint described his life with Erica as "the American dream"—two kids, a house, a great job. In only their mid-20s, they seemed to have already achieved so many of their goals, yet they continued to have, as Clint says, "big plans."

Clint's somewhat reticent personality was more than balanced out by Erica's gracious charm. When the family moved to a new neighborhood, Erica was the one taking cookies around to meet the neighbors rather than waiting for them to welcome her to the street. In five years of marriage, the couple never had one fight, never were frustrated with each other, never even raised their voices with each other, a dynamic that Clint readily attributes to Erica's kindhearted, selfless nature. Although Clint himself was easygoing, he realized that Erica was responsible for fostering the exceptional harmony in their relationship.

At age 25, in addition to her family and nursing classes at Idaho State, Erica's focus was on charitable work, donating her time to people in need. Clint would mock-complain about this aspect of her character to friends—"Well, Erica brought some homeless people home again, gave them food, gave them my clothes"—when it was obvious how much he admired her for it.

Sitting on the top of the pitch, squeezed close against his wife, Clint contemplated the lakes and canyons below, a brilliant expanse of scenery encompassing a panorama of majestic mountains sweeping down to the Wyoming plains. The Montana countryside and the geysers of Yellowstone sprawled out to the north; to the west, the Snake River wound throughout both the deserts and the fertile pasturelands of Idaho.

Despite the wind rushing around them, Clint and Erica existed only in a private cocoon of silence and stillness. The cold and the exhaustion of the day fell away. Lost in the rawness of their seclusion, Erica's face revealed only an absolute and un-qualified connection to the jubilation Clint was feeling.

"It was worth it," she said. The view was worth the climb.

Even though they were heading down without reaching the top of the mountain, those minutes alone together, the two of them inexorably linked, granted them a more profound joy than merely touching the summit ever could have. Some of the last words out of Clint's mouth to his wife before lightning struck were how surreal, how dreamlike, the whole adventure seemed, how beautiful it was to share the experience with her.

Erica leaned into Clint's shoulder as she expressed how much it meant to her that they were there together . . . and then the moment was over.

In unison, Clint and Erica transferred their attention and their eyes down to Rod, climbing on a belay line below them, about halfway up the pitch. Erica shifted her weight ever so slightly away from her husband, thighs still touching but her upper body leaning back a bit, freeing the rope up to give Clint space to focus on Rod.

When Erica had nestled in next to Clint, she had not unroped or clipped into the anchor. Clint had to take Erica's rope out of the Black Diamond–ATC belay device, then put the device on the rope below her knot so he could belay the rope leading to Rod.

This procedure would take Erica and Rod off belay for the time it took Clint to relock the carabiner back into his harness. If he had had more time, Clint would have done things differ-ently, but it was just going to take a second. A quick unclip and reclip, the matter of a blink of an eye. He yelled down to Rod, asking him if he had a good hold. All three of them were tied to one rope, and for a second, the belay device was not going to be holding the rope anymore.

In the instant Clint unhooked the equipment, Rod was still connected to the rope but completely detached from the belay device. If, for instance, lightning were to have struck in the split-second before Clint was able to reclip, ripping Rod off the mountain, there would have been no device to stop the rope from running out its full length. Best case, without a belay, Rod would have fallen until his rope played out, in fast motion, and came tight against Erica, hurtling him 200 feet down the mountain until he was jerked to a stop on the end of the rope. He almost certainly would have suffered fatal injuries when he hit the ledge at the bottom of Friction Pitch. In addition, since Erica wasn't anchored, she would have been yanked off the ledge as well, and fallen half the length of the rope. The rope would have then spun out until it came tight against Clint, pulling him off the mountain and stranding him, suspended in air, near the top of the rope.

More likely, however, the anchor would have failed from the violence of the weight of all three people straining against it so abruptly, and everyone would have plunged to their deaths.

Clint reclipped the belay device. He heard the metallic scrape it made as it clicked into place securely. The next sound he heard was the reverberation of his own screams.

As Clint began to come to, the sensation was not at all like waking up from sleep. He was alone in the dark, not knowing where he was and not understanding why he didn't know. His eyes were closed at first, then, when they did open, utterly unfocused. He could not grasp onto an idea of where he could be or what he was doing.

Clint finally caught a glimpse of the valley and realized that he had been climbing. The next thought he had was *What is that piercing noise, and where is it coming from?* He slowly began to realize that it was him shrieking as loudly as he could. He had no idea why he was screaming. He did not know that he had just been struck by a bolt of lightning. He hadn't yet felt the pain, at least not consciously. He hadn't had the time or the capacity to understand anything about Erica. In any event, he yelled until his breath ran out.

Only then did Clint look down at his left side, and Erica was sprawled against him, leaning on him, and she was not moving, and she was not breathing. The events, the timing, began to blur for Clint at that point. Erica remained on the rope connected to Rod, with her rope in his belay device. She was pressed up against Clint's body, and they were tied together with ropes and harnesses, and she lay limp next to him, and *on* him, and he couldn't move.

He held his wife in his one good arm, his right arm, the only arm he could feel, and shook her. He still could not comprehend what was going on with her.

Smoke filled the air, and the acrid smell of burned hair and scorched flesh was all around him.

And then he was screaming again, his throat aching, screaming in confusion about what had happened to Erica, what had happened to him. He had no feeling in his lower body, both of his legs were completely numb, he couldn't move his left arm. His left thigh, where it had been touching Erica's right leg, was torn up, and his foot was badly burned.

He screamed Erica's name, he screamed at her to wake up, he screamed for Rod, he screamed for help.

Clint couldn't see or, more accurately, couldn't accept the physical injuries to Erica. Without processing the actual condition of her body, however, he realized within a matter of seconds, long before he had stopped shouting for help, that she was gone. He could tell that there was no responsiveness, no spirit, no life. This wasn't Erica anymore. He knew with certainty, as he phrased it later, that Erica was simply done.

All of a sudden, Rob appeared from the other side of a

Grand Teton.
(Photo courtesy of Lanny Johnson)

(Photo courtesy of Leo Larson)

Lightning in the Tetons.

(Photo courtesy of Lanny Johnson)

Leo Larson.
(Photo courtesy of
Lanny Johnson)

Renny Jackson.
(Photo courtesy of
Brandon Torres)

Laurence Perry.
(Photo courtesy of
Laurence Perry)

Jenny Lake ranger rescue cache, 2003.
(Photo courtesy of Brandon Torres)

L to R: Scott Guenther, Dan Burgette, Renny Jackson,
Chris Harder, Brandon Torres.
(Photo courtesy of Brandon Torres)

Erica Summers, with Adison and Daxton.
(Photo courtesy of Clint Summers)

Clint and Erica
Summers.
(Photos courtesy of
Clint Summers)

L to R: Justin Thomas, Rod Liberal, and Reagan Lembke.
(Photo courtesy of Jake Bancroft)

Aerial recon photographs.

(Photos courtesy of Leo Larson)

Brandon Torres in the
rescue cache, July 26, 2003.
(Photo courtesy of Lanny
Johnson)

Leo Larson being inserted into the scene, taken as Jim
Springer ran up the mountain.
(Photo courtesy of Jim Springer)

Laurence Perry flying helicopter 2LM.

(Photo courtesy of Leo Larson)

Chris Harder and George Montopoli being short-hauled together.

(Photo courtesy of Leo Larson)

Chris Harder providing
medical assistance at
the lower scene while
Jim Springer awaits the
short-haul rope.
(Photo courtesy of Jim
Springer)

Jake Bancroft at the
lower scene.
(Photo courtesy of Chris
Harder)

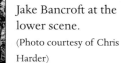

Jim Springer reaching for
the short-haul rope.
(Photo courtesy of Jim Springer)

Jake Bancroft being flown off the Grand.

(Photo courtesy of Leo Larson)

Craig Holm rappelling down Friction Pitch to reach Rod.
(Photo courtesy of Leo Larson)

Jack McConnell and Marty Vidak hauling Rod up Friction
Pitch. (Photo courtesy of Leo Larson)

Craig Holm with Rod approaching the top of Friction Pitch.
(Photo courtesy of Chris Harder)

Shadows moving over the mountains, July 26, 2003.
(Photo courtesy of Chris Harder)

Craig Holm with Rod at the top of Friction Pitch.
(Photo courtesy of Chris Harder)

Sunset over the Grand.
(Photo courtesy of Lanny Johnson)

Craig Holm attending Rod in short-haul
off the Grand.
(Photo courtesy of Chris Harder)

Laurence Perry's final flight of the
evening.
(Photo courtesy of Chris Harder)

Laurence Perry next to blue helicopter, Rick Harmon next to yellow helicopter. Rangers (in uniform) L to R: Tom Kimbrough, Jim Springer, George Montopoli, Chris Harder, Helen Larson, Craig Holm, Leo Larson, Helen Motter, Andy Byerly, Renny Jackson, Jack McConnell, Brandon Torres, Dan Burgette, Scott Guenther, and Marty Vidak.

(Photo courtesy of Leo Larson)

Rod's homecoming from the hospital. Standing, L to R: Reese Jackson, Bob Thomas, Rob Thomas, Dave Jordan, Reagan Lembke. Sitting, L to R: Clint Summers, Rod Liberal, Sherika Thomas, Steve Oler, Justin Thomas, Jake Bancroft.

(Photo courtesy of Jody Liberal)

Jody and Rod Liberal with sons Brennan, Easton, and Kai, 2011.

(Photo courtesy of Rod Liberal)

granite outcropping. From his perspective, Erica initially looked unharmed, leaning up against Clint. Clint was still howling, ungodly sounds coming out of his mouth. Then Rob saw Erica up close, and everything started to unravel.

Unlike her husband, Rob had no illusions about the way Erica looked. Her eyes bulged out of her head, her lips were black. The right side of her face was badly scorched. Her windbreaker and green zip-off pants were shredded and melted. Her clothes were blown outward, as if her skin had exploded. Where the rips were, revealing her legs and her stomach, it was as if a force had burst from the inside out.

Rob slid in next to Erica, and Clint released his hold on her. She fell motionless across Rob's lap. Rob checked for a pulse and found none, then he unclasped Erica's shiny black helmet. Her hair was matted with blood, and fluid leaked from her ears.

As Rob began to perform CPR on Erica, it became evident that the lightning had sucked the moisture out of her body. Her throat was dry and blackened, and it felt as if there was a rock in her chest. Rob actually rolled her over to see if there was a stone underneath her back before recognizing that she had experienced massive internal injuries. At first, the skin on the right side of Erica's body was burned bright pink and red, but as Rob worked over her, it soon turned black and blue. Her body quickly began to swell and puff up, making her appear as if she had been beaten.

Rob had a difficult angle to give Erica CPR, as Clint was twisted in his harness and crowding the space. Clint's fingers were not working well, and he couldn't stand on his legs, so Rob helped Clint out of his harness and moved him away from the edge of Friction Pitch, away from Erica.

Not wanting to move the gear, they left Clint's harness where it was. Clint's anchor had sustained the weight of Rod's fall off the mountain. Rob could see where Rod had fallen, precariously belly-up below, and he yelled down that he would get help to him. From the top of the pitch, Rob was able to hear him moaning, but he wasn't sure whether Rod was actually responding to his voice. In triaging the situation, he focused on trying to revive Erica.

The two men continued CPR together, Clint forcing air into Erica's mouth, Rob compressing her chest. At some point, sitting next to each other on the ledge, the friends admitted the truth to each other. They held Erica's lifeless form and closed their eyes and shared a moment of reflection.

Even though Clint and Rob already knew that Erica was dead, they traded off giving her mouth-to-mouth for approximately 45 more minutes, trying somehow to save her, to bring her back. Long after the climbers had contacted the rangers on the phone for help and the rangers advised them to check her vitals again and then be done, stop CPR, they continued to labor over Erica's body.

After first gently pushing her eyes back into their sockets, Rob's father, Bob, began a second series of attempts to resuscitate her, followed by Sherika, who took a turn for almost 20 minutes. In the aftermath, it became clear that Erica had been hit by a direct bolt of lightning that entered the top of her head and stopped her heart instantly. She never took another breath. The lightning had then jumped into Clint, snapping his leg, and wound down the rope to blast Rod into his inverted position.

As evidence of the level of shock the climbers were experiencing in their fight to save Erica, they had given barely a thought to Rod and the three climbers lost below them. When Rob's dad took over mouth-to-mouth on Erica, Rob walked away and took a minute to himself.

Before the lightning had struck, just before Rob was knocked unconscious, he had a sensation of being crushed, of every single muscle in his body contracting at once. He had been climbing roughly 15 feet up a face, with Sherika scrambling up below him, when he heard a vibrating hum. He couldn't determine the source of the sound, but at high altitude, climbers sometimes hear a ringing in their ears, so Rob yelled down to Sherika, asking her if she had heard anything. She couldn't catch what he had said and asked him to repeat it, but before he could answer, the ground-current charge slammed him, convulsing his body, and he was falling, he thought feet-first, sliding down. In reality, he was plummeting face-first, the weight and momentum of his backpack spinning him off the mountain.

It wasn't until months later, when Sherika heard Rob describing the accident, that she told him about the actual details of his fall. Sherika, climbing below Rob, had seen him falling and slammed her hands into his chest. She shoved back on him, forcing him onto the ridge, throwing him down onto the three-foot ledge. She had been shocked by the dissipating current herself but was aware enough of what was going on to yell, "Rob, don't you dare fall!"

Long after the tragedy, Rob teased Sherika that she must have some sort of superpower, because when she had felt the voltage coming up to her hips, shocking her like an electrified fence, she shouted "No!" at it, and it stopped. While the section of rock where Rob had been climbing at the time of the strike wasn't completely vertical, the slope was greater than 45 degrees, not a place to meander. He might have landed on the ledge on his own, but more likely, his wife broke what would have been a deadly descent off the face of the mountain.

When Rob roused himself after the strike, he was lying on his back with Sherika standing over him, a horrified expression on her face. As he stared back at her, it only took him an instant to figure out what had happened. He couldn't move his left arm at all. The trekking poles tied on his back had burn holes at the top, and some of his cams had melted and welded together. Fearing another strike, he immediately tore off his gear and his harness so he wouldn't have any metal on him. Within a few seconds, he heard Clint's wails and went to find him.

With Rob having been higher than Erica on the mountain, he was theoretically the more likely candidate for a direct lightning strike. In addition, as Erica sat on the edge of the ledge, there was an outcropping of rock above her that the lightning missed entirely. It seemed almost as if lightning didn't play its role correctly in the scenario. It should have hit Rob; it should have aimed for the other parties of climbers nearer to the summit; it should have collided with the mountain itself. According to the science of the phenomenon, as opposed to the mysticism, lightning should not have struck where, or who, it did.

As Rob paced the edge of the pitch, his dad still performing mouth-to-mouth on Erica, he didn't even try to make sense of the situation. He did, however, try to take stock of it: one friend dead, another one dead or dying, three missing.

Sherika had placed the initial 911 call for help, using Bob's cell phone. When the rangers began asking a bunch of questions that she felt she couldn't or didn't want to answer, she passed the phone off to Bob to continue talking to them. Bob had left his phone on during the day, so his batteries only held out for the initial call. After that, Bob switched to Clint's cell phone and used that to communicate with the ranger station. The climbers understood that their rescue was under way.

Until this point, Rod and the other members of his group on the top of the pitch had been focused on Erica to the exclusion of helping anyone else. While they felt helpless to do anything for Rod until help arrived, it was beginning to sink in with Rob that they hadn't yet located the three climbers on the fourth rope team who had disappeared from the base of Friction Pitch, one of whom was his brother, Justin.

"Hey, Just!" he yelled over the side of the mountain, first tentatively, then again and again, gaining in volume each time. There was no response. He tried to raise Justin on the radio but did not receive an answer.

He began frantically shouting "Can you hear me?" out over the mountain, his words adrift on the wind. When his brother's voice failed to come back to him from below, Rob hesitated in the unknown. Minutes before, they had all been heading off the mountain to safety, and now his brother was lost out in the ether, somewhere Rob couldn't see him or hear him. Uncertainty loosened its grip on Rob's psyche, and fear laced with panic slithered in to take its place.

Clint, who had dragged himself over to another crag of rock, felt that he needed to make a decision as a spouse. He was the one who made the call to stop CPR, acknowledging out loud that Erica was gone. With his injuries, he had limited resources to help physically, but he knew that there were other people in danger and that they needed to focus on saving the people who potentially still could be saved.

Clint's feelings were mixed at that point; he was strangely calm, clearly in shock. He was not out of his mind, not hysterical. The idea of concentrating on helping someone other than Erica seemed to channel his energy. Despite having just lost his wife, Clint did what he could for the group by acting as the positive element. He flashed determined and optimistic spirits, telling Rob that they had Web sites to build and they were going to get off the mountain.

Clint's left leg and foot, as well as his backside, were badly burned. There was an entry wound in his thigh where lightning had passed from Erica to him. His shorts were in tatters. Rob was worried that Clint was becoming hypothermic. Clouds had moved in to shroud the entire ledge, the wind had swelled sharply, and the temperature was dropping rapidly. Rob retrieved his extra clothes from his backpack and helped Clint pull on long underwear and a windbreaker.

Rob was still having trouble maneuvering his left arm, so Sherika took his climbing shoes off for him and put his boots on for him and tied them. The rangers had communicated to the group that because of the weather and the time of day, they should be prepared to spend the night on the mountain. Rob knew that the temperature on the top of the mountain would soon dip into freezing territory. He was certain that if they had to stay there all night, several more of them were not going to get off the mountain alive. As Rob snuggled with Clint to keep him warm, he thought it was likely that Clint would die before morning.

Clint tried to persuade his friend to climb down to check on Rod, but Rob believed that there was no way to do it safely. In addition, the rangers on the phone had made it clear that people who had been hit by lightning should not be moving around.

In an attempt to shield them from the wind, Sherika's dad, Steve, began piling up rocks to build a low wall. Steve did his best to keep everyone occupied so that they could only dwell on the discrete tasks in front of them. Bob kept himself busy yelling a steady stream of support and encouragement down to Rod.

Meanwhile, the members of the first rope team, who had been proceeding down the mountain when lightning hit, had seen the flash but did not know that it had struck members of their climbing party until Rob contacted Dave on the interfamily Motorola radios. Rob couldn't bear to use the word "dead" to describe Erica, instead telling Dave that she was "down."

Dave was by that point at the Upper Saddle with Reese and Kip, but he came back up to do what he could to help. Since he had fixed his rope at the main rappel to speed the group's progress, he had to run down toward the Lower Saddle to borrow a rope from the climbers from New York who had summited. Dave then hurried back up to the Upper Saddle to climb a soaking-wet Owen-Spalding route, traversing over and down the Exum Ridge to arrive at the scene.

By the time Dave arrived, the other climbers had received evidence of life from below, as the radio finally crackled to life with Reagan's voice, rambling incoherently. As Rob desperately asked about Justin and Jake, no straight answers, or answers of any kind, were forthcoming. Eventually, Justin himself got on the radio, and his father and brother heard for themselves that he was alive. Justin conveyed that Jake was with them, too, though unconscious. He continued to talk, but his voice was garbled as he listed the injuries the three climbers had suffered: paralysis, deafness, blindness, broken bones, lacerations. In the midst of a flood of relief that the three men were alive and the confusion of trying to process how badly they might be wounded, Justin's next chilling report rocked the climbers. Slowing his tempo down, he haltingly explained that he had a deep laceration to his thigh. He couldn't stem the blood flow, and it continued to hemorrhage severely.

By this time, a helicopter had twice hovered within 100 yards of the climbers' location and then had apparently given up and left the area. It was extremely tough for them to watch it turn and fly away. In their grief and trauma, the climbers hadn't completely understood that the first flight was only a reconnaissance mission and that the rangers never intended to land that time. It seemed to them that there had been two failed attempts to reach the scene, that the helicopter was *right there* but couldn't help. Frustration was replaced by despair after Leo's insertion attempt was called off.

The rangers contacted the climbers to say that the rescue had been impeded by clouds enveloping the ridge at 13,000 feet. Bob communicated the status of Justin's leg injury, clearly terrified that his son would bleed out from a wound to his femoral artery before help could arrive. The rangers reiterated their commitment to reaching the scene as soon as possible but again indicated that given their inaccessibility, the weather, and the time, spending the night on the ledge might be inevitable.

Before the lightning strike, Bob had been extremely shaken by slipping on wet rock while ascending Friction Pitch. Still, he began to rope back up. His son's voice was weak and strained, and the snatches of phrases that Bob could make out were terrifying. He felt he had to climb down to assess the gravity of the injuries and try to stop Justin from losing any more blood if he could. Rob asked his dad if he thought he was strong enough to climb back up. In response, Bob merely looked at Rob, stricken. Both men were choking up, tears welling in their eyes.

Despite having been struck by lightning and instructed by the rangers not to exert himself, Rob anchored himself to belay his dad. As the climbers above had no idea where the fourth rope team had ended up, Bob did not have a sense of how far he would have to rappel. In fact, the combined length of Friction Pitch and the distance the climbers had fallen totaled well more than 200 feet. Every three to four seconds on his descent, Bob paused to yell out, "You got me, Rob?"

Every time, Rob shouted back down that he did, the unspoken answer to his earlier question to his dad cycling inside his head. Bob was not planning on coming back up. He just had to get to his son.

TEN

At 6:09 P.M., two hours and twenty-three minutes after the initial call for help, a rescuer arrived on-scene. The clouds had abruptly cleared off the Exum Ridge, and within minutes, rangers had rerigged the short-haul rope, and Laurence was back in the air with Leo again on the end of the line. Leo touched down on the ledge about 30 feet east of the accident site, but by then, darkness was closing quickly. Nightfall was less than three hours away.

Leo saw members of the group at the site waving to him as he landed. The disturbing scene that he took in after he unclipped was like something climber's would have expected to see in the old days, horror stories from the Alps, notorious peaks where a climber's body could dangle for weeks.

A couple of the climbers were hunched over, bloody and huddled. It was clear that a tragedy had hit. It appeared as if a bomb had gone off, like the pall after a storm. They were all very quiet, some of them crunched under rock outcroppings, a few sitting close, clinging to one another, knees up, arms pulled in, dazed. They looked shattered.

To the climbers, Leo's appearance was like the cavalry arriving, as if they were no longer without hope. His appearance—extremely tall, blond hair to the middle of his back, blue eyes, slightly nonchalant demeanor—certainly fit the part of a prototypical rescuer. His air of total confidence and control made his first question to the group all the more surprising.

"Does anyone have a flat-head screwdriver?" he asked.

The climbers looked around at one another and shook their heads. Rob answered for the group that they didn't have one. Undaunted, Leo opened his pack, pulled out a butter knife, and used it to adjust what looked to be a 1950s radio.

It was initially difficult for Leo to triage the climbers. In order to determine what needed to be done, he first had to sort out who had been hurt. Even the uninjured seemed shell-shocked, so it was hard to ascertain who had been hit, and the climbers kept telling him that there were three men below them.

Although Leo, with one of the heaviest flight weights (body weight plus gear) at 225 pounds, had only been short-hauled in a nontraining scenario once before, he had responded to hundreds of accident scenes. In his experience, the victims were often so pleased to see a rescuer that they were overly talkative, repeating phrases like "Thank God you're here," but this group was stunned. The lack of talking was fine with Leo—as he says, he "would rather deal with that than hysteria."

When Leo landed, Clint had one boot off and couldn't walk. He was standing on his right leg and obviously in considerable pain from injuries to his left leg and foot. Although Leo's arrival on the scene was quick by rescue standards given the circumstances, there had been a time delay of almost two and a half hours since lightning had struck until he got there. Enough time seemed to have gone by that they had adjusted to their situation and gathered themselves together somewhat.

Leo had a flash of seeing members of the climbing party on the lower trails just the day before, when they were happy, joking, laughing. He shook off the image and concentrated on managing the scene. Everyone had stood up near the ledge, with Erica just a few feet away, still in the location where she had been struck.

Leo asked questions, assessed the situation. He asked Rob if Erica was dead, and Rob responded in the affirmative. Clint did not appear to have heard this exchange.

"Erica is dead," Clint told Leo.

Although Clint did not have the use of his left leg, he was standing, balanced on his right leg, closest to Erica. Leo wasn't positive right away what his relationship to her was, and he asked Clint a question to establish husband and wife.

Still in shock, Clint was not crying or angry or emotional. At that stage, he was numb, lucid, stoic; it seemed to Leo as if he had had enough time with Erica that the full gravity had not yet sunk in but that he had started to accept her fate.

Leo's first job was to assess whether Erica actually had been killed. He turned to where she lay crumpled on the rock, looking almost peaceful, as if she was sleeping. He noted that some of her helmet had melted, that there was superficial spidering on her body. Her eyes were closed, her face swollen and bruised. Her hair was badly singed, and there was a strong burning scent. Rigor mortis had already set in. Leo bent down over Erica. He had no doubt that she was dead, but he checked for a pulse before he quietly pronounced it officially.

Even though Clint was resigned to the reality of what Leo would find, Leo's confirmation that his wife was dead still seemed surreal to him.

"You must know what true love is," Clint said to Leo. Leo

told Clint that he didn't understand what he meant, to which Clint responded, "You save lives for a living."

At that point Leo felt that it was important to move Clint away from Erica. He brought all of the climbers back behind a boulder to finish evaluating them. He walked over to Rob, paused in the midst of the madness, and seemingly in slow motion, he put his hand on Rob's shoulder, looked directly into his eyes, and said, "I'm sorry about your friend."

Leo deemed Rob, Sherika, Steve, and Dave to be walking wounded. He then turned his attention to Rod, pointing at him hanging limply from the rope.

"Is he still alive?" he asked the climbers.

At this question, the group of climbers showed their first real signs of animation, insisting that he was, explaining that when they yelled at him, he would move in response. To prove their point, they all began screaming Rod's name down at him, urging him to gesture with his hand.

There was no movement from Rod, and Leo got on his radio, now operable after the butter-knife adjustments, to call for a body bag for Erica. Fearing that he was ordering two body bags and had given up on Rod, the climbers redoubled their efforts to elicit a response from their friend. Finally, whether related to the commotion above him or not, Rod groaned feebly.

The possibility that there was still a chance to save Rod's life ignited the climbers' energy and instantaneously swung Leo's focus to the logistics of his rescue. He radioed Renny asking for more rangers, fast.

In triage for mass-casualty incidents, patients are coded according to the urgency of their need to get to the hospital. Green is ambulatory with perhaps a broken arm. Yellow is serious but not immediately life-threatening. Red is high priority, needing quick intervention to save the patient's life. Black is dead. Making those triage decisions can be tricky, and it is usually done by one of the most experienced doctors or medics at the scene. Leo was eminently qualified to gauge triage levels.

At this scene, Erica was the lowest priority. Rod was the top priority, being in the most desperate condition. Since saving him would involve such a complicated rescue, however, Leo determined that the evacuation of Clint—in the yellow triage category and in combination with the loss of his wife—should be conducted simultaneously with the efforts to rescue Rod.

By this time, Laurence had inserted Craig Holm—flight weight 200 pounds with his medical gear—into the scene. The time was only 6:15. Immediately after inserting Leo, Laurence had returned to the Lower Saddle, Craig had connected to the short-haul line, Laurence had flown back up to the accident scene, and Craig had unclipped from the short-haul rope, all in six minutes.

As Craig was inserted, he had called out his distance to the ground and his rate of descent, giving Laurence and Renny a reference off the ground. He waited until the rope bag hit the ground to call up, "Down and comfortable," while still clipped in. He then unhooked himself, quickly spinning the 'biner off, making sure the ropes didn't tangle, trying to hold the line for the least amount of time possible. He radioed that he was "Unhooked and clear" and gave Renny the lift signal with his hand.

The weather had cleared somewhat by the time the second flight arrived. That was a fairly typical weather pattern in the Tetons—it was still extremely windy, but the storm seemed to have moved through. The winds were 24 mph straight from the west, but Laurence took this into account, dropping Craig and then, once the weight bag was on the ground, letting the helicopter drift slightly in the currents as Craig unclipped from the line.

As Leo discussed the accident scene and patient priorities with Craig, Laurence continued placing rangers on the rock, now two at a time. While short-hauling generally involves the insertion of one ranger on a rope at a time, in a multiple-victim accident like this one, every second was critical. In addition, it was possible that the storm hadn't moved on after all, and if the clearing sky was merely a break in the weather, it couldn't be counted on to last long. Based on load calculations at that time, the helicopter was able to carry more weight, so to cut down on the number of trips, Laurence agreed to put rangers on the mountain in sets of two.

Earlier, between Leo's aborted short-haul attempt and his successful insertion, Laurence had made three Lower Saddle–Lupine Meadows round trips, bringing Renny, Jim, and Craig in the first flight, then a total of six more rangers in the next two trips. The plan was for Laurence then to short-haul the rangers from the Lower Saddle to Friction Pitch one at a time. Dan Burgette was on the pad ready to receive the rope when Renny radioed down that Leo needed more help as fast as possible at the upper site to reach the Folded Man.

Once Laurence confirmed that he had enough power to fly two rangers at a time, Marty Vidak, the ranger who almost had to stay behind to find the lost boy at Spring Lake, came to the landing area to short-haul with Dan. When the rescue call had first come in, Marty was just concluding a search for a lost hiker after trekking 17 miles. He was in Paintbrush Canyon, two miles up, and he could tell from the call-out that this was a rescue he didn't want to miss. This was what he trained for, and to make sure he was included, he went belting down the trail toward the rescue cache. It initially looked as if his effort was wasted when he was diverted by the situation with the missing child, and then he got lucky when the fire crew offered to handle it.

Outside of training exercises, Marty had only been short-hauled to a scene once before, and he had never been on the line with another ranger in a real rescue. He and Dan, with flight weights of 185 and 190 pounds, respectively, were some of the lightest rangers for Laurence to haul.

Some rangers were obviously thinner than others, and even 15 pounds could be critical. There was also the factor of later trips being able to haul more weight because fuel had been burned off. While the pilot is responsible for the load calculation of how much weight a helicopter can lift given the elevation and the temperature, the Jenny Lake rangers also had the benefit of ranger George Montopoli's genius. He had created a computer program that acted as a check on the pilot.

The contents of Marty's pack included his harness, sticky rubber approach shoes, a climbing helmet, Snickers bars, granola bars, nuts, carabiners, and cordelettes. Marty, like most of the rangers, also carried some prusik cords, loops of cord that are tied in a friction hitch knot and put around a rope to grab it. Named after Karl Prusik, the Austrian mountaineer who developed this knot in 1931, "prusik" refers to both the cords and the hitch. Since they are lighter than other options, climbers often carry prusik cords for emergency use. They are handy for rope-rescue techniques, as they can work around multiple rope grabs (used, for example, in hauling systems) and provide a strong connection that will not damage or break the rope. The rangers are able to place prusiks on a rope extremely quickly and with only one hand if necessary.

Marty had come to Jenny Lake in 2000. He grew up on the south side of Chicago and first started climbing peaks in his late teens. He initially climbed to get to the views, but climbing soon began to mean more than that to him. There was the fitness aspect and the ability to share the experience with friends and an amalgam of sensations that Marty describes as "body, mind, judgment, the pleasure of feeling movement through the mountains." Most important, however, climbing for Marty was a faithful and trusted escape from the world. On even his most hellish days, the mountains were always there to clear his thoughts, refocus his perspective, take him away from the stress.

Having gone to school to study forestry, Marty's career progression went from running the trail crew in the Tetons, to wilderness ranger, to wildlife biologist, to wildland firefighter, to Jenny Lake climbing ranger, all while working as a ski guide (in British Columbia for a Canadian guiding service) in the winter off-seasons. As a ranger, he experienced freedom, camaraderie, teamwork, and climbing merged with a rescue dimension. He flourished in the tight grasp of the ranger family, welcoming the idea that the rangers didn't simply clock out and head home at the end of a tough day but stuck around together afterward to reflect on a harrowing rescue. He would have tried to become a climbing ranger sooner if he'd understood.

Unlike some of the more solitary rangers, Marty prefers the parts of the job that involve interacting with the public and instantly lists "helping people" as the aspect he likes best about the position. He does the work for a motivation beyond himself, in keeping with his philosophy that his skills can make a difference, can effect change for the better.

After Laurence successfully inserted Marty and Dan at the top of Friction Pitch, he went back for George Montopoli and Chris Harder and brought them to the scene on the short-haul line together.

To the injured climbers who had anguished over the sight of the helicopters flying away earlier, it was spectacular to see the rangers flying in suspended from a long rope, stacked two on top of each other, landing on a precarious little mountain ledge. They felt that they were truly being saved.

After Leo's initial failed insertion, Laurence was aware that other rangers were, as he says, "humping" it up the mountain, and he was assuming that they would be climbing with bivy gear (short for "bivouac") for the rangers and victims to set up an overnight camp. Instead, the weather cleared, Laurence "roared up" the mountain, and the mission turned into an intricately choreographed air ballet.

If the thunder cells hadn't moved away and the clouds hadn't lifted, the rescue would have gone in a much different direction. Many of the rangers realized much earlier in the day that the weather was going downhill, had seen the purple wedge of a heavy-duty storm in the early afternoon. As it was, the rangers kept scanning the skies and listening closely for signs that lightning had passed out of the area completely, racing not just darkness but the ominous threat of being trapped in a storm on the mountain themselves. At the end of the day, there would be no other flashes of lightning observed in that part of the sky on July 26 before or after the bolt that struck down the Idaho climbers.

The rangers were moving incredibly swiftly and efficiently, and Renny led a discussion with the rangers about whether the pace was too fast. They agreed that it was quick but not too quick, and each ranger managed it the best he could in his own head.

When the rangers were being short-hauled two at a time, since they were short on flight helmets, Marty flew with just his climbing helmet. Flight helmets are beefier and, in the event of a crash, provide better protection than a climbing helmet, which is mainly designed to allow rocks to bounce off the rangers' heads without cracking their skulls.

More significant, flight helmets are outfitted with radios so that the ranger or rangers on the end of the rope can be in communication with the people in the helicopter. Although there are backup procedures if radio communication was lost, the ability to communicate orally is extremely important. While it is only essential that one of the rangers on the end of the rope have a flight helmet, both rangers on the line ideally have the capability to be in voice contact with the spotter and the pilot. On this operation, where there were not enough flight helmets to go around, only Dan, assigned as the communications guy for the short-haul, had a flight helmet. Marty, therefore, could not hear what Renny and Laurence were telling Dan about where to land, when to unhook, and so on.

Dan had a pretty heavy pack, loaded with oxygen, a C-collar, and a medical kit, plus he brought along two sleeping bags in a large stuff sack. Early into the incident, the rangers had realized that battling hypothermia would be a serious issue for the climbers on the mountain. The lightning storm left the climbers wet and cold, and they had been stationary on the mountain for more than two hours before help arrived. To reduce the risk of hypothermia, Dan was taking up supplies he had packed from the Lower Saddle cache, including the sleeping bags and a stash of heat packs. He attached the bag to his waist and dangled it beneath him as he was short-hauled in.

As Dan and Marty started down toward the landing site on Friction Pitch on their short final approach, Dan was facing away from the mountain. He couldn't see the landing site, so he couldn't call out the two-zero, one-zero commands as they got close to the ground. As soon as he became aware of the situation, he radioed the rangers on the ground to ask one of them to provide the distances to Laurence and Renny from his position. Craig was on his radio ready to give distances, but by then, Dan and Marty had slowly rotated around in the air, giving Dan eyes on the landing spot.

The two rangers landed in a comfortable bivy site, a protected area built up with rocks walls to deflect some of the wind should a climber have to spend the night. Ideally, the floor of such a site is relatively flat so the climber can stretch out and sleep. The bivy site Laurence set them down in *was* flat, had rock walls a couple of feet high, and was roughly six feet by five feet.

Dan was feeling a little behind the curve, having been backward on the rope on the approach to the landing. Once he was on his feet, he remembered that he was the coms guy. He looked over at Marty and saw that he was already on the ground. Dan yelled to Marty about being down and comfortable, and Marty said that he was. In trying to catch up, Dan radioed the helicopter that they were both down and comfortable. As he was calling that in, he saw the weight bag in front of his face and instantly realized that it should have been on the ground before he called the down and comfortable signal. Renny called down to Dan that he was rushing it.

They unhooked without incident, and Dan caught his breath. Marty and Dan were just to the north of the big boulder on the traverse ledge at the top of Friction Pitch. Leo and Craig were dealing with anchor issues near the ridge crest. Dan went around the boulder to where some of the climbers were and saw that they were all hypothermic to some degree. The temperature had been 35 degrees on the flight. Dan gave them the sleeping bags he had brought and started questioning them about their ability to get down the mountain.

Realizing how cold both the injured and the uninjured patients were, the other helicopter, 4HP, flown by Rick Harmon, delivered a sling load of rescue equipment on a remote longline hook. Included in the load were down parkas, sleeping bags, a tarp, technical lowering kits, two anchor kits, extra morphine, and extra IV fluids.

The rescuers were forced by weather and fading sunlight to make several triage and treatment decisions to rescue the patients. They knew that evacuations would have to occur the following day unless they took immediate action to extract the climbers from the mountain. Two members of the climbing party—Kip and Reese—had stayed down in the Upper Saddle. That left only four ambulatory climbers—Rob, Sherika, Steve, and Dave—at the top of the pitch. In the end, given Rob's and Dave's knowledge of climbing, their familiarity with the route, the lateness of the day, and a shortage of rescue personnel, the rangers made a determination that those four climbers could safely climb down the mountain. They ideally wanted to send a ranger with them to escort them, but they didn't have one to spare, so they sent them off down the mountain by themselves before it got too dark.

The Folded Man, although the most inaccessible, remained the rangers' top-priority patient. As medic for the upper site, Craig's first priority was to get to Rod and assess his condition. Equipped with a rope and anchor gear, he began to construct a rappel anchor to access Rod below. He looped the rope around a huge block and ran a couple of extra loops. Leo helped him, even though doing so compromised his operations role.

As operations chief, it was Leo's duty to organize and delegate. He was supposed to sit back and look down on a scene, make sure it was coming together. He did not have the vision to oversee a mission while he was helping hands-on with the rescue. The moment a ranger in that role got sucked into actually assisting with the operation rather than directing it, he had lost control of his operation. Leo's feeling was that he couldn't do both jobs well, but here, he didn't have that latitude. In this accident, he had to get involved. After a short time, Marty and George were able to jump in and help Craig with the rappel anchors.

Meanwhile, Dan had been assigned as medic for the lower site, responsible for assessing the three climbers more than 200 feet below them. By that time, Rob's dad, who had successfully reached his son and the other two climbers, called up on his radio to confirm that Justin had what appeared to be an open bilateral thigh fracture that was still bleeding significantly. Femur fractures can result in life-threatening bleeding, and it had been several hours since the climbers had fallen. The rangers knew that if the climber's femur injury was still actively bleeding externally, he would be extremely shocky by that time. Based on Bob's information, it seemed likely that Justin was the next patient in priority after Rod, and it amped up Dan's desire to get down to the scene as quickly as possible.

Dan and Craig reconfigured the med gear a bit, with Dan taking some of the supplies from Craig's medical kit as well as his drug kit. Craig felt that they wouldn't be giving the Folded Man a great deal of treatment on the mountain if they were to have any chance of getting him out before dark.

While Dan was determining how to rappel safely down to the lower site, Rob told him that the rope going over the edge had been used by his dad to rappel to the climbers below. Dan looked at the anchor and saw two cams, metal mechanical spring-loaded devices that fit into cracks and crevices to protect a lead climber by securing the climbing rope, which is then clipped to a cam with a carabiner. The devices come in varying sizes, from half an inch to eight inches to fit different-sized cracks. One cam looked and felt solid, but the other appeared a bit unsteady.

Dan jiggled the anchor, and it seemed relatively stable, plus he knew that it had held the dad when he rappelled on it. Still, the events continued to move very quickly, and when the pace was too fast, the rangers were concerned about getting loose or careless. It took just one bad decision to injure or kill a rescuer. Dan didn't trust himself to think straight with his tunnel vision focused on the injured people below, and he wanted a second opinion before he rapped on the anchor. He called to Leo, but he was still busy out near the ridge crest. Dan then asked Craig to check the anchor, and Craig deemed it unacceptable. The second cam had a bad placement, and when Dan wiggled it, he had probably pushed it further into the crack, which flared wider. As a result, the cam was no longer firmly seated.

Craig constructed an entirely new anchor tied together with a cordelette, a long loop of accessory cord used to tie into multiple anchor points. When Craig was satisfied that it was rock-solid, Dan clipped in and started rapping.

Dan's pack was heavy with the extra medical supplies in it, and he was climbing down on a single rope. Intent on dealing with several snarls in the rope, he passed within 20 or 30 feet of Rod. He wasn't rappelling straight down the climbing route, as his rope would have added confusion to Rod's location. In addition, his 200-foot rope wouldn't have reached the climbers nearly 240 feet below him.

Instead, Dan rappelled down the gully just to the east side of the rock ridge that Rod was on, such that he couldn't really see him when he got to his level. He was looking for where to put his feet and paying attention to what he was doing while rappelling, so he didn't look over in Rod's direction, but he did talk to him on his way down.

The rangers, Dan included, feel that hearing is the last sense to fade away, and they are generally big believers in talking to unconscious people. Dan knew it hadn't been that long since Rod had moaned when his friends called to him, but he didn't respond to Dan. Nonetheless, Dan chose to assume that he was alive and told him to hang on, to fight, that people were up above setting anchors and would be down to help him as soon as possible.

Dan rapped to the end of the 200-foot rope, which put him in a gully just to the north of the base of the Jern Crack. Having rappelled through the steepest section of the climb, he landed on a ledge that he was able to downclimb until he could climb up and over to access the three injured climbers.

Just seconds before he reached them, Dan was shocked to see Jack and Jim pull themselves up and over the ledge where the climbers were trapped, exhausted but exhilarated after having completed their incredible run up the mountain from the Lower Saddle. Dan radioed up that he had arrived at the location of the three patients plus a fourth climber and that Jack and Jim were also there. The three rangers began to evaluate Justin, Jake, and Reagan as Chris Harder rappelled down from the top of the pitch to join them.

Back in the air, Laurence brought an extraction suit to Marty via the short-haul rope. The rangers are not supposed to go chasing after the equipment dangling from the rope. They want the pilot to bring the line to them, as close as he can without the rangers having to run around. They reach out a little, but not over a precipice. Here, Laurence placed the end of the rope right *into* Marty's open palm. He then departed for a couple of short revolutions in the air while the rangers attached the suit to Clint.

Within an hour of Leo arriving on the scene, the rangers had secured Clint in an evacuation suit—the slinglike harness also known as a screamer suit—to ready him for extraction. In the rangers' experience, most patients are fairly relaxed about the idea of being flown off a mountain on a rope 100 feet below a helicopter. For one thing, it happens fast. For another thing, climbers are, in general, less afraid of heights than the average person.

Moreover, rangers begin their explanation of the process by saying, "What's going to happen next is . . ." They describe the procedure, then announce that they are park rangers and this is the way it's going to go. The rangers tell patients in a firm and clear tone what they can and cannot do in the air. The basic instructions are to sit back and go for a ride and don't fidget.

No one in the park has ever turned down the ride or even

registered much in the way of resistance or complaining. There are stories of victims becoming unglued in the air and trying to leap from rescue litters in fright, but it has never happened to the Jenny Lake rangers. The patients they are loading into screamer suits are in dire situations so far out of their element, removed from their own experience, that they often can't even process flying under a helicopter. As the rangers say, it beats walking out.

The evacuation harness has a clip and a backup, two points of attack. Clint clipped in by himself with a daisy chain, a length of webbing with sewn loops that run the length of the chain. One end of the daisy is usually permanently girth-hitched to a climber's harness to provide a safety attachment by quickly and easily clipping into an anchor with a carabiner.

After orbiting nearby for a few minutes, Laurence returned to pick up Clint. To lift off with him from the top of the pitch, Laurence had to come back and hover directly over him. He couldn't swing back into the mountain. The wind velocity was still very strong, and to keep the helicopter still, he had to pull up on it very slightly, watch what was going to happen, and then correct for it almost in advance.

Once Marty had the rope in his hand, he hooked Clint's screamer suit to the short-haul line via an O-shaped ring. He called, "Hooked and ready," up to Renny and Laurence in the helicopter and, just in case radio communication had failed, also gestured with a finger over his head.

As Clint was lifted up and off the mountain, he understood that Rod's rescue was fully under way. His left leg had been badly scorched, 70 percent of it covered in second-degree burns and a five-inch spot of third-degree burns on his thigh where lightning had transferred from Erica's body to his. Blood and pus and bodily fluids were oozing out of him every-where. He was freezing and drained to the point of emotional and physical exhaustion. As the shock set in that he was actually getting away from the scene on Friction Pitch, his primary feeling was relief.

Knowing that Erica was gone, he had moved through a lot of processing being next to her in that situation. He believes that if there is a 12-step program for grief, he went through the first eight steps of it in those three frigid hours up on the mountain.

Clint's ride out was exactly at the point of twilight over the Tetons. The flight circled around the mountain range, displaying the view and the setting sun in a way that Clint had never seen before. His thoughts were on his children and what the events of that day signified for him as a father, what it would mean for the kids to grow up without their mother. As he flew, he took in the enormity of the dazzling orange and backlit horizon, looking forward rather than back.

ELEVEN

"Hooked and ready."

—

Jim Springer, Jenny Lake ranger

When Jim Springer arrived on the tiny ledge on which Justin, Jake, and Reagan were crouched and asked, "How's everybody doing?" he viewed it as an encouraging sign that all three of the climbers answered him.

Jim knew only that three members of the climbing party had fallen in the Jern Crack area below Friction Pitch and that at least one of them was busted up, but he had no sense of the specifics of their predicament or their medical condition. He was relieved at least to discover that none of them was unresponsive.

The lightning bolt had ricocheted down the mountain, knocking the three climbers off their stances at the base of Friction Pitch and sending them somersaulting down 100 feet of rock face. Two young men were crumpled up back in a tiny corner, one of them with bloody legs sitting on the lap of the other one, with rope looped around them everywhere. Another guy was clinging to a knob, directly above the abyss. He looked as if he was just about ready to flip off the pitch. They lay tossed upon the rocks and ledges where they had happened to land, not moving.

Sometimes when a climber falls, his ropes will tangle and slow his fall. In this case, the ropes had not only snarled but also virtually tied themselves together. Since they had been anchored at the bottom of Friction Pitch when the lightning hit, the climbers should have been swinging in the air off the side of the mountain, suspended from their ropes like Rod, dead or dying.

As they were hurtling 100 feet down through space, however, bashing against the rocky cliffside as they fell, the climbers' ropes had entwined themselves around some pointy rock horns and jammed into cracks, providing a counterweight and stopping their descent. The event was totally random, a one-in-a-million shot. Their survival was sheer blind luck.

These climbers were not in any way hanging from their ropes or harnesses but had simply collapsed, pinned on top of a steep sweep of rock. They had hardly moved at all since. Either none of them knew what to do to try to help himself, or they were hurt too badly to attempt to better their positions.

While some of the other rangers were trying to reach the Folded Man, Dan Burgette, Chris Harder, Jack McConnell, and Jim Springer—two medics and two ski patrolmen—were all at the lower scene evaluating the condition of the three climbers trapped there. Dan had arrived from above just after Jim and Jack climbed on-scene from below, and shortly after Dan reached the site, Chris also rapped down from the top of Friction Pitch to help out.

Before his ranger career, which began in 1990, Chris had migrated from Wisconsin to Montana to work on oil rigs. In 2003, he was a full-time ranger in Gros Ventre, another subdistrict of the park (he has since become a Jenny Lake climbing ranger). He was off duty on July 26th but heard the call from home and volunteered to come in.

The rangers assumed that the climbers' ropes were still anchored to the mountain, but they couldn't figure out where or why all of the various ropes went. The cord was wedged in among the rock fixtures and the climbers' bodies and legs, a twisted mess of coils. It was chaotic rope, a junk show. The rangers didn't know what lines to trust, and they felt that if they waited to sort out the ropes, the climbers might lurch off the mountain. As the rangers said afterward, these climbers wouldn't have had to look too far for a disaster. Their lives at that point were utterly in the hands of the rangers.

It seemed impossible that the climbers had fallen down that kind of terrain on the mountain and weren't crushed to death in the process. If one of the climbers' heads had bounced against the mountainside on the way down, if they had not stuck their landings, they would certainly have been killed.

As it was, they were all bleeding from blunt-force trauma injuries from their 100-foot plunge down the mountainside and their sudden stop on hard, sharp rock. They had a collection of broken bones, ripped tendons, and severe burns. Here and there, lightning had run on the surfaces of their bodies, blistering some of their skin.

All of the climbers were in various stages of paralysis and had a questionable mental status, whether because of hypothermia or the effects of the lightning strike. Each of them was in somewhat of a trance, almost as if they were under the influence of drugs or alcohol, and, given the circumstances, were a little too casual in response to their rescuers.

The first action the rangers took was to anchor the climbers to the ledge where they were located. Jack set an equalizing anchor above Justin and Jake, while the other rangers seamlessly split up the medical assessments. A focal point to keep them all connected to the mountain together seemed immediately to give the climbers something to trust, a step toward feeling safe. The rangers clipped into the new anchor as well.

When Dan had rappelled down to the lower scene, he had had to downclimb a bit of rock to reach the victims. The first person he encountered was Bob Thomas, the dad who had rappelled down to his son, Justin, and the two other injured climbers. He told Dan that he wasn't hurt and identified himself as the father of the man with the bleeding legs. Bob admitted that he wasn't an experienced climber but that he had done what he had to do to try to save his son.

Dan took off Bob's pack and told him to stay on a ledge in a small area known as a chimney, a rock cleft with mostly parallel vertical sides, that was large enough to fit his body. When climbing such a structure, a climber uses his head, back, and feet to apply opposite pressure on the vertical walls. While Dan was getting medical gear out of his pack and talking to Bob, Chris climbed over to do an initial evaluation of the two men sitting on top of each other in the corner, Justin (Bob's son), age 29, and Jake Bancroft, age 27.

The climbers had landed in an incredibly awkward location on the mountain, and it was obvious that there was no place for a ranger to stand to work on the lower two. Chris had to stem across in front of them, meaning that he simultaneously assumed two widely spaced footholds and supported his body by using the opposition created when he pressed his feet outward in opposite directions. Chris's left foot just smeared with friction on the steep rock, and his right foot found a hold on a small ledge a few inches wide. There was clearly no room for a second ranger. Chris asked Dan to stay where he was and write down the information he called down from the assessments of Justin and Jake.

The predicament of Justin and Jake can be illustrated with a large book standing open on a table, with the pages riffling slightly and a muffin crumb dropped into the crack between the pages to represent a rock. Justin would be sitting on Jake, both of them atop the crumb. Then the book would need to be tipped backward at about a 70-degree angle.

In order to reach the patients trapped at that angle, after Chris had stemmed the crack with one foot on the left rock face and one on the right rock face, using counterpressure to hold himself in place, he then had to bend over at the waist to assess and treat the patients.

Upon initial exam, Chris determined that while Justin had bled a great deal from his legs, the source was a series of deep lacerations on his lower legs and knees rather than his thighs. The bleeding had nearly stopped. Jake, on the other hand, was extremely disoriented. He barely seemed to be able even to recall his own name, and he didn't know where he was or what had happened.

Meanwhile, Jim assessed Reagan Lembke, age 25, the man on the small ledge above Justin and Jake. Their ropes appeared to run up into the rock leading to Reagan, but it was impossible to decipher the progression of the lines. Jim conveyed the details of Reagan's condition down to Dan. After checking him out, Jim felt that Reagan was stable and not hurt too badly, given the situation. He was significantly burned on his upper body and one leg, and he had a large laceration on his shin. His main complaint was that his backside ached from landing violently on a knob on the chimney.

All three climbers were becoming severely hypothermic in the cold mountain air, and the rangers quickly covered them with sleeping bags. When one of the rangers put a sleeping bag around Jake, it seemed to him like the warmest, most comfortable thing he had ever felt. He hadn't realized until that moment how cold he was and how much he was shaking. As the rangers started warming and reassuring the patients, the mental status of each of them began to improve, making it easier for the rescuers to evaluate their injuries.

As they worked, the rangers radioed the information about the severity of the injuries down to Brandon in the rescue cache. While Jack later stated that the rangers at the lower scene were "well within what we were doing," he also admitted that the situation was "pretty wild." There was a lot of helicopter action above them, beneath them, around them. The noise was extremely loud and very distracting, and the abrupt appearance and disappearance of the helicopter dashing around so close to them jangled their nerves and added to the general chaos of the scene. In addition, it looked as if another storm might be brewing off to the west, so the rangers had to keep looking over their shoulders to see if they were going to be struck by more lightning.

Chris initially felt that Justin was the top priority at the lower scene and that he would need to be extracted from the mountain in a litter. Jake was very cold, and his mental deficiency was his most pressing visible symptom. His position was problematic because he was tucked into a corner behind a flake of rock (a thin slab of rock detached from the main face) and was partially covered by Justin. Chris felt that Jake would also require a litter.

As Chris completed his secondary evaluation, it became evident that Justin wasn't as bad as he first appeared. He had initially feared that Justin had fractured both legs and his back, but after checking more closely, Chris determined that his legs were not broken after all. He was in a lot of pain from his upper back, but he probably could move a little. Chris examined his spine as best he could in the cramped space and deemed it likely clear of fractures.

Justin had been beaten up terribly from the fall, shattering his shoulder blade by bashing it against the mountain, with the bones essentially in chunks. His face was obliterated—he had chipped a tooth and broken his nose, and there was a deep grove running through his helmet and indenting his face. He had cheese-gratered his legs and injured the ACL on his left leg. There was blood all over him, and he was still partially paralyzed. He had had trekking poles in his backpack like his brother Rob, and his whole body had been shocked by the lightning. He kept offering to do what he could to help, even though he could barely move, but despite that behavioral quirk, he did not appear to have lasting neurological deficits.

Jake had been knocked unconscious following the lightning strike. When he regained consciousness, he was paralyzed. He had smashed his head brutally and repeatedly on the rocks, and he had a stupid smile on his face and a lot of blood on his socks. He was making a funny kind of exaggerated looking-around motion, repeatedly saying things like "Well, where are we? Sure is a nice view."

Jake had left his wife and baby girl at home in Rigby, Idaho, to climb the Grand. He had grown up camping, backpacking, and hiking in Utah, but this was only his first climbing trip. A self-described computer geek, Jake knew Rod from work, and they clicked when they discovered a shared love of hockey. Jake had never climbed before, but Rod had been talking about the trip, and Jake felt he was in decent enough shape to come along. When Rob took him sport climbing on a bolted route on a cliff a few weeks earlier, it was the first time Jake had ever been roped up. Rob led Jake's climb up a 70-foot wall, and Jake found it thrilling, but, as he says, "it turns out that sport climbing and mountaineering are two different things," and he admits that he didn't know what he was getting into by joining the Grand trip.

While Jake was waiting at the base of Friction Pitch tied together with Justin and Reagan, watching Rod climb, it had started to sprinkle. He heard one thunderstrike in the distance, and then it began to rain harder. All three members of the fourth rope team were sitting down, and Jake had his hands in his lap. Suddenly, the hair on his left arm stood straight up, a strange and tingly sensation, and when he looked down at his arm, he heard the sound of an explosion. It was an insanely loud crack, and it occurred *right* on top of them.

Jake was instantly rendered blind and deaf and experienced an immediate desire to get away from something very painful. He had time to wonder if he had been hit by lightning, then he realized that he was no longer sitting but was standing up, and then, just before he blacked out, he had the overwhelming feeling of falling forward. He became conscious long enough to register an eerily painless impression of bouncing and rolling down the rocks out of control before he slipped into blackness again.

Jake was lying down when he woke up. His limbs were sluggish and seemed frozen in place, but he was able to manipulate his body into a half-upright sitting position before he sank back into unconsciousness. Reagan was above Jake, and Jake could hear him, but he had a hard time seeing him. Jake and Justin were mashed together, and one of the times Jake woke up, he saw Justin's lower face and mouth bloodied and broken. He realized at that point that a big thing had happened, and he tried to stand up, but he couldn't. He didn't have any sense of what was going on with Erica or Rod, and he assumed that the three of them were the only ones affected.

Despite having worn a helmet during the fall, Jake had suffered a serious concussion. He kept replaying the same scenario—he would come to, ask Justin and Reagan what had happened, be told that they all had been hit by lightning, then pass out. A few moments later, he would wake up again and, as if he had never posed the question, ask Justin and Reagan what had happened. This pattern occurred over and over, with his friends' answers getting progressively shorter, until finally they told him they had had enough and to give it a break.

Jake knew he was coming out of his stupor when he was able to process the thought that he had been hit by lightning and that these guys were being *rude* to him. Even then, he kept fading in and out of consciousness. He threw up at one point and later, in the midst of the rangers' lifesaving heroics at the scene, made a point to tell them to be careful not to step in it.

After approximately an hour, Jake could move his arm, although he was still numb and had no fine motor skills. He could hear voices on the radio in his pocket but could only paw at the zipper. His body was splotchy, and he had burn holes from the lightning coming down the rope. The bolt seemed to travel a path beginning at his wrist (where the hair had stood up on his arm) and then coursed through the rest of his body—arm, waist, leg—until it surged out through his toes, leaving black, charred skin.

Jake and Reagan had essentially ridden Justin's body down the mountain when they fell. Justin and Reagan were aware of what had happened, and they were fighting the fall, trying helplessly to prevent it somehow. Jake, like a drunk or a baby, was limp and relaxed and tumbled down the mountain with no resistance. As a result, he had rolled through the experience with the least bloodshed. He was hurting in places he couldn't see, and he had deep bruising in the area of his ribs that would only show up days later.

Chris was still trying to appraise Jake's injuries, but Justin was sitting on his lower body, making it hard to access him. Chris spread his legs wider, stretching over to Jake, trying his best to evaluate him on the steep section of rock where he was jammed. It was, as Chris says, "a delicate kind of situation." After a few minutes, Chris was able to feel Jake's spine well enough to be reasonably sure that he had not broken his back.

Dan was worried about Jake given how spacey and bewildered he was acting. In addition, Dan was cognizant of the fact that a massive electrical-shock injury could have residual problems, and he was concerned about spending the night with Jake on the mountain given the limited cardiac medical capabilities they had. Chris reversed himself regarding the severity of Jake's injuries compared with Justin's, and the other rangers agreed that Jake was the top-priority patient.

A problem existed in that Jake was wedged into the ledge and blocked by Justin, and the rangers couldn't extract Jake until they had removed Justin from his position. Treating the trapped patients in the remote and hazardous terrain was frustrating for the rangers—the most serious patient was the most difficult to reach and therefore had to be the last to be extricated. That wasn't by the books or the EMT manuals of how to triage—those hurt the worst are supposed to be the first to get help. In this case, however, they had to be pragmatic, and their goal was to get people off the mountain.

The rangers needed to gain access to the more seriously injured climbers and also create more room to work. It was essential for them to remove as many people as quickly as possible in order to simplify the problems they were dealing with in the confined space. They were concerned about risk and exposure, weather and rockfall, not only for the patients but for themselves as well. Therefore, the rangers did not fly the climbers off in the order of injury severity but rather got to whom they could when they could.

The rangers were faced at that point with a potentially life-or-death decision. The mechanism of their injuries suggested full spinal immobilization for all three patients. If a climber fell farther than one and a half times his body height, the rule of thumb was to evacuate him on a backboard. In this case, of course, the patients had fallen more than 16 or 17 times their height. The choice was to extract them on a litter, a considerably more time-consuming rescue, versus putting them in screamer suits and flying them off the mountain more quickly.

Despite the length of his fall, Reagan appeared to have only isolated extremity injuries, and the rangers determined that a sitting position in an evacuation harness would be an appropriate way to transport him.

The options with regard to Justin and Jake were more complicated. The primary concern was that one or both of them had a back injury that would result in permanent injury or paralysis if they were not spread out flat in a stretcher. Chris was fairly certain that the backs of both men were clear. He had run his hands down their spines. There was no numbness or tenderness, no point tenderness, no distracting injury or pulling pain. There was a lot of blood but no bones sticking through their skin.

If the rangers erred on the side of caution and attempted to fly the patients out on a litter, given the time of day, the danger was that only one or neither of them would be able to get off the mountain at all that night. If the rangers were not able to fly them out of there before the morning, there was an enormous risk of cardiac issues and hypothermia complications. There was also the possibility of another storm brewing, and the rangers were very aware of the need to move people away from the area before the next thunderstorm rolled in.

The rangers weighed patient care against conveying the climbers out that night and to a hospital as soon as possible, measuring the pros and cons, leaning toward rapid extrication with the patients flown unattended in full body harnesses. There was a consensus among the rangers that if there were fewer victims and/or more daylight, they would have packed the victims into litters for removal from the mountain. In this case, however, there were only so many minutes before darkness set in, and every one of those minutes was essential. Looking around the corner from their vantage point, the rangers could see Rod's rescue playing out. Although those rescuers were working feverishly, their efforts to maneuver a litter on the steep mountainside didn't seem to be happening as fast as the four rangers at the lower site thought it needed to given the dwindling daylight.

Jim, who had a vast history of quickly assessing victims based on his extensive experience as a ski patrolman, was insistent from the start that in order to save their patients, they had to stabilize and transport them as fast as possible.

"We don't have time. We gotta scream these guys," he said to the other rangers at least 10 times. "We're getting this done, we're running shuttles. We're gonna clean *our* scene up."

In the end, it came down to a decision by the rangers that if they opted for a litter extraction, the patients would never get off the mountain that evening, and the chances of them surviving the night were too slim.

Once the choice was made, it was made. The rangers all realized what the game was and they knew that some compromises had taken place. After reaching their decision, the next step was for them to justify it by successfully executing their plan. They flipped into action, instantaneously focusing on the individual tasks they needed to accomplish to short-haul the climbers out. Time seemed to be sprawling out before them, the minutes ticking away. They were constantly checking the level of daylight, but the rangers all considered themselves skillful mountain people. They knew that if they could just get their patients off, they could always handle themselves, could speed out of the scene and find their way off the mountain in the dark if need be.

The rangers thought of the rescue in terms of lots of small steps, just like climbing, and they did not let themselves get overwhelmed by the big picture. With the limited time and the group of patients they had, there was little room left over for problems. There was so much to do that the rangers mainly dealt with their own discrete jobs, but an equally vital aspect of streamlining the process was their willingness to jump in and pick up loose ends for one another, to see something that needed to be done and unselfishly move in to complete it.

Reagan was the easiest patient for the rangers to extract since he was on a bit of a pedestal. He was surprisingly calm and uncomplaining and the most coherent of the three climbers. Jim radioed Renny requesting a screamer suit for him. Laurence had already short-hauled Clint from the top of Friction Pitch to the Lower Saddle, and as soon as Clint was removed from the screamer suit on the Saddle, Laurence flew it back to Jim at the lower site. When it arrived, Jim and Jack got Reagan ready to go.

As they packed him in the suit, the rangers referred to it as a giant deep diaper. The rangers did their best to use humor to lighten up the show. They pointed out the helicopter, telling the climbers that it would be the greatest ride of their life, the best ride in the park, better than the roller coaster when they were six.

The injured climbers seemed amenable to the idea of the suits. They realized that they were getting out of there, and they were very accepting of all that the rangers were doing toward that end. They were obedient and cooperative, ready for anything, anxious to get off the mountain. They didn't ask a lot of questions.

As he was being strapped into the harness, Reagan did ask Jack why the rangers called it a screamer suit. Jack's answer: "Because you can scream if you want to."

The rangers explained what was going to happen—"You *are*

going to dangle"—so as not to surprise their patients. They made it clear that it was a snug harness and that all of the connections were doubled up, so there was no way for a patient to fall out of it during flight. The general attitude of the rangers at an accident site was that they wouldn't need to be there if the victim(s) had done the right thing, and they tended to approach the extractions from that perspective.

As taught by Renny, the two points for a ranger to emphasize to a victim on-scene were (1) I know what I'm doing, and (2) I'm going to get you out of here. Crammed together on the side of the mountain, the rangers took complete charge of the situation, and the wounded climbers responded by compliantly doing what they were told.

In his shock and resulting skewed perspective of reality, however, Jake was making light of the situation, in no way appreciating the gravity of their circumstances. He seemed to have no concept that he, or anyone else, was in danger. He was, as he later said, in "La-La Land." He was in good spirits, laughing and joking around, and he seemed vaguely offended that no one seemed particularly amused by him. He quoted a line from the Jim Carrey movie *Liar Liar*—"You're all doing a wonderful job"—but to his disappointment, the rangers didn't seem to get, or at least acknowledge, the reference.

When Laurence came to pick up Reagan, Jake was nearly giddy to see a helicopter flying overhead. Justin and Reagan had been frustrated earlier when the helicopter kept coming and going and leaving them. To Jake, for whom time was malleable, it seemed as if the aircraft had arrived simultaneously with the accident.

Short-hauling the patients off that location was definitely a risk, especially given the altitude. The air was thinner, and the helicopter didn't have as much reserve lift. The area had little protection from the wind, and the currents wrapping around the peaks in that location could be both strong and squirrelly. During the time of the extractions of the climbers at that lower site, however, the weather happened to be as clear, and the air as relatively still, as ever could have been expected.

In order to hook a patient up to the short-haul line, the ranger has to reconnect with the rope hanging from the helicopter, but at that precipitous location on the mountain, there was no place for Laurence to set down the 10-pound weight bag. That eliminated the ranger's wiggle room should there have been a badly timed gust of wind, but they couldn't take a chance of the bag catching on anything. As it wasn't an option for Laurence simply to drop the bag somewhere at the scene, Jim had no choice but to grab the rope as it swung under the helicopter. While clinging to the side of a cliff, however, he obviously couldn't reach out very far to snatch it.

With Renny coordinating from the helicopter, just as he had done earlier on the top of Friction Pitch, Laurence sustained a hover and maneuvered the line directly over the ranger ready to receive it. Laurence was moving so slowly that Jim later described it as "almost annoying perfect." Caught up in the deliberate pace of Laurence's motion, Jim was concerned that Laurence was being so careful, so absolute, that he was almost taking too much time. And then Laurence deposited the orange weight bag precisely and softly into Jim's outstretched hand.

Laurence flew Reagan off the mountain at 7:24 P.M., deposited him at the Lower Saddle, then immediately returned for another victim.

The next-easiest person for the rangers to get off the mountain was Bob Thomas. It was obvious to the rangers that they would have to help Bob get off the mountain one way or another. With him hanging out nearby in the chimney, they didn't know what he was going to do or where he was going to end up.

Bob had been immensely helpful to the injured climbers earlier, warming Justin as best he could and making sure that Jake stayed awake. When Reagan had first seen Bob appear, he declared in his delirium that he saw Christ and knew he was going to be saved.

Jake had experienced a soothing feeling of wanting to go to sleep, to drift off and not worry, but Bob tried to keep him alert and talking. In one exchange, Jake acted confused and frantic about how Bob could possibly know his middle name was Wade, even though Jake himself had just told it to Bob two seconds before. Jake later credited Bob's efforts at preventing him from slipping into unconsciousness in the time before the rangers arrived as likely saving his life. Looking back, he feels that if he had lapsed into sleep, he would never have awakened.

At that point, however, from the rangers' perspective, Bob was a loose cannon, and they needed him out of their responsibility. Since they were at the lower site more than 200 feet below Friction Pitch, Bob would have had to reclimb the Jern Crack and Friction Pitch before he could rejoin the other uninjured members of his party. That wasn't going to happen in time for him to meet up with the others. It wouldn't have been safe for him to climb down the mountain by himself, necessitating the dedicated time and energy of a ranger to lead him. Since they didn't have any rangers to spare and Bob, being uninjured, was low-priority, a ranger wouldn't be available to guide him down until all of the injured parties were helped first. By that time, it would likely be after dark, which would make the climbing dangerous and slow and might take more than one ranger to get the job done.

In addition, Bob was physically and emotionally exhausted. When Jim asked him if he thought he could climb up out of the lower scene, he first replied that he wasn't sure, then said that he couldn't. The rangers decided that they just needed to get him off the mountain, that it was time for him to go. It was such a clear-cut way to proceed that Jim made the decision to "stick him in a suit" in about three seconds. Bob was flown off the mountain in an evacuation harness at 7:52 P.M. In essence, it was triage by short-haul.

That left only Justin and Jake at the lower site. Justin was in a lot of pain when he tried to move, and the rangers requested an order of morphine from the park's medical advisor, who was at the rescue cache during the mission. Morphine is one of the drugs that the rangers carried in their drug kits, but before it could be administered, the ranger had to get permission from the medical control doctor at St. John's Hospital in Jackson or the park's medical advisor. The rangers received the order, but Justin ended up declining the injection. He felt that he could deal with the pain, and he wanted to be lucid for the flight out.

The rangers had a tough time maneuvering Justin into the screamer suit, since Chris wasn't able to cut his Camelback water pack totally off of him. Given the tight space, it was awkward for them to slash his clothes away and very difficult to get the crotch strap under him.

When he was finally in the suit, the rangers cut free every rope leading to Justin. An extracted patient must obviously be unclipped from all anchors before being hooked into the helicopter's long line. As a sign of how messy the scene was, the rangers told Laurence, in a less than confidence-inspiring way, that they couldn't isolate where all of the ropes were anchored but that they were pretty sure they had the patient cut loose. While they thought they had gotten all of the ropes, they weren't certain, and they were afraid of ripping someone else off the rock or tying the helicopter to the mountain. Their solution was to ask Laurence to lift Justin off extra-slowly while they held knives at the ready. It turned out that they had, in fact, cleanly sliced through all of the ropes, and, untethered, Laurence flew Justin away to the Lower Saddle.

With only one extraction left to go, Jack's attention was drawn to the top of Friction Pitch. Craig, Leo, George, and Jim had set up a raising system in an attempt to save the Folded Man, but without enough rescuers to pull on the ropes, their progress was excruciatingly slow. Jack saw a need, and every mountain instinct he relied on compelled him to fill it. He looked at Jim, and Jim knew intuitively what he was thinking.

"Go," Jim said.

That was all the encouragement Jack needed. He free-solo-climbed up the mountain to reach the top of Friction Pitch to provide extra manpower, an act that was to become ultimately pivotal in the rescue. There was a gully off to the right of Friction Pitch that was slightly less exposed, and he scrambled up that route. Having made the climb a thousand times before, Jack did not pause to rope himself up.

Following Jack's quick departure, the three remaining rangers were alone with Jake on the mountainside. As time passed, his thought processes improved somewhat. He was able to remember Chris's name, and he started to retain information about where he was. His chief complaint was of severe pain in a section of ribs high on his back.

Jake had watched Reagan, Bob, and Justin taking off one at a time under the helicopter, and the process had seemed to him "pretty hairy." When it was his turn, he had a hard time sitting up as the rangers hooked him into the harness, and he kept repeating that he was concerned about his ability to hold on to the reins. The rangers told Jake that if he was spinning, he should stick his arm out to balance himself. Jake responded by asking the rangers to take his picture as he was flown off (which they did).

Then Laurence gently lifted him off, and within seconds, he was flying thousands of feet above the ground. He was not frightened, as he had expected to be, but tranquil and then happy. As he flew away, he turned and looked back and saw the rangers in the place where he had just been. From that angle, it seemed to him like so small an area, such a little ledge. When he was stuffed in there, he hadn't realized how incredibly steep that part of the face was, hadn't thought of the spot as being treacherous. He was surprised that he had felt secure in the space, and his last thought as he left the mountain was that he couldn't imagine how they had all fit.

As Dan, Chris, and Jim cleaned up the area where the climbers had clung to the mountain face, they finally solved the mystery of where the various ropes went. To their shock, they discovered that none of the climbers' lines had, in fact, been anchored.

Upon further investigation, it became clear that the anchor that had held the climbers to the mountain face at the base of Friction Pitch had failed, blown out of the wall by the force of the lightning strike. It turned out that every bit of rope draped over the rocks at the lower scene was loose, not tied to the mountain, not connected to anything at all.

As they plunged 100 feet, the climbers' falls had been arrested merely by the dumb and nearly miraculous luck that their rope looped around some spiky rock protrusions on their way down. In addition, as the rangers inspected the rope, they could not find any evidence of melting. The cord had been hit by lightning and flew free of the mountain, but it had kept the three climbers all tied together. Despite the electric current that had flowed through it, the rope remained strong enough to snag on some cracks as the climbers free-fell as well as support their weight until help could arrive. Their survival was secured by an unbounded rope, a true lifeline that prevented the three climbers from taking, as the rangers said afterward, "a big ride."

A trick rope had conjured the shimmering illusion of safety, performing a sleight of hand in which, while attached to three men plummeting to certain death, it abruptly unfurled itself at the precise moment necessary first to catch and then inexplicably to coil itself in tangles around a series of unremarkable rock spurs peppering the sheer mountain face. It was the fantasy of desperate men grasping at wishes and engaging in wild flights of imagination as they lay dying at the rocky base of the Grand. But in the end, the rope stunt turned out not to have been a chimera at all; it was the straight story, the unvarnished reality of what had actually happened to those climbers, and whether it was in fact a magic rope or faith in a higher power or the spirit of the mountains wielding its force to balance tragedy, the only unassailable truth is that Jake, Justin, and Reagan were not destined to die at that time, in that lonely place.

TWELVE

"Pumpkin Hour is 9:23."

—

Laurence Perry, helicopter pilot

The 30 minutes before official sunrise and after sunset are subject to long-standing visual flight rules enforced by the Federal Aviation Administration for aircraft under government contract. It is not safe for a pilot to fly, and it is especially not safe for a pilot to land, a helicopter in the dark. The makeshift heliports at mountain rescue headquarters do not have the lighting required to ensure a successful landing at night.

On July 26, 2003, the National Weather Service indicated that sunset would be at 8:53 P.M., making 9:23 P.M. the drop-dead time beyond which a pilot was forbidden to fly. The rangers refer to this mandatory cut-off time as Pumpkin Hour.

Jake had been screamer-suited off the lower scene to safety by 8:20 P.M., leaving only the Folded Man (and Erica's body) to be evacuated from the mountain.

Earlier in the evening, Craig had rappelled down mid-rock face to Rod, reaching him at 6:54 P.M. By that time, Rod had spent more than three hours dangling on his rope, exposed to the elements as he hung upside-down from his seat harness. When the lightning bolt blasted him off Friction Pitch, he dropped a dozen feet or so, and falling even that far with a dynamic rope severely jolted him. He was barely alive. His pulse was so weak that Craig could detect only a faint beat from his carotid artery.

As an EMT-1, an intermediate emergency medical technician, Craig had been assigned to assess Rod. Along with Dan and Chris, he was one of the rangers with a higher degree of medical interest and training (for which the park paid). Craig was able to dispense medication and was qualified to do the same things a paramedic could do, although the classes he took mainly focused on an advanced level of backcountry medicine.

Craig obtained extensive experience with patient care and trauma in the mid-'90s, working at the Eldora Mountain Resort outside Boulder, where he treated about 50 skiers every season. At that time in his life, Craig was based in Boulder without a career plan. When he showed up in Jackson in February one year, all of the good jobs had already been taken. Despite having studied biology, ecology, environmental science, and geology at college in Santa Barbara, Craig took a job as a dishwasher. His mom was worried, but Craig viewed the cheap lodging and free ski pass as a means to an end. He didn't yet know what it would be, but he understood that he was searching for a job he was positive about, work that would have depth and meaning. It turns out that he found the purpose he had been seeking at Jenny Lake.

As a practical matter, Craig was not often required to give an immense amount of medical care to patients in the mountains. His main goal at an accident site was to assess the seriousness of the injuries and then set the pace required to get the wounded party to definitive care (a hospital or a doctor). The questions he was generally tasked with answering on-scene were "How bad is he?" and "How fast do we need to move him?" Occasionally, Craig was called on to buy time, to give fluids or whatever else was necessary keep a victim alive until rangers could get him off the mountain.

In this case, having surveyed his patient on his short-haul ride in, Craig was not anticipating a need to do much of any medical treatment. As it appeared clear to Craig that, in EMT-1 parlance, Rod "was not in a position consistent with life," he basically wrote the Folded Man off.

After viewing the photos from the recon flight of Rod suspended from his rope, the rangers had essentially been in agreement that no one could survive that situation, yet suddenly, Craig was faced with a viable patient. Rod was most certainly dying, but he wasn't dead yet.

It seemed almost certain that Rod's rope had been seriously compromised after lightning traveled through it. While suspended from his own line, Craig secured Rod with a fresh rope and new anchors. He then began a medical assessment, checking Rod's vital signs and slipping an oxygen mask over his face. As best he could, he tried to support Rod's torso to ease his breathing and take some of the weight from his harness.

Rod's clothing was melted to his wrists. The back of his rain pants was burned and partially dissolved. He had gashes from the lightning and other trauma sliced across his body and on his head. Craig determined that he didn't have feeling in his legs.

Craig had never seen a patient in that position before, jackknifed in his harness, bent backward in two. Craig tied himself off on his rope so he could have his hands free. Then he did the only thing he could think to do in the situation: he propped Rod up and unfolded him.

Craig put his knees against the wall facing the mountain and came up underneath Rod. He built a platform with his body, Rod's torso on Craig's knees, his back and head on Craig's thighs.

Despite all of the training the Jenny Lake climbing rangers

endure, Craig had never trained for this particular situation, had not learned what to do when he encountered a man doubled over upside-down. He had never conducted an assessment and administered medical care while hanging from a rope.

He didn't even know if unfolding Rod was necessarily the right thing to do, but given the damage to his airway when he was bent, it seemed worth the risk to Craig. When Craig lifted him up onto himself and straightened him out, Rod's breathing seemed to improve slightly. His feet were still hanging down, but Craig was able to support his torso and neck. As he sat there with, as he said later, "a lapful of Rod," Craig was committed to staying underneath him, providing him with the least possible amount of movement.

When Craig first reached him, Rod was barely conscious, and even when Craig talked extremely loudly and squeezed him a little, Rod's only response had been to moan. The agony Rod experienced when Craig first moved him, however, increased his level of consciousness by creating pain. Craig hadn't hurt him on purpose to elicit a response, but it was a positive, if small, indication of Rod's condition. The brain recedes backward with head injuries, and responsiveness to pain is the most primitive reaction. A better sign would have been for Rod to be able to respond to verbal commands involving person, place, and event.

Craig asked Rod his name, and Rod was able to come up with it. Rod didn't say much else during the course of his rescue, other than to plead weakly with Craig to get him out of there because he had a three-month-old son.

That piece of news was particularly disturbing to the ranger attempting to save his life, in that it instantly made the situation, and Rod, real in a way he would rather not have confronted. All things being equal, Craig had no interest in getting to know a victim's family. He was upfront about his queasiness and resulting lack of interest in humanizing his patients, feeling that it jeopardized his objectivity. Nevertheless, for the rest of the day, Craig latched onto the information about Rod's son as a wedge upon which to pin his survival. He asked Rod what his son's name was, and the last clear word that Rod uttered on the mountainside was "Kai."

Craig was responsible for continually assessing Rod's status, which was deteriorating rapidly. His blood pressure was extremely low. The pulse in his radial artery in his wrist was so weak that Craig couldn't even feel it, and he was compelled to monitor Rod's pulse from his femoral and carotid arteries. When Craig wasn't directly interacting with Rod, Rod's eyes remained closed. It helped Craig considerably if his patient was conscious while he evaluated him, so he tried his best to keep Rod focused on staying awake. Once Rod regressed to mumbling as his only form of communication, Craig kept up a patter of one-sided conversation. He told Rod that as a relatively new ranger, he himself was nervous about the rescue. He explained that he had never seen a lightning strike or electrical injury before but that the purple spidering on the skin surrounding Rod's bruises was a classic symptom. The lightning appeared to have entered his torso on the left side, then exited out his right leg.

One topic Craig did not talk about with Rod was his medical condition. Unlike many rescuers who believe in rotely assuring a patient that he was going to be OK, Craig was not interested in giving Rod false hope. Craig felt that Rod would probably get off the mountain alive but would die in transit before he could reach the hospital, and Craig couldn't live with himself if he lied to Rod while he was dying.

Craig's alternative strategy was to give Rod a reason to go the distance, to put the burden on him to fight. To that end, rather than mislead him with platitudes, Craig took a brutally honest approach. He told Rod that the odds of him getting out of the situation were slim but there was still a possibility. He said that all of the rangers were doing the best they could, that Rod would be off the mountain in another couple of hours and he needed to stay awake in the meantime. For the remainder of the time Craig worked on Rod that evening, whenever he felt Rod slipping away, he murmured, "Think of Kai," to him for motivation, over and over again.

Rod was born in Brazil in the fall of 1975. He came to the United States with his mom when he was 15, and his sister followed them three and a half years later. He first settled in Florida, then lived briefly in New York, then moved to Boston for high school. Through contacts in her tight-knit community in Brazil, Rod's mom had a friend in Boston, and Rod lived with him while he attended school. As part of his upbringing in the Church of Jesus Christ of Latter-day Saints, Rod traveled to California for Mormon missionary work and to Utah for training.

It was when Rod was back in Florida to be with his mom that he met Jody, a friend of a friend of his mom's. He first saw her on an ice-skating rink, while she was skating and he was playing hockey. She was a small-town girl from Michigan who had been living in Florida since she was seven. Rod had a crush on her for a year before he did anything about it. Finally, when she was 16 and he was 18, he asked her out. They were married five years later, in South Pembroke Pines near Fort Lauderdale.

A year before their wedding, Rod and Jody had visited the Tetons for a couple of weeks. They loved everything about the place—the focus on the outdoors, the slower pace, the snowboarding. Jody cried on the plane home to Florida because she didn't want to leave.

During part of a cycle in which the couple moved 12 times in 10 years, they relocated to Salt Lake City for Rod's job as a software developer. In the year they lived in Utah, they bought their first house and Jody got pregnant, all before Rod got laid off. Jody was on bed rest during her last trimester, while Rod commuted to the only job he could find, in Idaho Falls, where he rented an apartment. In May 2003, Rod found a new position in the IT department of Melaleuca as a software developer, and he and Jody—and baby Kai—moved to Idaho Falls.

Billing itself as the Wellness Company, Melaleuca develops, manufactures, and sells, according to its marketing, effective, safe, and natural products, including cleaning products. Melaleuca advertises that its products are both good for the environment and cost-effective for its customers. Rod made friends quickly at the company, hanging out with Reagan Lembke and Jake Bancroft, who he initially thought was a bit of a jerk but who turned out to be what Rod deemed the "nicest redneck."

He also got to know Clint Summers and Rob Thomas. Rod had taken some classes and done some sport climbing in Utah on bolted routes, but he hadn't climbed anything extreme or technical. Rob had been planning and training for the late-July 2003 trip to the Grand for the past year with his family, but he supported the late addition of new climbers to the venture once he saw them on a practice climb, two weeks prior to the trip, on Guide's Wall in the Teton range.

Despite the success of that outing, Rod was busy working and taking classes in computer science at the University of Idaho. He initially tried to opt out of the Grand climb, but Reagan and Jake ultimately persuaded him to come along. While Rod was climbing the Grand, Jody, who was afraid of heights, drove down to Salt Lake City with Kai and a friend visiting from Florida. She was riding the carousel with her three-month-old son just about the time Rod was ascending Friction Pitch.

When Rod first regained consciousness after the lightning strike wrenched him from the mountain, he tried to replay the previous few minutes. He remembered falling, and then everything turned pitch black. In his head, he kept repeating, *This is it, I'm going to die right now.*

Then he felt a sandy, gritty feeling in his mouth. As he ran his tongue over the rough edge of his front tooth, he figured that if he was aware that he had chipped a tooth, he couldn't be dead. He had fallen about 10 or 15 feet until his rope jerked him to a stop, and he recalled bashing his face into hard rock on the way down.

He opened his eyes, and all he saw was sky and his feet. Then he noticed a rope going straight up. He was swinging in his harness, face-up, hundreds of feet of open air below him. He was aware of his belly-up position, yet he felt oddly detached from his body.

His lower back felt as if it was breaking, and given the sharp pain, he figured he had snapped it. He couldn't move his right leg or his left arm at all. He attempted to right himself, but he couldn't. It was hard enough just trying to breathe.

He screamed for help, but it turned out that he was only screaming in his mind. It was nearly impossible for him to make any sound with his voice; what he thought were screams came out only as moans.

Every part of his body was hurting, and in an attempt to ease the pain, he unclipped his backpack and shrugged it off his shoulders. Just like that, it was gone, crashing to the ground hundreds of feet below, along with the food and water in it. Earlier in the day, Rod had snapped several photos on his Fuji digital camera—a sunrise bathing the entire valley in pink, a view of the Idaho side of the park from the Lower Saddle, two climbers in his group perched at the base of Wall Street. The camera was lost along with his pack, although the rangers were later able to recover it.

He had no sense of time; he couldn't see anybody, and his sense of hearing seemed to come and go. He did catch snatches of radio communication, of Bob Thomas calling for help, relaying that the group had been hit by lightning. He didn't know where anyone was. He also heard some of the climbers trying to talk to Justin, but he did not hear Justin respond.

As Rod swam in and out of consciousness, he was aware of Bob's voice on the phone, referring to one dead, maybe two. He didn't understand if he was being included in the body count.

As time went by, daylight began to fade, and the temperature dropped dramatically. Rod knew with utter clarity that he would not survive the night. He began to see visions of his baby boy. His eyesight blacked out entirely, and he frantically tried to resist the urge to go to sleep. Even though Rod, like his friend Jake, recognized that if he fell asleep, he might not wake up, that knowledge was still not enough to keep him fully awake.

He was feeling weaker by the minute, and he kept hearing the blades of the helicopter so close and so loud, deafening, overwhelming, directly on top of him. In response, he tried to scream and flail to let the rescuers know where he was, to assure them that he was still alive. He thought the aircraft was coming to save him, but it went away, again and again, and while the sound he was hearing was actually the rangers being short-hauled in to rescue him, the effect of the rotors repeatedly fading into the distance escalated his desperation, nearly causing him to give up hope.

Then, in the darkness, he heard Craig's voice. He still couldn't see anything, and the noise was mostly coming out as a blur, but as the ranger identified himself Rod heard the word "Craig" repeatedly, and he understood that the rescuer was encouraging him to battle.

At that point, Rod no longer had any negative thoughts. He simply felt relief. The sound of Craig's voice was a release from panic for him, an unassailable conviction that he was going to get out of there. He felt the distant sensation of his body jerking a little, gently scraping against rock.

When Craig was inserted at the top of Friction Pitch and constructed an anchor for the rangers to rappel down, he had fallen right back into his training. There was so much going on around him, but at another level, he was just working on his assigned piece of pie. That dynamic seemed to have completely reversed itself once he reached Rod. He had not been taught how to set up shop on the end of a rope, and the on-the-job training made him feel as if he was flying by the seat of his pants. Even the process of putting Rod on oxygen was treatment that a ranger would normally perform on a ledge, not in the air.

Craig was concerned about keeping his movements to a minimum so as not to jostle Rod, but even more so, he was intensely focused on trying not to drop anything. If a piece of equipment accidentally slipped out of his hand, it could potentially collide with any of the seven people (three victims and four rangers) below him. An oxygen bottle released from his location could have killed someone at the lower scene. Very little of the equipment that he carried in his medical kit—an IV, for example—was capable of being clipped off onto a rope.

In addition, the tools he needed access to weren't necessarily on the top of his kit, and he couldn't unpack it because he had nowhere to set the items he was recovering. He found himself holding more things than he could balance or attach to the ropes. The whole situation was incredibly awkward, and in response, Craig briefly walked himself into a silent stream of consciousness about how some training in this aspect of a rescue would have been nice.

He radioed to the top of the pitch asking George Montopoli to rappel down and help him by providing more hands to hold things. George, who had a photographic memory and could remember the distribution of pins he had placed on a mountainside 20 years earlier, came down to Craig's location immediately to assist.

The weather had cleared for the most part, but the air was freezing, and George's yellow Nomex flight jacket provided only limited warmth and protection from the wind. George viewed the whole rescue mission as one huge improvisational experience. It involved a set of circumstances that the rangers could never have specifically trained for because they wouldn't ever have thought of it, but without the techniques developed in practice, they would have had no chance of pulling it off. In most operations, including many facets of this one, the rangers knew exactly what needed to be done and how to do it, and they just got to it. In this case, however, the rescue also show-cased the rangers' highly developed ability to adapt, to shift seamlessly as a team into components of a situation they had never encountered before. To that end, George focused on his role, which was to help Craig. At one point, he held an oxygen bottle between his legs.

George, age 54, grew up in Corning, New York, and moved out west at age 17 after high school. He worked for the Air Force Academy for 10 months before he resigned. He then moved to Boulder and met a climber who invited him out to Wyoming. To that point, he had done some scrambling back on the East Coast, including Mount Marcy in the Adirondack Mountains, the highest peak in New York, but had not performed any tech-nical rock climbing until he arrived in the Tetons. As he says, "It kinda grows on you . . . it kinda grew on me."

He held jobs as diverse as car mechanic, fruit picker—pears, cherries, apples—and carpenter. He can build a house from the ground up, including cutting down the trees for the wood. George did whatever was required to feed his climbing habit, working and traveling from Wyoming to Washington to Colorado, even heading to South America after reading an article in the *American Alpine Journal* about climbing in Colombia.

What appeals most to George about climbing is the adrenaline rush, the endorphin high that kicks in on the rocks. For him, it is about overcoming fear, controlling fear, surviving. He has had a few extremely close calls and as a result has learned to trust his instincts unfalteringly.

In the '70s, he worked as a climbing guide, a job he detested because of the pressure to get clients to the top. He was guiding a slow-moving party up Mount Rainier at the base of Gibraltar Rock when he had an overwhelming sensation that they needed to get off the section of the mountain they were climbing *that instant*. He cleared his climbers off (by yelling, "Jump, or I'm gonna push you!" at them), then shouted down to the party below that they had better not come up. Everyone vacated the area moments before a tremor shook the mountain and tons of rock descended in the place George and his group had just been climbing.

After determining that guiding involved too much responsibility and risk in connection with elements that he had no control over, such as clients who proceeded too leisurely up the mountain, George instead became a climbing ranger. He first came to Jenny Lake in 1977 and remained there for several seasons. In 1980, while pushing his limits on the Rock of Ages (a fine granite wall in Rocky Mountain National Park in Colorado), he had a serious accident solo-climbing a thousand-foot cliff. When a ledge pulled out, he fell inward and was pushed into the rock, rotating his calf and blowing out his fibula.

After being laid up, he traveled to Chile to work in the Peace Corps for a couple of years, then headed to Ecuador for a couple more. He lived at the end of a road on an ocean, totally isolated. He built water systems, constructed schools, and climbed 10,000-foot walls. He got married in Chile, brought his wife back to the United States, had a daughter. In 1984, he returned to Jenny Lake and has essentially not left since.

In the midst of his climbing career, George managed to fit in an extensive formal education from the University of Wyoming, receiving his undergraduate degree in applied mathematics, then going on to get both a master's in math with an emphasis in statistics and a PhD in statistics with an emphasis in math. He has been a professor of statistics and math in Yuma, Arizona, at both Arizona Western College and North Arizona University.

Still, George believes that being a climbing ranger is the best job in the world, and in his prime, he went on 30 to 40 climbs a summer in between supporting operations and running rescues. When he slowed down on the frequency of the climbing a little, he started spending his days off running a research study on bald eagles in the Tetons, studying mercury poisoning and possible sources of contamination.

Even with George on-scene to help him with Rod, Craig was still forced to consider whether the absence of certain care was going to kill Rod and weigh that belief against the danger of clumsily maneuvering the equipment. He decided that the administration of IV fluids and the bandaging of Rod's burns could wait. In any event, the priority was to get Rod off the mountain before nightfall, and that process was in the works above him.

When Craig had first conveyed to Leo that Rod was still breathing, Leo quickly conducted a risk analysis concerning how best to extract Rod from the mountain. A few aspects of the rescue were clear: first, he was much too seriously injured to be transported in anything but a litter, and second, before Laurence could hook the short-haul line into a litter, it had to be on a ledge where it wasn't attached to the mountain. Therefore, Leo needed to make the critical decision about whether it was better to raise or lower Rod on the mountainside to reach a flat area for extraction.

Lowering a patient on a litter is generally preferable, in that gravity is the rangers' friend in rescue scenarios, and they try to use it to their advantage whenever possible. The primary downside to a technical lowering is that it is possible for the rope to dislodge rocks from the mountainside that can crash down on top of the patient.

Raising techniques are rarely used in rescue work, in that gravity is working against the rescuers. The process requires a device for gaining a mechanical advantage and is practically impossible except on vertical or near-vertical rock where the litter can be held away from the face by one or two rangers. In addition, raising a patient generally requires more manpower and time.

In this case, however, the rangers would have had to lower Rod as far as 150 to 200 feet. The rangers at the top of the pitch would have then had to rappel down to that location and transport Rod away from the vertical aspect of the Grand to a suitable extraction site. The distance and type of terrain they would have had to cover to find an area with adequate rotor clearance were uncertain. In contrast, Leo knew that once Rod had been raised, the top of the pitch would be an ideal location for extraction, with great clearance and maneuverability for the helicopter. After considering the options, Leo decided that given the relative placement of Rod on the mountainside, about 50 feet down, it would be faster to bring him up to the ledge at the top of Friction Pitch.

The main problem with raising Rod was a shortage of personnel. Craig needed to be down with Rod guiding the litter, and George was assigned to belay, a full-time job by itself, leaving just Leo and Marty to raise a rescue load—patient, rescuer, and litter—of approximately 450 pounds. The rangers needed to assemble a specialized mechanism to make that possible, and they didn't have a lot of room to work. In addition, with only the two of them raising, the process was destined to be lengthy, and time was getting away from them, the light starting to fade.

Leo had earlier radioed Renny asking Laurence to deliver a litter to the top of the pitch. While it was on its way, Leo and Marty constructed a raising system, building additional anchors for the two ropes necessary, the litter main line and the belay line, so that they could drop the litter down to Craig and George. As the terrain was exceptionally rough and entirely vertical, the rangers wanted a separate line attached to a different anchor in the event that the main line failed. They rigged a mechanical advantage system involving pulleys, friction breaks, and a complicated combination of knots.

The litter arrived soon enough on the end of the short-haul rope, and Laurence carefully set it down on the top of Friction Pitch. Delivered in packaging full of medical gear, the rigid litter weighed about 100 pounds. The rangers at the top of the pitch unpacked and assembled it so that it could move down the mountain intact and ready for a patient to be inserted. There was no ledge for the rangers to rest the litter on when it got down to Rod; the litter was simply fixed on a line and sent down to rangers hanging off ropes for them to load a patient into in midair.

Just after 7:30 P.M., Leo and Marty began lowering the litter on the main line down the rock face to Craig and George.

As they worked together in perfect synchronization, both Leo and Marty couldn't help but consider the potential futility of the operation. Neither of them expressed any doubts aloud at the time, but much later, when they reflected back on the events of that evening, each independently used the same phrase to sum up what his expectations had been for getting Rod off the mountain that night: they had a shot. The color they used around those words made it clear how slim they believed that chance to be—Leo didn't think it would actually happen, and Marty felt they were likely out of time.

For his part, George, who was right next to Rod at that point, believed that the timing of his extraction was probably moot. George didn't understand why Rod wasn't already dead and gave him at most an hour to live. With the combination of the vastness of his injuries, the level of destruction in his body, and the increased trauma from hanging inverted for so long, George fully expected Rod's heart to fail at any minute. With no sense of irony, George later referred to Rod's predicament on the rope as "walking dead."

Then again, George was also a big believer in the will to live, and he knew from experience that many people in Rod's position would have given up and died before the rangers had even arrived. A rescue he conducted in the '70s always stayed with him, in which two climbers in the same circumstance, lost and frozen in the mountains, huddled together waiting for help to come. George never considered it a coincidence that the married man was the one who survived.

At one point or another while the litter was being lowered, each of the rangers turned to check on the intricate array of shadows splashed across the surface of the Grand. They knew that when the silhouettes vanished, they were within a shout-out of the time they would be forced to shut down the operation. Leo was intensely aware of what minute Pumpkin Hour would occur, but as he played out the rope to advance the litter down, he couldn't twist his wrist to get a look at his watch. Instead, he measured the rangers' remaining time in the pattern of the shadows deepening over the mountains.

THIRTEEN

*"It will put a damper on the rescue if his head
is cut off by the rotor."*

—

Dan Burgette, Jenny Lake ranger

Clint had been airlifted off the mountain at 7:13 P.M., and within
one hour and seven minutes of that time, four more climbers
had been flown off the mountain to safety. That level of precision did not happen without the coordinated efforts of dozens
of people at the Lower Saddle, 1,500 feet below Friction Pitch,
as well as at the rescue cache at the base of the mountain in Lupine Meadows.

The support team beneath the scene unfolding on Friction
Pitch consisted of one air ambulance, three ground ambulances, two full interagency helitack crews, several more rangers, a medical unit, almost every member of the Jenny Lake
subdistrict staff, and more than 20 assorted park personnel. At
one count, 49 people had responded to assist with the rescue in
one way or another.

The fluid and fast turnaround from patients in helicopter

2LM to helicopter 4HP at the Saddle was especially crucial to the orchestration of the rescue. That part of the operation functioned like a high-stakes assembly line, with rangers at the Lower Saddle (including Scott Guenther, one of the four permanent climbing rangers) efficiently unhooking each patient from the long line and extricating each from the screamer suit so that Laurence could fly the suit back up the mountain to extract the next victim.

A ranger then conducted a rapid trauma assessment of the patient and moved him out of the landing zone to make way for the next incoming patient. At that point, a ranger swiftly transferred each injured climber to 4HP, the second helicopter, so that Rick Harmon could fly the patient (riding on the inside of the aircraft this time) down to Lupine Meadows. Another ranger was onboard 4HP to attend to the patient during flight.

At Lupine Meadows, medical team members assessed and treated the injured climbers and arranged their transport to various hospitals. Clint, Reagan, and Justin went to St. John's Medical Center in Jackson via Teton County EMS ambulance, and Jake, who was in more serious condition, was prepared for an air-ambulance flight to the Eastern Idaho Regional Medical Center in Idaho Falls.

The Friction Pitch incident officially qualified as the 11th major search-and-rescue (SAR) mission in the park that summer. It was the third fatality, with the first two coincidentally also involving female victims killed in climbing-related accidents. None of the other SAR operations, however, had involved so many members of the ranger team, and rescue personnel in general, working so closely together for such an extended period of time.

In addition, in the Friction Pitch rescue, the show in the air was a full-blown and unprecedented spectacle. For example, at 6:57 P.M., Rick Harmon in helicopter 4HP delivered a sling-load of rescue equipment and sleeping bags to the upper scene. Six minutes later, Laurence, in 2LM, flew the litter to the upper scene, leaving the mountain within 10 minutes with Clint on the end of the short-haul rope. By then, Rick had returned to the Lower Saddle in time to ferry Clint from the Saddle down to Lupine Meadows. And that pattern wove in and out throughout the evening, as the two helicopters soared and dipped through the dusky Teton sky.

In order to keep Laurence in the air for so long—between inserting the rangers and extracting the injured climbers, he and Renny had already been flying for more than four hours while awaiting word on the status of Rod's rescue—he had to refuel his helicopter repeatedly. He flew down to the valley to fit in the refuels between trips up to Friction Pitch.

The official government rules require a pilot to shut off a helicopter when it is being refueled. The pilot then has to wait approximately two minutes for the aircraft to cool down, and once the temperature has stabilized, the helicopter can be filled with fuel. In this case, the rescuers didn't have two minutes. They needed absolutely every minute they could get, which meant that they also didn't have the additional three to four minutes it took for a pilot to start a helicopter back up after refueling.

From the very start of the rescue, Laurence made a determination that he wanted to hot-fuel, meaning that he would keep the rotors running throughout the refueling process. As the rules can be waived in a life-threatening situation, Laurence let Renny know how he wanted to handle it, and, predictably, Renny's response was "Sure."

To implement the process, there was an entire helitack crew on the ground acting as a safety check on the way procedures were followed as well as the pace at which they occurred. During the hot-fuel, everyone cleared away from the helicopter except for Laurence and a fuel guy in a full protective suit that

was somehow supposed to protect him in the event of an explosion. As Laurence explains, "It's just the two of us if anything
goes wrong."

Between the hot-fuels and the staggering number of people
Laurence was short-hauling in and out of the accident scene,
Laurence and Renny had simply not taken one minute of
downtime during the entire rescue. The helicopter had been
running in excess of four hours straight. While he was awaiting
word on Rod's status, Laurence even made a trip up to the
lower site with a cargo net suspended from the helicopter and
removed the gear and medical equipment that Jack, Jim, Dan,
and Chris had used in that part of the rescue.

Air support was often an integral part of a rescue in Jenny
Lake, but for it to be involved in the operation for the entire
time, from start to finish, was extremely unusual. Rather than
becoming fatigued by the extended air time at altitude, Renny
felt as if his powers of observation had been heightened. He
could see all of the events unfolding in extreme detail. As he describes the orchestration of the acrobatics in the sky, "It was the
most remarkable thing. There was meshing, synchronization
that I hadn't seen in a long time . . . or ever."

Laurence's feeling is that he could make what he did look
like magic by holding it together for one day, but in reality, he
was in a plastic bubble, a shell, with Renny's voice coming to
him from behind his back while he performed for remote and
disjointed people. He sums up his perspective on the day by saying, "That day, I never felt like I was on the edge of reason or
the edge of my abilities." In Renny's opinion, the standard Laurence set during the Friction Pitch rescue put a nearly insur-
mountable amount of pressure on future pilots.

The whirlwind pace of extractions and transfers that the
two pilots maintained throughout the evening did not allow the
victims much chance to process or even reflect on what was

happening. As they were conveyed from helicopter to helicopter at the Lower Saddle, the climbers all continued to appear fairly dazed. Clint seemed particularly stunned, telling rescuers over and over that it was his wife up there who had been hit.

During his second helicopter ride, Jake overheard something about a party of 13 being struck by lightning, and he realized for the first time that he was involved in a major catastrophe that affected more than just the three members of his rope team. Even as he became a little more cognizant of the scope of the disaster, it was clear that Jake was still in deep shock. His foot was on fire, burned all over, and his socks were crusted with blood and largely melted away. He had bought brand-new hiking socks for the climb, and as the paramedic was cutting away his scorched, tattered clothes, Jake indignantly asked him if he could please just take the socks off and save them instead of ruining them.

The transfer process proceeded flawlessly for five climbers in a row. Jake, the fifth person to be extracted that evening, was removed from the mountain at 8:20 P.M. and five minutes later had already been loaded into the second helicopter on his way to Lupine Meadows. Once Jake departed from the Lower Saddle, the brisk pace of controlled tension that had been sustained for hours by the rescue personnel finally slowed somewhat.

Jake arrived at Lupine Meadows at 8:32 P.M., and because of the extent of his injuries, the medical staff determined that he should be flown in an air ambulance to the hospital in Idaho Falls. As the rescuers at Lupine Meadows prepared Jake for a ride in yet a third helicopter, the urgency that had infused that atmosphere since midafternoon gradually began to slacken.

Twilight descended fully, and then a stunning sunset came and went. As the minutes continued to slip by, rescue operations stalled in both locations while everyone waited to see whether there was another patient coming down off the mountain that night or not.

FOURTEEN

"Rod, we're flying."

–

Craig Holm, Jenny Lake ranger

For how smoothly they pulled it off, it seemed as if loading a nearly unconscious patient with a probable spinal-cord injury into a litter in midair while hanging from ropes was a rescue maneuver that Craig and George had practiced repeatedly together in training.

It was a complicated and time-consuming operation, although time seemed to slow down for the rangers as they executed it. After Leo and Marty lowered the litter so that it was alongside Rod, they tied it off and secured it from above to allow the rangers to package Rod into it. Leo sent down a belay line, secured to a separate anchor, which George attached to the litter. Craig and George slid the backboard portion of the litter out into space, then lowered the front end of the litter. George stood on the litter, one leg on each side, grabbed Rod's legs, brought him up, and heaved him onto the backboard. The two rangers then straightened the litter and shoved the backboard back in.

Rod was essentially fragile dead weight and could not help with the process. He tried to speak, but he wasn't making much sense. It was obvious from his grimaces and whimpers that he suffered a tremendous amount of pain when they moved him into the litter.

After hanging from his harness for more than four hours, Rod's weight was finally fully supported. With the temperature having dropped into the 30s and his low blood pressure decreasing his peripheral blood flow, it was apparent to the rangers that he was freezing. Craig and George covered him with their jackets to keep him warm, Craig stripping down to just a lightweight fleece. Between the adrenaline of the moment and the pace at which they were working, the rangers were not feeling the cold. Craig piled his Nomex clothes, as well as an extra down jacket he had pulled out of his pack, on top of Rod's torso. George folded his yellow Nomex jacket over Rod's legs.

They then put a red Benham bag around him. Named after the man who designed it, the medium-weight sleeping bag Velcros 360 degrees with no zipper. It allows rescuers to access a patient to reassess him, take his blood pressure, reach his leg, and so on, and it has a hole in the center by the belly button where a patient attachment can come out.

As the rangers tucked him in, Rod experienced the sensation of his body settling in the litter and moving up the rock. Then, all of a sudden, he couldn't remember Craig's name anymore, a realization that made him panic, although he couldn't communicate his fear to the rangers helping him.

Once Rod was secured, Craig briefly assessed him again and then, using the litter as a ledge, transferred to the litter and strapped himself into it with Rod. His task at that point was to keep the litter from catching or bouncing as it was raised. Above him, Leo and Marty began to convert the ropes on which they had lowered the litter to a raising system to bring it back up with Rod in it.

As they began the technical raising operation, all of the rangers understood that they were pushing up against nightfall, and they began to accept that the four of them were likely not going to be enough to raise Rod as quickly as was necessary. There was no doubt that Rod would not survive the frigid night in the open air if he couldn't be evacuated. As it was, he had hovered not far from death for several hours.

George was manning the belay line, feeding the rope through the tension system as a backup in case the hauling line broke. It was a great deal of work for him to be doing all by himself; if Leo had access to unlimited manpower, he would have placed two rangers on rope management. From the top of the pitch, Leo and Marty were pulling the main line. The litter tried to turn and scrape into the face as they hauled it up, and Craig had to stabilize the litter as it ascended the mountain, about half a foot at a time. The litter was between Craig and the mountainside, and it took a tremendous amount of arm strength for Craig to pull the litter to himself continually to keep it from snagging on the rock.

Their movement was efficient but deliberative. Rod was tied securely into the litter, but 50 feet was a long way to hoist him up in six-inch increments. A variety of catastrophic events could occur between their location and the top of the pitch, including another lightning strike, rockfall, or, especially given the amount of force being expended on the rope, anchor failure.

While the rangers were raising Rod, Laurence took a quick flight down to Lupine Meadows to hot-fuel.

The combination of Rod, Craig, and the litter was an incredible weight for the rangers to haul, and it was dangerous for the rope to rub against the rock as it went over the edge of the pitch. In addition, using the mechanical-advantage device after a rainstorm was a mess. Static ropes are meant to be dry, and the wet rope they were using kept jamming. It was proving much too difficult a job for just Leo and Marty, so George went up to help with the raising.

It was at that point that Jack appeared up over the ledge. From the lower site, he had scrambled up a gully, traversed in to the south, downclimbed five feet, then jumped over a rock step to land. His last move required him to leap directly over Erica's body, which he felt was disrespectful, but he forced himself to "push away the sad" and focus on his task.

Jack quickly scanned the main line, the belay line, and the pulley system and felt it all looked solid. As he clipped in, he knew that he was trusting his life to the anchor. Jack had a strong preference for systems to be constructed with redundancy so that if one aspect failed, there was a backup structure to prevent disaster. While he was worried about the catastrophic failure of the anchor, Jack's question to himself was, *Would I lower my mother off this anchor?* and his answer was that he would.

Jack's added strength dramatically increased the speed of the raising. The rangers maintain that they would never work so quickly as to compromise the safety of the group, but in this case, it didn't seem possible that they could have performed any faster.

They were moving together in unison, like, as it were, clockwork, a particularly apt metaphor given that time was their enemy at that moment. They knew that they could move their patient up to the top of the pitch, but they couldn't control the setting sun. They weren't sure they would be able to get Rod off the mountain by nightfall, but they were convinced that if it was physically possible for them to accomplish it in time, they would get it done.

Craig made a radio call at 8:44, stating only, "Pretty hectic here . . ." before his voice faded away. A few minutes after that, Leo received a radio communication that there was only 35 minutes of flight time left. The light dimmed as the sun began to dip below the horizon. All of the rangers saw the beginnings of the sunset . . . and none of them said anything.

Laurence was doing his part to stall, generally staying in air, flying around the scene. Flight regulations required all contract helicopter operations to be *concluded* 30 minutes after sunset. Initiating a flight too close to Pumpkin Hour was not permissible. In Laurence's mind, the way around this rule was simply to remain in the air. He made the decision on his own to hang out in the sky, fearing that if he returned to the Saddle, the Forest Service might not let him back up. From the air, attuned to Laurence's thought process and able clearly to visualize the only chance the rescue had of succeeding, Renny relayed the details about their status down to Brandon in Lupine Meadows.

It would have taken Laurence two to three minutes to fly back to the Saddle, then another minute to get back off the ground with a long line, and there was a good chance that those minutes would be enough to ground him. Laurence knew that if the rangers were able to raise Rod in time to be extracted but the helicopter wasn't in the immediate vicinity at that moment, the whole operation might fail. Rather than take the risk that he would be prevented from returning to the scene, Laurence chose to hover off to one side of the mountain in the dusk for a solid 10 minutes or more.

As the litter approached the ledge at the top of the pitch, all of the rangers were acutely aware of the time clock on the mission. Still, one of them couldn't help but comment on the obvious, calling out, "When's Pumpkin Hour?"

Leo's response was simply a terse "Close."

As soon as the litter crested that edge, the rangers, spent with exertion but tensed for more effort, deferred to Craig for the next step.

Meanwhile, Laurence was staving off pressure of his own,

in the form of a "chippy guy" from the Forest Service who kept "screaming about Pumpkin Hour" on the radio. In response to the repeated warnings and admonishments, Laurence pushed the rangers to get Rod packaged. In consummate LP style, his version of exerting time constraints on them—which they understood implicitly—was calmly, quietly to radio the message, "Let's not worry too much about packing this guy."

Craig calculated the math as to what remained to be done before Rod could be flown off the mountain while concurrently conducting another quick medical assessment of him. Rod's condition had continued to degenerate; he was both sluggish and delirious, his mumbled responses to questions coming slower or not at all. Craig could hear the helicopter nearly on top of them, and when he looked over, he was surprised to be able to see right inside the aircraft. Renny and Laurence were directly at his eye level.

Craig knew that it was time for him, as the medic responsible for Rod, to make a decision. It was getting dark, Rod was getting worse, and there were only so many more minutes of flight time. Standard procedure before a litter patient was attached to the short-haul rope was to package him in a position known as left lateral recumbent. The patient was supposed to be tipped at a 90-degree angle in the litter onto his left side, then packed in and strapped in that pose. The purpose behind the position was to reduce the risk that the patient would drown in his own vomit if he threw up during the short-haul flight. If the patient threw up while on his side, he would generally clear his own airway with gravity.

Craig knew that if he worked as fast as possible, with no missteps, it would take him at least 15 minutes to repackage Rod securely into the correct position in the litter. He did not feel that he had that time. It was potentially possible, but if anything went wrong, the timing was much too tight. On the other hand, if he did not tip Rod onto his side and sent him off flat on his back in the litter, he would be taking an immense risk that Rod would choke to death in the air.

Craig was trying to maintain his clarity, but it was difficult to concentrate with the helicopter ratcheting right in his line of sight. There seemed to be an immense amount of obstacles impeding his ability to reach a solution. Craig took a deep breath, blocked out the stress of the rotors roaring at the level of his head, insulated himself from the immense time pressure, and took a few seconds to review the options once more. Taking the time to repackage Rod on his side might destroy any chance he had of getting off the mountain that night. Allowing Rod to fly out on his back was too risky.

He looked back over at Renny, leaning out of the doorless helicopter. Craig's heart was pumping madly, but he knew what he had to do, and he did not hesitate. He pushed the button on his radio while simultaneously attaching himself to the short-haul line.

As he clipped in, Craig requested Renny's permission to fly Rod out "attended." If Rod vomited while on his back in the air, Craig would be there to step on the litter rail and flip the litter upside-down as they flew.

Craig hooked into the litter, parallel to Rod's head, so he would be able to check his airway throughout the flight. He tried to explain to Rod that he was going to stay with him, but Rod had stopped communicating, and Craig wasn't sure what information, if any, he was taking in. Craig did not expect him to live much longer. He still assumed that Rod was going to die in transit, but Rod would not be alone when it happened.

At 8:49, Craig sent out the following radio transmission: "Patient attached with two daisies to litter and two to the God ring. Partially strapped to scoop, scoop strapped to litter. Comfortable with this configuration to valley. Will need to put him in better C-spine position. ETA 10 minutes."

The "God ring" was the large metal O that clipped a rescuer or patient to the short-haul line. It was referred to by that name, depending on which ranger is answering the question, either because they put all of their trust in it or because if it breaks, you see God.

Although Craig had never flown with a litter during a rescue before, he confidently swung one leg up and hooked it onto the bar of Rod's litter just seconds after they took off.

In the end, Laurence lifted Rod and Craig off the mountain at 8:57 P.M., with darkness coming on fast. Given the time and Rod's condition, Laurence was not going to mess around flying Rod to the Lower Saddle and then transferring him to the second helicopter for transport down to Lupine Meadows. This flight, Laurence's last trip of the day, was going straight down the Grand to the rescue headquarters at Lupine Meadows.

As a result of this strategy, which doubled the time Rod and Craig dangled 100 feet below the helicopter, the procedure was not technically a short-haul. The purpose of a short-haul is to move a patient the shortest possible distance, then put the patient *inside* a helicopter where his safety can be more easily controlled. This flight covered 6,300 vertical feet and lasted 12 minutes. Through it all, Craig monitored his patient's airway, checked his carotid pulse, and hoped.

FIFTEEN

"I was just so proud to be a Jenny Lake
ranger."

–

Jack McConnell, Jenny Lake ranger

From the rangers' perspective, there was immense and utter relief at watching Rod fly. The intense focus and immense tension they had labored under for hours lifted up and away from them along with the helicopter's twirling rotors. This completely chaotic thing had just unfolded before them, and they had seen it through together without the slightest hitch. They looked around at one another, shaking their heads, almost laughing, as if to say, "What just happened?"

The rangers realized that Rod might not be alive by the time the helicopter landed in the valley, but regardless, they had completed the rescue. From that point on, whether or not their patient died was out of their control. They were secure in the knowledge that they did their job and as a result gave him the best possible opportunity for survival.

Rather than celebrate immediately, the rangers spent the final few moments before darkness descended packing up Erica's body. They had assumed that they wouldn't be able to get her off the peak that night, and some of them would need to stay with her to protect her from animals in the night and shield other climbers from encountering her body early the next morning. None of the rangers wanted to spend the night with her on the mountain, and as they discussed who would remain at the scene to tend her body, several of them looked at their watches, seemingly in unison. If they operated as a team for just a little while longer, it was possible that there could be enough time to fly her off.

The atmosphere remained calm and respectful, but there was a controlled sense of urgency. Packaging Erica for her flight off of Friction Pitch fit with the remainder of what the rangers had to do. At the very end of the day, the moment had finally become about her.

As the rangers worked, hoping that Laurence would somehow have time to return to the scene, the second helicopter, with Rick Harmon piloting, suddenly appeared right over their heads. As it turned out, he was summoned by a brusque radio communication from Leo. In response to Rick stating, "Thought we were waiting on deceased until A.M.," Leo responded, "Negative. Make it happen."

As the rangers loaded Erica into a body bag, Jack was especially conscious of the juxtaposition of the chaotic helicopter rotors and the peaceful woman lying prone on the mountain. The rangers expertly clipped the bag to the cargo net hanging beneath the helicopter, and with just minutes to spare before darkness descended completely, the final flight off the Grand that night was made at 9:09 P.M., to transport Erica home.

Once she was in the air, the rangers at the top of Friction Pitch began gathering up their equipment. As the helicopter receded in the distance, the atmosphere on the pitch turned extraordinarily quiet and still. The rotor blades that had spun relentlessly above their heads for hours were no longer active, the action of the rangers' repetitive hauling movements had ceased. The whole experience had shifted from a river of movement and flow to pure serenity. As Jack later described the moment, "It was just this calm thing. It connected me beyond words, beyond time and place, to these people forever."

It was too late for any of the rangers to be short-hauled off, so they all had to fend for themselves getting down the mountain. By this time, it was just about pitch black. Dan and Chris climbed up from the lower site to help break down anchor systems and coil ropes, while Jack and Jim headed off to set up a fixed rope in the V Pitch to rappel down. The rangers left hundreds of pounds of gear in a pile to be removed the following day and headed over to the escape route.

In order to get down the mountain, the rangers first had to scramble up the V Pitch, the last technical exposed pitch on the climb. The ensuing rappel is about 140 feet, and climbers tend to drift off course as they descend it. Navigating it in the dark, even for climbers as experienced as these rangers, was not an insignificant task.

The V Pitch is an open book on the crest of the ridge, with the 100-foot rock pages forming a V that is a little less than 90 degrees. The rangers had to climb the left page of the book, often along the edge, with a drop straight down several hundred feet of vertical rock. As Dan Burgette says, "It's a place to pay attention, and in the dark, it is more of a challenge."

The rangers constantly checked themselves—this way, no, wait, this way here—as they climbed. According to a plaque on the wall of the ranger station, more climbers die on the way down than on the way up. This was their mountain, and the terrain was achingly familiar when the sun was shining, but by this time the corners were pitch dark, the cracks and crevices were black, and they could barely make out the knobs for handholds and footholds. Adding to the adventure, the rock was still wet from the rain.

Still, as Leo said, "We all knew we could get home." As the conversation drifted and lulled, the rangers occasionally lapsing into silence, the scope of what they had accomplished in such a short amount of time, the fusion of precision and teamwork, began to sink in. A total of 13 people (six rangers and seven victims) had been flown on and off the upper reaches of the mountain in the span of just over three hours. By the time the rescuers waited their turn to rappel through the chilly mountain air, headlamps bobbing all over the pitch as they descended in darkness, there were whoops of triumph and constant chatter.

Once down the rappel, the other rangers waited until Leo and George, bringing up the rear, pulled the rap rope, then they all downclimbed the Owen-Spalding route. At that point, the eight of them—Leo, Craig, Dan, Jim, Jack, Chris, George, and Marty—hiked down the mountain together under a starless sky, reliving the details of the rescue, talking it up, admitting out loud that no one upon arriving at the accident scene had truly thought that the mission could be completed by nightfall.

Adrenaline was still surging when they reached the hut at the Lower Saddle at midnight. Two other rangers, Scott Guenther and Darin Jernigan, who had been helping with the rescue from the Saddle, made them a bunch of food, which essentially consisted of pasta and slugs of Jim Beam. They were drained but also wound up, so they kept the impromptu slumber party going until two in the morning, then slowly drifted off to sleep.

Meanwhile, in the Lower Saddle, Jake Bancroft, goofy smile still on his face, had been transferred to the air ambulance and was awaiting his flight to the hospital. He was lying down on a gurney when paramedics set another patient next to him. Jake looked over at his friend Rod, drained of color, life seeping from his body, and thought, *I'm glad I'm not that guy.* Not only was

Rod unrecognizable to his friend, but he was, as described by Lanny Johnson, a former Jenny Lake ranger helping out in Lupine Meadows as a medic, "the most dead person I have ever seen that was still alive."

The air ambulance took off from Lupine Meadows bound for Eastern Idaho Regional Medical Center in Idaho Falls at 9:21 P.M., two minutes before Pumpkin Hour. With better instrument flight capabilities and a landing scheduled at a well-lit hospital heliport, that aircraft was legally allowed to fly after dark.

A nurse from Idaho Regional called Rod's wife, Jody, catching her in her car in Salt Lake City, where she had been visiting a friend. She asked Jody, using the past tense, "Was your husband's name Rod?" Nothing the nurse could say to Jody from that point on could convince her that her husband was still alive. Near hysterics, Jody pulled the car to the side of the road to continue the conversation. The nurse told her repeatedly that Rod was there with her in the hospital, but Jody was beyond reason by that time. Jody finally demanded to speak to her husband on the phone, and the nurse obliged, although Rod made little sense and recalls nothing about the call.

Jody was then told, or thought she heard, a slew of inconsistent information about Rod's accident. She understood that he had been hit by lightning but thought that he had fallen a great distance (which was incorrect) and then was told that he was badly burned, with various percentages thrown around—18 percent of his body scalded, 47 percent, 57 percent. She didn't expect to be able to identify him when she saw him.

The nurse told Jody to stay where she was, that once Rod was stabilized, he would be flown to the burn ward at the University of Utah hospital in Salt Lake City. Jody finally saw Rod at the hospital at 1:00 in the morning; he was weak and burned and broken but still breathing. That night, a nurse told Jody that

Rod was going to get a little worse before he got better. The truth was, he got a lot worse.

As Jim Springer described Rod's prospects, deliberately downplaying the agony to come, "After being in that position for that long, there's got to be some damage." Rod wore an oxygen mask at first, but when his breathing became worse, he was intubated and put on a ventilator, where he remained for several weeks. In addition, doctors placed him in a medically induced coma for three weeks, which spared him excruciating pain but caused him to experience terrible nightmares.

One night while he was in the coma, Rod's doctors called Jody in the middle of the night, telling her to get to the hospital right away because Rod had crashed and they didn't expect him to make it through the night. His blood pressure was 20/12, and the doctors had a cart and paddles ready to shock him back to life. His survival was day-to-day far beyond the immediate time period after the accident; he essentially could have died at any time in the following six weeks.

Rod's oxygenation was initially 70 percent, and his doctors relied on the tracheotomy tube in his throat to help him breathe. Just about everything that happened with his body was life-threatening. When he was eased off the ventilator, his kidneys shut down.

His right leg was swollen so tremendously from the hours he had hung from his climbing harness that the doctors considered amputating it. He experienced circulation problems and blood-releasing toxins, and his liver stopped working. He developed pancreatitis. Every time he was put on dialysis for his kidney damage, his blood pressure would drop precipitously.

Rod had a chest tube inserted to drain the fluid filling his right lung. Inexplicably, he did not have a broken back, but his right hip was severely dislocated, causing internal hemorrhaging, calcification, and nerve damage. He also contracted pneumonia while he was in the hospital.

Finally, by the end of his time in the coma, Rod began to improve. With repeated dialysis, his kidneys eventually kicked back in. By the end of six weeks, his lungs and pancreas started to function normally. He regained the use of his left arm, and his engorged right leg shrank back to normal size. He underwent mobility therapy. His father-in-law recorded hockey scores for him and sent them to him every day, and Jody posted them in his hospital room. His favorite nurse put fresh slices of green apples by his head each morning so he could smell them.

Meanwhile, the doctors were heavily involved in another aspect of Rod's treatment. He had second-degree burns from his left arm across his body, extensive but not deep, for which he spent 43 days in the burn unit. There were burns on more than 12 percent of his body, including his right leg, stomach, and chest. He had a lightning exit wound on his foot, and the underside of his left arm, expanding across his chest, was stained with a particularly gruesome purplish, spidery, six-inch lightning burn.

Following his release from intensive care, Rod was moved to the Salt Lake Regional Hospital for three weeks of rehabilitation and physical therapy. After spending nearly a month and a half in the burn unit with no windows, Rod was desperate to view the outdoors. There was a big window in his room at the rehab facility, and he redesigned the furniture to push his bed up against it so he could see out. The second night of his stay, the sky lit up with a huge lightning storm. The staff was forced to move Rod's bed completely to the other side of the room, where he spent the night cowering under the covers.

Undeterred, Rod asked his doctor to write him a prescription stating that he was required to be taken outside every day. To fill that prescription, the hospital staff had to move his whole bed outside, where he spent time near a fountain and a bunch of rose bushes. It was during one of these outdoor visits that a medical helicopter landed at the facility, and Rod experienced a full-blown panic attack. He heard the sound of the rotors and he was instantly back at the scene, dangling from that mountain, grisly memories streaming back to him unbidden, forcing him to relive the horror—*They're leaving*—looping on the dread.

By the time Rod was discharged from the hospital, his five-foot-eight frame was down from 155 pounds to 115, yet he walked out with just a cane to support himself, in good spirits, feeling that he had done something right.

Rod left the rehab facility on the two-month anniversary of the accident, just days before his 28th birthday. When he got to his house, the other climbers from the Grand trip were in his backyard to surprise him and welcome him home.

In an effort to regain his strength, Rod did squats, lifted weights, went bicycle riding, and stretched constantly. He felt that he had a good attitude, he was grateful for his family, he was ready to get back to his life. His company, going well above and beyond, kept his paychecks coming, sent flowers, and paid his rent, despite the fact that he had no disability insurance.

While those facts are all true, the reality of Rod's aftermath is actually a much darker story. After being discharged from the hospital, he still suffered from major nerve damage. He had internal scar tissue that restricted his mobility and prevented his leg from straightening completely. He had essentially lost his proprioception, the sense of knowing how one's own limbs are oriented in space, and consequently had to concentrate intensely to be able to take steps or reach for things.

When Rod got back to his job, he couldn't sustain his attention long enough to complete his work, and his company had to let him go. He had significant memory loss and lapses in his attention span. He tried to skate again a few months afterward, when his brain thought he could do something for which his legs were not prepared. He got out on the ice, took two steps, and collapsed.

Rod was scared that Kai would struggle in his lap and hurt him, so he wasn't ready to hold or even touch his son. Once when Jody was in the bathroom and Kai was crying, Rod felt utterly helpless to comfort his child. He began suffering from dramatic mood swings, alternately enraged and fearful. He was easily agitated and impatient and became quick to anger, aggressive to a point. His behavior was hard on Jody, tough on the marriage. He turned to depression medication and painkillers, then quit cold turkey and crashed.

Rod's healing process has come full circle in the years since the accident. In the summer of 2004, a year afterward, he took a job as a software developer in Utah for a change of scenery, a fresh start. He went back on medication and developed a plan with his doctors to wean himself off of it gradually. He stopped relying on his cane, and despite constant pain in his hip, he continued with physical therapy. His body adjusted to the changes the lightning had wrought.

Rod has made a nearly complete physical recovery from his injuries, so much so that he has competed in three marathons. He is back to playing hockey. Kai now has two younger brothers: Brennan, born on Rod's birthday in 2006, and Easton, born in the summer of 2010.

There are obviously remnants of the accident, both physical and psychological, that will always remain with him. He still feels uneasy when he glimpses lightning in the sky, and he makes his boys come indoors during rainstorms. He has a large scar on his right leg and unrelenting numbness in his right leg and foot. His nerve endings are permanently damaged. His left leg is hypersensitive when his kids knock into it. Despite these limitations, Rod says there is nothing that he can't do.

The year after the accident, Rod had not been physically ready to participate in a memorial climb up the Grand with members of the original group, but in 2005, he summited the mountain with Jake. While he doesn't blame climbing for what happened to him, he has chosen to do no other climbing since.

Rod's short-term memory problems persist, but Jody has put this issue in perspective in the scope of their lives together. When he loses his keys, for example, she is likely to respond by teasing him, "How long are you going to use the I-was-hit-by-lightning excuse?"

Regarding the rangers who saved his life, Rod has this to say: "They told me over and over that they don't risk their lives . . . but I think they do."

Rod is acutely aware that neither of his younger sons would exist, and Kai would have grown up without a father, if it weren't for the heroics of the Jenny Lake climbing rangers. He questions how he could possibly make them understand what their actions mean to him, how he could ever repay them for his second chance at life. The best answer he has come up with is for him to raise his three boys to be good men. That is the most, and the least, he can do to thank them.

In a move definitely departing from standard procedure, the climbing rangers have followed Rod's recovery. Most of them see themselves as one cog in society's safety net; they prefer to do their job and save people's lives and never know anything else about them. Occasionally, an injured party will send a thank you to the rangers afterward. One time, a woman twisted her ankle on the east face of Static Peak and wanted to pay for her rescue—when Renny explained to her that the rangers cannot accept monetary compensation but mentioned that they do drink whiskey, a case arrived at the doorstep of the ranger station the next day. After another rescue, a package of steaks was delivered to the rangers from Kansas City.

Rod, however, thrust his gratefulness right into their world. He came back to Jenny Lake and walked straight into the ranger station, not giving them a choice of whether or not to see him. He

introduced them to Jody and Kai. Craig, who only likes to monitor the progress of his patients anonymously, said that it made his
"skin crawl" to see Rod—then followed up that comment up with
the explanation, "You can't do your job if you're crying."

All of the victims struck by lightning that day on the Grand
still bear the remnants of charred entrance and exit wounds
where the current coursed through their bodies. Jake Bancroft
was in intensive care for three days, then emerged, as only Jake
can twist a phrase, "100 percent except for my injuries," by
which he means that his heart and internal organs were intact.

Initially, it wasn't clear that would be the case—when Jake
was given an EKG at the hospital around midnight on the night
of the accident, his heart's rhythm and electrical activity were
extremely irregular and his creatine phosphokinase level was
astronomical, indicating stress or damage to his heart and muscles. There were aspects of the ordeal that he remembered and
talked about that first night in the hospital that he completely
forgot by the next morning.

On the mountain, the only pain Jake felt was around his
ribs, but it turned out that there was a hole in his arm as if a
chunk of meat had been ripped out of it by a hungry predator.
Specific portions of his feet were blown off, and he lost most of
one pinkie toe. He still has round holes basically tattooed on his
body, scars larger than a silver dollar. He also suffers from permanent nerve damage, a feeling like numb or dead spots on his
skin. He's become used to the sensation. He remains unaccus-
tomed to the migraines, the worst aftereffect for him, which
have shadowed him—sometimes as many as two to three a
week—since the summer of 2003.

For the first six months after the accident, if the skies were
overcast or there was a light sprinkle, Jake's feet would begin to
tingle, and he would start to go into shock. One time, when a
storm came in during a fishing trip, he sat out the entire excur-

sion in his car. Lately it seems to faze him less, although he has adopted a vast respect for the weather. Still, Jake describes the Grand climb as "It was a good time except for the outcome."

Like Rod, Jake watches his kids play—Kylie, born the summer before he climbed the Grand, and Cody, conceived almost immediately after the accident and born nearly nine months later to the day—and he remains convinced that if he went to sleep on the mountainside, he wouldn't have woken up. He realizes that he was so deeply in shock, so hypothermic, that his body was shutting down. He knows that he would not have made it through that night, and consequently Cody would not have been born, if not for the climbing rangers.

Rob Thomas sometimes looks to the sky and the mountains with anger at what was taken but always also with gratitude for what was given, which he defines as a greater sense of life. He has continued to climb and at last count has summited the Grand 13 times.

Rob's brother Justin, who experienced a premonition of death on the mountain, as a member of the Church of Jesus Chris of Ladder-day Saints was wearing garments, essentially sacred underwear, on the day he was hit by lightning on the Grand. The two-piece white garments are worn under clothing at all times as a constant reminder of faith and devotion and a symbolic gesture of the promises that Mormons have made to God. The top resembles a T-shirt, covering the shoulders completely and hanging below the waist, and the bottoms resemble boxer briefs but extend to the knee. In the hospital, the nurse attempting to cut off Justin's clothing recognized that he was wearing garments and wondered aloud about them protecting him from more serious injury. Before proceeding any further, she called a bishop to give Justin a blessing regarding their removal.

Clint Summers's recovery, which he carefully distinguishes as his "physical" recovery, took about six months. He endured intensely painful skin grafts on his leg, taken from flesh on the other side of the same leg, a couple of inches over. After the hospital in Jackson, he was transported to a hospital in Idaho Falls for two days. He was discharged, still in a wheelchair, in time for Erica's funeral, held on their fifth wedding anniversary.

When Clint told his daughter, Adison, at age four that her mommy was with Jesus, he realized that she didn't fully comprehend the enormity of the loss. The first Valentine's Day without their mom, Adison and Daxton went to her grave with cards for her. They taped their messages to a white balloon and released it into the sky for their mom to catch.

Two months after the accident, Rob Thomas went back to the Grand to set a cairn at the top of Friction Pitch for Erica and to carry down a 15-pound piece of granite from the area where she was struck by lightning. Clint had it engraved with "Touched by God" and Erica's initials and dates of birth and death. The two men took the memorial stone up the Grand the following summer and put it where they knew it would be safe.

Clint remarried the year after the accident, to a woman with two girls of her own, and in 2005, they had a baby girl, McKenna, together. His physical recovery from the lightning strike is complete, save for a scar on his leg, and an area, where his thigh was pressed against Erica when she was struck, that may never have feeling again.

Eight rangers, the ones who were on the Grand that day— Leo Larson, Dan Burgette, Craig Holm, George Montopoli, Jim Springer, Jack McConnell, Marty Vidak, and Chris Harder— received Department of the Interior Valor Awards in Washington, D.C., the highest honor a public servant can receive. They are given only to employees of the department who demonstrate unusual courage involving a high degree of personal risk in the face of danger and risk their lives while attempting to save the life of another.

Following the incident, the Jenny Lake climbing rangers received a letter from Fran P. Mainella, the director of the National Park Service, U.S. Department of the Interior, stating in part, "One lost life is a tragedy. Your staff and partners, however, kept that tragedy from blossoming into a catastrophe."

Both pilots, Laurence Perry and Rick Harmon, were named Pilot of the Year by the Helicopter Association International for their part in the rescue, the most prestigious award given by the HAI. Laurence also received a Canadian Meritorious Service Decoration, bestowed on individuals who have performed an exceptional deed or activity that brought honor to Canada.

Renny can still climb every peak in the Teton Range faster than most, but after 35 years as a ranger, a National Park Service rule for law-enforcement employees forced him to retire in 2010 at age 57. The provision was meant to relieve employees in physical or stressful careers and help maintain a vigorous workforce, and there was no exception for Renny, despite his obvious physical fitness.

Renny did not go quietly into that good night. At his retirement party in July 2010, when formally presented with a memento of his service by a park representative, he responded, "Ah, the dreaded plaque." Postretirement, Renny took a position as a commercial guide in the Tetons with one of the local tour companies, and Pete Armington hired him to work with Denali National Park to reestablish its short-haul program with new helicopters.

Dan Burgette was also forced to retire, at 57, in 2005 ("They never got a pole long enough to pull me out of there") and is now a master woodcarver based in Tetonia, Idaho. He recently returned to his childhood home in Indiana to log three walnut trees, a hard maple, and a cherry tree for use in his carving. Leo Larson retired in 2008 and has not "touched rock" since he left. He and his wife, Helen, now run their printing business out of

La Jolla, California. Craig Holm left Jenny Lake to pursue a position with the fire department in Boulder, Colorado. Brandon is currently a ranger at Zion National Park in Utah.

George, Jim, Jack, Marty, and Chris all remain Jenny Lake climbing rangers.

Scott Guenther, one of the rangers who unloaded short-haul patients in the Lower Saddle during the Friction Pitch accident, now leads the team.

In general, the mountains continue to be oddly forgiving in relation to lightning strikes, given the harsh, unpredictable storms and the number of people caught unprepared. And yet, on the afternoon after Erica's death, lightning struck a couple hiking along the Willow Creek Trail just east of Crestone in the Colorado Rockies, killing the 25-year-old woman and sparing her husband.

Renny says that the Friction Pitch rescue was, "As good as we've ever done it and perhaps as good as we ever will." Every rescue in the Tetons is, at its core, about these rangers and the missions for which they prepare, but somehow it almost seems as if the lessons learned from each operation in the 53-year history of the Jenny Lake rangers converged to groom them for this one epic rescue.

Climbing rangers bristle at the mention of the word "hero"—"We do what we do, we don't need recognition." "We don't see ourselves that way. At all." "Just doin' our job is kinda cool for us."—but this was a mass-casualty incident at extreme altitude in vertical terrain with unsettled weather and only five hours of daylight. The operation simply would not have succeeded this spectacularly anywhere else in the country. This triumph, their victory, required a confluence of the specific backgrounds and skills and judgment of each of those men at that particular time in that exact place.

Decades of groundwork, training, and technological advancements—the cell phone, the short-haul procedure—

allowed the rangers to progress to the point where they were able to pull off a pitch-perfect rescue against all but impossible odds. One climber had died instantly, but five others were severely injured and undoubtedly would not have survived without help.

Saving them all, some might say, was like trying to catch lightning in a bottle.

As a mathematician, George Montopoli believes in two types of luck, the self-created variety and the by-chance kind. In this rescue, there was clearly a phenomenal amount of each. The rangers were trained expertly and performed selflessly, but they still required virtually every element of the operation to fall their way, and that is precisely how it played out. The accident was reported promptly by a cell phone that had both batteries and service range. The two pilots and the two helicopters were in the immediate vicinity. The weather broke in time for the rescuers to reach the scene and get everyone safely off the mountain by nightfall.

Then again, all of the experience and bravery in the world wouldn't have helped the climbers if the lightning had struck a split-second earlier, before Clint had reclipped the belay device. His anchor would have almost certainly failed, knocking the third and fourth rope teams down off the mountain on top of one another, likely resulting in six fatalities. The rangers would have come in and cleaned up the carnage, but it would not have made for nearly as good a story.

You need both kinds of luck.

ACKNOWLEDGMENTS

My first thank-you goes to Lanny Johnson, my idea guy and a true Renaissance man. I could not have told this story in such depth without the multiple doors he opened for me. Thank you also to each of the Jenny Lake climbing rangers involved in this rescue—every one of them was a reluctant hero during our interviews, and one of them even required a Renny Jackson–style ambush to speak with me (I'm talking to you, Jack). In the end, however, they were all not only exceedingly helpful but also incredibly responsive.

I am especially grateful to Leo, Chris, Brandon, and Jim for giving me access to such phenomenal photographs, and to Dan for enduring many a late-night e-mail request for additional minutiae about the climbing world. Over one very long cup of coffee, Craig was shockingly honest with me about the events of a day that forever changed him—a conversation that no doubt added a crucial intensity to certain passages in the book. A special thanks to Laurence for an above-and-beyond willingness to meet with me that extended to a California house call.

My appreciation as well to the Idaho climbing party, particularly Clint, who endured my need to prod at the most painful wound imaginable. Jake and Rob willingly filled in details from invaluable perspectives, and Rod allowed himself to relive the horror of July 26, 2003, with me over and over until I was convinced that I had the details of that day (and beyond) exactly right.

I owe an enormous debt to my agent, Scott Hoffman of Folio, who steadfastly believes in my writing and also regularly feeds my ego by making me feel like I am the smartest person in the room (next to him). Thank you also to Sarah Durand of Atria, who embraced this project and showed an infinite amount of patience with an author who is something less than tech-forward.

I would not have been able to give this story the focus it deserved without my husband, Nick, who was nothing but relentlessly encouraging throughout the past two years, readily accepting my penchant for quirky work hours, wrangling our kids with reckless abandon, and rarely venturing into my office without bearing black licorice or peppermint tea. In the final few months of the project, he proved to be every bit the staggeringly gifted editor that I suspected him to be, as well as a much more indulgent listener than I had any right to expect. His unwavering support takes my breath away.

And finally, thank you to my children, who always manage to assist with my manuscripts in their own special ways: Tess, who displayed a surprising knack for photo layout; Griffin, whose unflagging fascination with the logistics of the rescue inspired me to dig deeper; Ellie, whose merciless calculations of how many pages I had yet to write spurred many productive nights; Owen, who never tired of having passages read aloud to him; and Jack, who was awed and delighted to meet a real-life rescue hero.